"Every so often a cookbook comes
along that raises the bar for food writing.
Think Nigella Lawson's *How to Eat*
or Samin Nosrat's *Salt, Fat, Acid, Heat*.
The latest chef to join the pantheon:
Anna Jones."

—*Vogue* (U.K.)

One:
Pot, Pan,
Planet

Also by Anna Jones

A Modern Way to Eat

A Modern Way to Cook

The Modern Cook's Year

One:
Pot, Pan,
Planet

A Greener Way to Cook
for You and Your Family

Anna Jones

Photographs by **Issy Croker**

Alfred A. Knopf | New York 2022

To Dylan, you outshine everything

THIS IS A BORZOI BOOK
PUBLISHED BY ALFRED A. KNOPF

Text copyright © 2021 by Anna Jones
Photographs copyright © 2021 by Issy Croker

www.aaknopf.com

Library of Congress Cataloging-in-Publication Data
Names: Jones, Anna (Food writer), author.
Title: One : pot, pan, planet : a greener way to cook for you
   and your family / Anna Jones.
Description: New York : Alfred A. Knopf, 2022. | Includes index.
Identifiers: LCCN 2021010010 | ISBN 9780593320327 (hardcover) |
   ISBN 9780593320334 (ebook)
Subjects: LCSH: Vegetarian cooking. | Cooking (Vegetables) |
   One-dish meals.
Classification: LCC TX837 .J5424 2021 | DDC 641.5/636—dc23
LC record available at https://lccn.loc.gov/2021010010

Cover design by Ellie Game © HarperCollins Publishers 2021

Manufactured in China
First United States Edition

One: Pot, Pan, Planet

Introduction

This book is a celebration of food, cooking and togetherness; of the principles that ground how we live, cook and eat; of showing love to those we hold dear, to our communities and to ourselves.

When I started writing this book in late 2018, the world was a different place. But now we are at a turning point, in a moment of crisis and great opportunity. The events of 2020 have proven that collective action can lead to radical change, both in ideology and behavior, and I hope that we can move forward armed with the knowledge that a different world is really possible. Many of us do not want to go back to the old patterns. This is a chance to be part of the urgent shift that needs to happen, especially helping to slow climate change.

My books have previously been gentle in their approach to putting plants at the center of your tables. And while food and cooking, for me, are absolutely about the joy and the connection and beauty of sharing a meal, I feel now it's time to stress the changes we need to make. I want to make it clear that how we eat can actually help to shift the world we live in.

All the information on the climate crisis, and what we as individuals can do, can feel overwhelming. While we need to be real about the seriousness of what's going on, I think it's important to focus on one manageable step at a time. We make 35,000 decisions a day; that's a lot of potential for making a change. What we need, of course, is a systematic change in our food system led by our governments; but each small choice we make matters, and it is up to us to make different choices as well as demanding action from those who hold the power and purse strings.

Our food system has the single biggest impact on the climate. It affects every inch of our planet and every creature on it. If we want to help slow, and one day (hopefully) begin to reverse, climate change, it is widely agreed that the most powerful thing we can do is eat fewer animals and more plants. For you, that might mean one meal a day without meat, or it might mean fine-tuning your vegan diet. However it looks, start from where you are and don't look back. Change comes from what we do next. Try to make sure as many of the food decisions you make line up with how you want the world to look.

We are all learning; I am learning too. While I try to live as sustainably as possible, I make mistakes. Sometimes I buy plastic-packaged goods and flown-in treats. If you look back over my books, you will see a shift in the ingredients I use to cook and, while I have always cooked seasonally, I have slowly moved away from some ingredients that have a bigger footprint. In my mind we should celebrate our successes, not focus on what we have not done.

The food we eat quite literally builds and fuels the bodies which we walk around in every day. The food and farming systems we support likewise determine the kind of world we live in. Food is the one thing we ALL have in common, that we all engage with three times a day. It's an important thing to focus on, inform ourselves about and celebrate.

We need to bring some connection and kindness back to the way we support our farmers and those who grow and harvest our food; the way we shop (from supporting local to reducing packaging); the way we store, prepare and waste food; and the way we honor our bodies and our families with the food we put into them. It is all a web of infinite connection. Let's put kindness and joy at the heart of how we cook and eat.

How this book can help

This book is, I hope, where thought meets practical action, and where theory is grounded in reality. I want to show you a way of eating that WILL help the planet.

I could have made this book more radical, asking you, for instance, to buy only food from sustainable agriculture or biodynamic farms, and to eat more wild and foraged ingredients, and to eat 100% seasonal, British-grown produce. And whilst I think we can and should aspire to all of these things and move toward a climate-friendly diet, this book takes more manageable, but equally important, steps.

I hope that for many of you this book will sit in a sweet spot among the time you can devote to shopping and cooking, ingredients that are accessible to you and that you can afford, and a way of eating which is kind to the planet.

None of us is perfect and the science is complicated. At times it feels hard to make the right choices. But every small change adds up.

It was proven to me over the months of the pandemic that we can make the time to cook, that we can waste less and we can be creative with recipes and ingredients. I think the past year has changed us all as cooks. We came to value food for the miraculous life-giving stuff it is. If we had been told in the months before the coronavirus crisis how much appreciation we would come to have for a simple bag of flour or an egg, I doubt any of us would have believed it.

One Pot/One Pan/One Tray/Quick

The recipes in this book are grouped by what they are cooked in. Stews, soups and curries fill the One Pot chapter. Fritters, pancakes and crispy-edged veg make up the One Pan chapter. Easy all-in-one dinners and desserts are in the One Tray chapter. And I've included a collection of quick recipes for when time and your willingness to stand at the stove are in short supply. There are a few slightly more complicated recipes which I have included, as they are things I love to cook for friends—you will find those at the end of each chapter.

I have simplified the recipes, cooking and ingredients as much as possible, to save you time and money, as well as reduce the washing-up and the energy

used (more on that on page 74). I am a working mother of a young child, so meals these days need to deliver on flavor without taking up too much time and energy. Limiting the pans and processes used keeps things quick and easy but still, I hope, knock-out delicious.

Ingredients

The book is focused around seasonal fruit and vegetables, low-impact grains and pulses, herbs and spices. The majority of the produce I cook with is available in the U.S. and the world over. I encourage you to eat with the seasons wherever you are. There are, though, ingredients that come from farther afield, from lemons to coconut milk. I use these mindfully and sparingly knowing that they are, as a bar of chocolate might be, a treat. These ingredients are part of how I learned to cook, and part of my flavor palate when I am writing a new recipe, so I wanted to continue to use them but with an increased awareness of where they are from and how they may have traveled to my plate. I have written extensively on pages 54–55 about how to shop sustainably for your food, so do read those pages before you shop.

I also wanted to be up-front about my sourcing of recipes and ingredients from traditions and cultures that are not my own. I do this with the greatest respect, and in no way do I intend my recipes to represent or even replace these culturally important recipes. The London I have grown up in is a tapestry of different people, cultures and food; it has informed how I cook and eat; these flavors, ingredients and techniques have become part of me and part of my innate instincts in the kitchen. I know, though, that while I draw inspiration from a wide variety of cuisines, they are not mine. They belong to the people and cultures who have been cooking them for time immemorial, and I celebrate them in my cooking with the deepest reverence.

More than ever, it's important to be mindful of how we spend our money. Eating without meat or fish will almost always be more affordable. I would encourage you to buy the best-quality food you can afford, from organic carrots to fair-trade-certified chocolate. But I also realize that even being able to consider these choices is a huge privilege, so I encourage you to buy the best that you can. Connecting, cooking and awareness is the goal of this book, not making sure all your carrots are organic.

I very much hope there will come a time when crops from organic and sustainable agriculture become the norm; until then, if you can, search them out. If that's not an option for you, then understanding where the food you buy comes from is an excellent place to start too.

Planet

As well as recipes, you will find a few sections about the issues facing us and our planet. I am by no means an expert in this area (though I have asked a few experts for help), but I wanted to weave in some of the urgent issues we face when it comes to the connection among food, our bodies and the planet.

While flavor is still the center of how and why I cook, I have felt the need to stress the importance and urgency with which changes need to happen to how we shop, eat, and cook. I hope that many of you, along with reading the recipes, will be reminded of some of these issues as you plan your meals for the week or get inspiration for your weekly grocery shop.

Waste

After eating mostly plants, ensuring that the food you buy does not go to waste is the next most impactful thing you can do. The book is peppered with ideas on how to reduce the foods which we are most likely to waste, from flexible recipes for using up any amount of your most-eaten veg, to a guide on how to use the everyday foods we often throw away. Not wasting food is an easy win and a very satisfying one too. Throughout the book I encourage you to buy the best food you can from farmers who care; I hope doing this will mean you have a deeper connection with the food in your kitchen and are less likely to waste it, saving time and money too.

It is with great hope that I encourage you to cook the recipes in this book, to eat with your families, to celebrate the enlivening brilliance of food. Joy should always be at the center of how we think about food, how we cook and eat. Food is the great connector and has immense power for change. Every meal is a chance to focus on the great joy of eating.

ONE POT

Corn & cauliflower chowder

In a chowder, corn is usually paired with potatoes to add creaminess and body, but I use cauliflower here instead. It keeps the soup a little lighter than the potato version. The basil, scallion, green chili and peanut topping make this soup sing. The often-wasted cauliflower leaves are crisped up in the pan, too, like kale. You could use other nuts, and cilantro would work in place of basil if you like.

———

Heat the olive oil in a large saucepan over a medium-high heat. Add the leek and a good pinch of salt, then cook for 5–10 minutes until soft and sweet. Next, add the garlic and cook for 2–3 minutes.

Add the cauliflower florets, keeping the leaves for later. Add all but a handful of the corn, a good pinch of salt, the coconut milk, stock cube or powder and 3½ cups (800 ml) of hot water. Bring to the boil and simmer for about 20 minutes. It's ready when the cauliflower is soft throughout and the soup has thickened a little. Blend with an immersion blender until it's about half liquid and half still textured. Add a little lemon juice and a good grinding of black pepper, taste, adding more salt, pepper and lemon as needed.

Heat a frying pan over a medium heat, add a little oil and then the remaining corn, sliced green chili and scallions, along with the shredded cauli leaves. Cook until the corn is charred and the leaves are deep green and wilted. Serve this on top of the soup with the basil torn over, a final scattering of peanuts and a drizzle of olive oil.

SERVES 4

2 tablespoons olive oil
1 leek, washed, trimmed
    and thinly sliced
4 cloves of garlic, peeled and
    thinly sliced
½ a large cauliflower (about
    1 pound/500 g), cut into small
    florets, leaves shredded
the kernels from 4 ears of corn or
    1 pound/500 g canned/frozen
    kernels
1 x 13.5-ounce/400 ml can
    unsweetened coconut milk
1 teaspoon vegetable stock
    powder or ½ a stock cube
the juice of ½ lemon, unwaxed
    or organic

FOR THE TOPPING
a little olive oil for frying and to
    serve
1 green chili, thinly sliced
4 scallions, sliced
a bunch of basil
a handful of roasted unsalted
    peanuts, roughly crushed

Late summer
corn & tomato curry

SERVES 4

2 teaspoons fennel seeds
2 teaspoons coriander seeds
2 teaspoons black mustard seeds
coconut or peanut oil
2 leeks, washed and roughly
   shredded
4 cloves of garlic, peeled and
   chopped
1 green chili, roughly chopped
1 x 13.5-ounce/400 ml can
   unsweetened coconut milk
2 tablespoons tamarind paste
2 pounds/1 kg tomatoes,
   small ones halved, big
   ones quartered, or
   2 x 14.5-ounce/400 g cans
   cherry tomatoes
the kernels from 1 large ear of
   corn or 1⅓ cups/175 g canned/
   frozen kernels
2 large handfuls of chard or
   spinach, washed, leaves
   roughly shredded, stems sliced

TO SERVE

lime-spiked yogurt (plain yogurt
   of your choice mixed with lime
   juice and zest)
rice (see page 193)
warm rotis or chapatis

This is a summer kind of curry. It's bright in flavor, with sourness from tamarind offsetting the sweet tomatoes and corn, all leveled off with the calming creaminess of coconut milk.

———

You will need a large shallow pan for this; a big frying pan would do.

Put the fennel and coriander seeds into a spice grinder or pestle and mortar and grind until you have a rough powder. Put your largest frying pan or wok over a medium heat, add the ground spices and mustard seeds and push them around the pan, toasting for a couple of minutes, then tip into a bowl.

Put the pan back over a medium heat, add a little oil, the leeks and a pinch of salt, then cook for 10 minutes until soft and sweet. Put the toasted spices back in the pan and stir.

Add the garlic and chili and stir around the pan for about another 5 minutes or so. Next, pour in the coconut milk, add the tamarind paste, tumble in the tomatoes and cook for 20 minutes on a medium-high heat. You want the tomatoes to lose some of their liquid and the coconut milk to intensify and thicken.

Next, add the corn and greens (sliced stems and leaves) and cook for another couple of minutes until the greens have wilted. Serve with lime-spiked yogurt and rice, or rotis or chapatis.

Seasonal variations

To make this in autumn or winter, which I often do, use canned cherry tomatoes, frozen corn and some roasted or very thinly sliced raw butternut or winter squash.

Quinoa, lime & jalapeño pilaf

1 tablespoon olive oil

1 tablespoon cumin seeds

2 cloves of garlic, thinly sliced

1¼ cups/200 g quinoa, rinsed

2 limes, unwaxed or organic

4 scallions, thinly sliced

2-3 tablespoons sliced pickled
    jalapeños, roughly chopped

a small bunch of cilantro,
    roughly chopped

1 x 15-ounce/400 g can black
    beans, drained and rinsed

a bunch of kale or greens
    (about ½ pound/200 g),
    de-stemmed and shredded

TO SERVE

½ pound/200 g ripe tomatoes,
    roughly chopped

3½ ounces/100 g feta or vegan
    feta-style cheese, crumbled
    (optional)

3 tablespoons toasted
    pumpkin seeds

Quinoa is one of those foods I love to hate. My sister Laura ate mostly quinoa for a lot of her twenties and we both got sick of it. But we are coming back around to it now, and, cooked right, it is a delicious protein-packed grain (though technically it's not a grain, it's a tiny seed and a member of the rhubarb family). Here I pair it with lots of lime, pickled jalapeños and black beans, which makes an all-in-one dinner. Quinoa is now grown in the U.S. and Canada too, so search that out if you can.

Put a saucepan big enough to hold your quinoa over a medium heat, add a little oil and the cumin and garlic, and cook for 2 minutes, until the edges of the garlic are beginning to brown. Add the quinoa and cook for a few more minutes to toast, then add 2¼ cups/500 ml boiling water and half a teaspoon of sea salt and lower the heat until the water is just simmering. Cover and let the quinoa cook for 8 minutes. While the quinoa is cooking, grate the zest of the limes into a bowl, then squeeze in the juice, and add the scallions, jalapeños and most of the chopped cilantro. After the quinoa has cooked for 8 minutes, top with the drained black beans and re-cover. Simmer for another 2 minutes, then turn off the heat, throw the kale or greens on top, replace the lid and allow to steam for 2 more minutes.

Chop the tomatoes, put them into another little bowl with a tablespoon of the lime zest mixture and a generous pinch of salt and mix well.

Check the quinoa and kale or greens—the water should be absorbed, the quinoa should be tender and the germ should have emerged from each grain.

When the quinoa and kale are done, fluff with a fork, stir in the lime zest mixture, then crumble over the feta (if using) and top with the pumpkin seeds and remaining cilantro. Serve in bowls with the tomatoes on top.

Lemon, tomato & cardamom dhal

SERVES 4–6

FOR THE DHAL

2 tablespoons coconut oil

2 red onions, finely chopped

1 red chili, finely chopped
(de-seeded if you like)

1 green chili, finely chopped
(de-seeded if you like)

1 tablespoon cumin seeds

1 teaspoon coriander seeds

1 tablespoon black mustard seeds

1 teaspoon ground turmeric

the seeds from 6 cardamom
pods, ground

1 cup/200 g dried split red
lentils, washed

1 x 13.5-ounce/400 ml can
unsweetened coconut milk

2 cups/500 ml vegetable stock

3½ ounces/100 g baby spinach,
washed

4 ripe vine tomatoes,
roughly chopped

2 lemons, unwaxed or organic

16 fresh curry leaves (optional)

1 teaspoon coconut oil (optional)

FOR THE TOPPING

1 cup/100 g toasted cashew nuts

1 green chili (de-seeded if
you like)

½ lemon, unwaxed or organic

a small bunch of cilantro

TO SERVE

rice (see page 193)

warm rotis or chapatis

We make dhal at least once a week through the colder months of the year. This one, though, has a fresher feeling that means I'd be as happy eating it on a summer eve as I would a winter night. If you make this in autumn or winter, you could leave out the fresh tomatoes and replace with some grated squash for the last 10 minutes of cooking.

—

Heat the coconut oil in a deep saucepan and fry the onions over a medium heat with a pinch of salt for 5 minutes, stirring regularly until they start to soften. Add the chilies and cook for another couple of minutes until everything in the pan is soft and fragrant. Add the cumin, coriander and mustard seeds, and when the mustard seeds start to pop, stir in the ground turmeric and cardamom.

Quickly add the lentils, coconut milk and stock to the pan. Bring the dhal to the boil, then turn the heat down to a gentle simmer. Cook for 25–30 minutes, until the lentils have softened and are cooked through.

Now make your herb and cashew topping. Roughly chop the cashews and green chili as well as the whole lemon half, discarding any seeds, then add the cilantro and chop the lot together with a good pinch of salt to make a rough lemon salsa.

Back to the dhal: stir through the spinach and the chopped tomatoes so the spinach wilts a little, then taste it and add the juice of up to 2 lemons, depending on your preference. Add salt and pepper to taste.

If you are using the curry leaves, melt about a teaspoon of coconut oil in a frying pan and when the surface is shimmering, fry the leaves for about 15 seconds to crisp up.

Spoon the dhal into bowls, top with the curry leaves and cashews and serve with rice or warm roti breads.

Sweet potato, ginger & coconut stew

This stew has its roots in the Rastafarian Ital stew. This is my take on it. It uses familiar flavors like coconut, ginger, bay and allspice, but in a combination that's new to me. I've suggested a quick topping here that I urge you to make, as it lifts the whole stew. For more recipes from the Ital tradition, check out British cooks Riaz Phillips, and Craig and Shaun McAnuff.

———

Toast the allspice berries for a minute or so in a large heavy-bottomed saucepan that you can use for your stew (skip this step if using ground), then put into a food processor with a tablespoon of the olive oil, the scallions, garlic, ginger, thyme leaves, cilantro stalks and the juice and zest of 1 lime. Season with salt and pepper and blitz to form a paste.

Put the saucepan back over a medium heat and, once hot, add the remaining oil and fry the paste, stirring all the time, for 3–4 minutes, until fragrant.

Add the bay leaves, half chili, coconut milk and 2¼ cups/500 ml warm water to the pan. Stir to combine, bring to a simmer and cook for a few minutes, then add the squash or pumpkin and sweet potatoes. Drain and rinse the beans, then roughly mash them in a bowl, add to the pan and cook for 30–40 minutes at a gentle simmer.

Make your topping. Mix the olive oil and pumpkin seeds with the zest of the second lime and season with salt.

Once the squash or pumpkin and potatoes are cooked, and are just holding their shape but soft throughout, and the sauce is rich and flavorful, scoop out the bay leaves, whole chili and any thyme sprigs, then add the greens to the top of the stew—don't stir them in—and cover with a lid. Cook for a couple of minutes until dark, bright green. Remove the stew from the heat and squeeze over the juice of the remaining lime. Taste and add more lime, salt or pepper if needed.

Use tongs to divide the greens among warm bowls before spooning over generous helpings of the stew. Scatter over the toasted pumpkin-seed topping and the reserved cilantro leaves. Serve with yogurt and rotis or rice on the table for people to help themselves.

SERVES 4–6

2 allspice berries or 1 teaspoon ground allspice
2 tablespoons olive oil
a bunch of scallions, white and green parts roughly chopped
4 cloves of garlic, peeled
a thumb-sized piece of ginger, peeled and roughly chopped
a few sprigs of thyme, leaves picked
a large bunch of fresh cilantro, stalks finely chopped and leaves picked and reserved
the juice and zest of 2 limes, unwaxed or organic
2 bay leaves
½ Scotch bonnet chili
1 x 13.5-ounce/400 ml can unsweetened coconut milk
½ butternut squash or pumpkin (about 1 pound 5 ounces/600 g), peeled and chopped into bite-sized pieces
2 sweet potatoes, peeled and chopped into bite-sized pieces
1 x 15-ounce/400 g can black-eyed peas or kidney beans
1 head of greens, (like chard, spinach, kale or spring greens), thick stalks removed, roughly shredded

FOR THE TOPPING
2 tablespoons extra virgin olive oil
½ cup/75 g toasted pumpkin seeds (or the toasted seeds from inside your squash)
yogurt of your choice
rotis or rice (see page 193)

Winter red cabbage & apple soup

SERVES 6

1 pound/500 g red cabbage, finely
    shredded
2 tablespoons red wine vinegar
a little butter or olive oil for frying
1 large red onion, finely chopped
3 stalks of celery, finely chopped
1½ teaspoons caraway seeds
2 apples (Coxes, a British variety,
    are my choice, but any sharp
    eating apple would work),
    cored and cut into chunks
6⅓ cups/1.5 liters vegetable
    stock
2 tablespoons balsamic vinegar
2 teaspoons honey or agave
½ cup/50 g walnuts, crumbled
a small bunch of dill, leaves
    chopped, with some fronds
    reserved for garnishing

TO SERVE

4 tablespoons oat crème fraîche,
    sour cream or thick Greek
    yogurt

This is a cheerful, vibrant soup that ticks all the flavor boxes. It's a soup I make all year, as it's both comforting in winter and vibrant enough to eat on a colder spring or summer day too (think borscht). Sweet red cabbage comes with a pickled edge, earthy caraway and freshness from a couple of apples. The crunch from buttery toasted walnuts, brightness from dill and some leveling creaminess from crème fraîche finish it off. I use an oat crème fraîche here (see recipe on page 308), but a dairy version or some thick Greek yogurt would work too for non-vegans.

—

First, put the cabbage into a bowl with a good pinch of salt and the red wine vinegar. Squeeze together in your hands, then put to one side to pickle, while you start on the soup.

Melt a little butter or heat some oil in a heavy-bottomed saucepan over a medium-low heat. Add the onion and celery and sweat until soft and translucent, stirring from time to time. It will take about 15 minutes.

Once the onions are soft and sweet, add the caraway seeds and stir for a minute. Turn the heat up a little and add the apples and three-quarters of the cabbage, then fry for a further 5 minutes until the cabbage begins to soften.

Add the stock, balsamic vinegar and honey or agave. Bring to a boil, then reduce the heat, cover and simmer for 30 minutes. Uncover and simmer for another 10 minutes.

Meanwhile, heat a frying pan and add some oil. Once it's really hot, add the remaining cabbage and cook until crisp. For the last couple of minutes add the walnuts and half the dill.

Back to the soup. Stir in the rest of the dill and season to taste with salt and pepper. You can leave this as it is, but I like to blitz it with a handheld blender to make a vibrant purple soup.

Ladle the soup into warmed bowls and top each serving with the fried cabbage and walnuts, a spoonful of crème fraîche, sour cream or yogurt and some more dill if you like.

Any-way congee

Congee, best known as a Chinese rice porridge, might be the ultimate comfort food and one-pot dinner/lunch/breakfast. It takes a while to cook, but it's worth it for the satisfying spoonable texture. I have kept this recipe very simple and suggested some different topping options, so this can be made a number of different ways depending on what you feel like eating.

——

Rinse the rice in a sieve or strainer until the water runs clear, then put it into a large saucepan or Dutch oven with the stock, the ginger and a good pinch of sea salt.

Bring to the boil, then reduce to a simmer and cook slowly, uncovered, for 1 hour, stirring often; you want just a little bubbling on the top of the rice. It should become really thick and creamy. Add a splash more hot water from time to time if needed.

Now is the time to prepare your toppings. I've suggested lots below, but think greens, crunch and a kick of chili or acid.

After an hour, the congee should be oozy like good rice pudding. Season with salt to taste and add the vinegar.

Topping options

— Crispy fried greens and tofu, toasted sesame seeds and soy sauce
— Thinly sliced scallions with kimchi and blanched broccoli
— Roasted root vegetables, a spoonful of miso with some toasted seeds
— Crispy kale with pan-fried golden garlic slices, chili oil and ginger

SERVES 4–6

2 cups/400 g long-grain white rice
12⅔ cups/3 liters hot, clear vegetable stock
a 1½-inch/4 cm piece of ginger, peeled and thickly sliced
a splash of rice vinegar

Persian noodle soup

SERVES 4

3 tablespoons olive oil, plus
  extra for drizzling
2 onions, thinly sliced
1 teaspoon ground turmeric
1 teaspoon ground cumin
3 cloves of garlic, peeled and
  thinly sliced
1 green chili, finely chopped
  (de-seeded if you like)
1 x 15-ounce/400 g can
  cannellini beans, drained and
  rinsed
1 x 15-ounce/400 g can green or
  Puy lentils, drained and rinsed
5¼ cups/1.25 liters vegetable
  stock
7 ounces/200 g spinach, washed,
  chopped
3 ounces/80 g linguine/spaghetti,
  broken into 1¼-inch/3 cm
  sticks
a small bunch of parsley, chopped
a small bunch of cilantro,
  chopped
a small bunch of dill, chopped
the juice of 1 lemon, unwaxed or
  organic (use the zest below)

FOR THE TOPPING
⅓ cup/50 g toasted pine nuts
1 green chili, finely chopped
  (de-seeded if you like)
the zest of 1 lemon, unwaxed or
  organic
3 tablespoons extra virgin
  olive oil
a handful of herbs

This is my take on Persian noodle soup, expertly guided by my dear
friend Mersedeh Safa. It's a deeply savory soup with spice, cannellini
beans, lentils and some pasta thrown in for good measure. This is a
great way to use up the ends of bags of pasta you have hanging around.
I have suggested a noodle pasta, but really any pasta bashed up a bit
will do.

———

Heat the olive oil in a large pot over a medium heat. Add the onions
and cook for about 10 minutes, until they're very soft, golden and
fragrant. Add the spices, garlic, and chili, and cook for another
2–3 minutes, or until the garlic is fragrant but not browning.

Add the cannellini beans and lentils, along with 4 cups/1 liter of the
stock and a good pinch of salt. Bring the mixture to a boil, reduce it to
a simmer, then cook for 15 minutes until everything has come together.

If you are not eating all of the soup now, put those portions aside
before adding the spinach, pasta and herbs. Add the rest of the stock
to the pot with the spinach and pasta. Simmer until the linguine is
tender but slightly al dente. This should take about 8–10 minutes.

In a small bowl mix the pine nuts and chopped chili with the lemon
zest and olive oil to make the topping.

Add the herbs to the soup and leave to simmer for a minute before
tasting and adjusting the seasonings. Stir in the lemon juice.

Spoon into bowls and top with the pine nuts, chili mixture and more
herbs, if you like.

White miso ramen

SERVES 4

FOR THE CHILI MISO PASTE

½ cup/150 g white miso paste

1 teaspoon dried chili flakes or
   1 tablespoon fermented chili
   paste or chili oil

a bunch of scallions,
   thinly sliced, including greens

a small thumb-sized piece of
   ginger, peeled and grated

2 cloves of garlic, peeled
   and grated

½ teaspoon ground turmeric

FOR THE RAMEN

10 radishes, thinly sliced

1 large carrot, peeled into ribbons

2 tablespoons rice wine vinegar

honey or maple syrup

1 teaspoon sesame oil

4¼ cups/1 liter unsweetened
   almond milk

12 ounces/350 g dried noodles
   (I use brown rice ramen
   noodles)

3½ ounces/100 g kale (I use
   a mix of purple and green),
   pulled from its stalks and
   roughly torn

1 tablespoon tamari or soy sauce

7 ounces/200 g firm tofu

This ramen is a favorite—more satisfying than a straight-up clear broth and packed with flavor thanks to the punchy ramen paste—and you can play around with what vegetables you add here. The paste will make more than you will need, but it will keep in the fridge for up to three weeks and can be frozen too (ice cube trays are useful for portioning).

———

First, make the paste. Combine all the ingredients in a small saucepan over a gentle heat. You just want to warm this for a few minutes, to get the ginger, garlic and scallions to lose their rawness. Leave the paste to cool, then transfer to a jar. Keep the saucepan to one side for later use.

Next, put the sliced radishes and carrots in a bowl with the vinegar, a squeeze of honey or maple syrup, the sesame oil and a pinch of salt. Toss together and put to one side.

Put the almond milk and 1¼ cups/300 ml water into the saucepan used for the paste. Bring to the boil, add the noodles and cook until al dente, adding a little more water if it starts to look dry.

While the noodles are cooking, massage the kale with the tamari or soy sauce and divide between four bowls. Cut the tofu into pieces and divide these among the bowls too.

When the noodles are done, take the pan off the heat, put 6 tablespoons of the chili miso into a small mixing bowl, add a little of the noodle broth and mix well to thin it out, then pour it into the pan. Taste and add more paste if you like. Divide the noodles among four bowls and serve with the broth and the pickled veg.

Ways to use your chili miso

— Use in soups or stews at the end of cooking
— Add to dressings
— Toss through roasted vegetables for last 10 minutes of roasting
— Spread on sandwiches for extra punch

Eggplant & peanut stew
with pink onions

This stew brings charred eggplants to a pan with peanuts, peanut butter and lots of chili and spice. The onions add a shock of acid and neon pink. I love red-skinned peanuts. They are a great source of protein, and in the summer we soak them in cold water, which makes them more nutritious, keeping them in the fridge to eat with fruit for our breakfast.

——

In a heatproof bowl, soak the peanuts in 2¼ cups/500 ml boiling water, leaving until they need to be added to the stew.

Put a large saucepan or Dutch oven over your highest heat, add the chopped eggplants and dry-fry, turning regularly, until browned on all sides. This will take about 5 or 6 minutes, and you may need to do it in batches, depending on the size of your pan.

If you have been cooking in batches, add all the eggplants back to the pan, then add the oil and fry for a further 5 minutes, adding more oil if it looks a little dry. Next, add the white onions to the pan and cook over a medium heat for another 10 minutes until the onions are soft and sweet.

Add the spices, bay leaves and cilantro stalks and fry for a minute more. Add the diced tomatoes and tomato purée and fry for a couple of minutes, stirring from time to time so nothing sticks.

Add most of the Scotch bonnet and all the vegetable stock. Drain the peanuts and add to the pan, then simmer over a medium heat for 10–15 minutes until you have a thick sauce.

While the stew is cooking, slice the red onion as thinly as you can and put in a bowl. Add the superfine sugar or honey and red wine vinegar and massage gently with your hands. Add the remaining Scotch bonnet and the cilantro leaves and stir well.

Once the stew is ready, stir in the peanut butter. Drain the liquid from the onions and stir it into the stew a tablespoon at a time until it is the right level of acidity. Add a little more hot stock or water if it's too thick. Taste and season with salt and black pepper, ladle into bowls, top with the pink onions and cilantro, and serve with rice or flatbreads.

SERVES 4

1 cup/150 g unsalted red-skinned peanuts
2 medium eggplants, chopped
2 tablespoons peanut oil
2 white onions, peeled and thinly sliced
1 teaspoon ground coriander
1 teaspoon smoked paprika
½–1 teaspoon cayenne pepper or chili powder
2 bay leaves
a small bunch of cilantro, stalks chopped, leaves kept whole
6 whole tomatoes, roughly chopped, or 1 x 14.5-ounce/400 g can diced tomatoes
3 tablespoons tomato purée
½–1 Scotch bonnet chili, finely chopped, depending on heat
2¼ cups/500 ml hot vegetable stock
3 tablespoons peanut butter

FOR THE PINK ONIONS
1 red onion
1 tablespoon superfine sugar or honey
2 tablespoons red wine vinegar

TO SERVE
a small bunch of cilantro, chopped
rice (see page 193) or flatbreads

Muhammara chickpea stew

This stew is based on the flavors of muhammara, a pepper and chili dip from Aleppo. It is a riot of flavors: musky sweetness from the peppers, earthy spice from the cumin and buttery depth from the walnuts. It was a happy collision of some leftovers, inspired by the cook and photographer Joe Woodhouse, that was so good I have made it again and again.

Pomegranate molasses is traditionally used here to add a sweet, piquant roundness. Most larger supermarkets and Middle Eastern shops stock it, but if you can't get your hands on it you can substitute a tablespoon of balsamic vinegar and a tablespoon of date syrup or honey.

———

Put the nuts and cumin seeds into a Dutch oven and toast until the nuts are just starting to turn golden and the cumin smells wonderful and has released its oils. Tip into a food processor and add the red peppers (make sure these are drained if you are using from a jar). Blitz to a paste, then add the tomato purée, pomegranate molasses, chili flakes, juice of half the lemon and a good pinch of salt and pepper. Blitz again for 2–3 minutes until completely smooth.

With the processor on, slowly pour in the oil and blitz until really smooth.

Taste, season if needed, and blitz again. Keep tasting and balancing the flavors—you may need a bit more lemon juice, molasses or seasoning.

Tip the lot into the Dutch oven with the chickpeas or cannellini beans and stock and bring to a gentle simmer for about 20 minutes. Once the stew has thickened and tastes great, put the greens on top, cover and cook for a couple of minutes to wilt the greens, then take off the heat.

Scoop the greens off the top, divide the stew among bowls, then top with the greens and some more lemon juice. Finish with the herbs. Serve with rice, flatbreads or sourdough.

SERVES 4

½ cup/75 g walnuts or almonds
1 teaspoon cumin seeds
1 × 7-ounce/200 g jar roasted red peppers (drained weight 5½ ounces/160 g), or 3 roasted red peppers, peeled, de-seeded and chopped
2 tablespoons good-quality tomato purée
2 tablespoons pomegranate molasses, plus extra to finish
1 teaspoon Turkish chili flakes or a pinch of normal dried chili flakes
1 lemon, unwaxed or organic
4 tablespoons extra virgin olive oil
2 x 15-ounce/400 g cans chickpeas or cannellini beans
2¼ cups/500 ml hot vegetable stock
7 ounces/200 g kale or greens, de-stemmed and torn into pieces

TO SERVE
a small bunch of mint, parsley, or cilantro, or a mixture, roughly chopped
rice (see page 193) or flatbreads or sourdough

Golden turmeric &
ginger udon noodle soup

SERVES 4

1 teaspoon coriander seeds

5 black peppercorns

1 large onion, peeled and halved

2 small carrots, halved

1 small whole head of
   garlic, halved

1 large thumb-sized piece
   of ginger, sliced

1 small thumb-sized piece of
   fresh turmeric root, sliced, or
   1 teaspoon ground turmeric

¼ red chili, de-seeded

8½ cups/2 liters clear vegetable
   stock

6 scallions, thinly sliced

the juice of ½ lemon, unwaxed or
   organic

soy sauce, or salt, to season

10 ounces/300 g thick udon
   noodles

TO SERVE

4 tablespoons chili oil

I love the uncomplicated simplicity of the golden broth with chewy udon noodles. You could add seasonal vegetables, too: shredded greens, sugar snap peas, even roasted squash, if you like. I eat this when I feel under the weather, and also when I want something satisfyingly warm and straightforward.

Turmeric is as delicious as it is nourishing, bringing sunshine yellow to everything it touches. We are used to jars of the bright yellow ground stuff, with its earthy flavor, but if you can get it, use fresh turmeric. Its light, almost citrus, notes add freshness here.

———

In a large saucepan, toast the coriander seeds and peppercorns over a medium heat for 2 minutes. Add the remaining ingredients, apart from a third of the scallions, the lemon juice, soy sauce, noodles and chili oil. Add 4¼ cups/1 liter of boiling water.

Bring to the boil, then turn down to a gentle simmer for 25 minutes, to allow the flavors to infuse, adding more hot water from time to time if needed. Strain the broth if you are serving straightaway, or, if you plan to eat this later, cool the broth with the vegetables left in for a more intense flavor and strain before reheating.

To balance the broth, squeeze in the lemon juice, taste and add more if you'd like, and add soy sauce or salt as needed. You should have a delicately flavored, fragrant broth.

When almost ready to serve, cook the noodles according to the package instructions and drain well. Divide the cooked noodles among deep bowls and ladle the broth over the noodles. Serve on its own or with the remaining sliced scallions and a little chili oil.

Green pepper & pistachio risotto

This is my all-time favorite risotto. It is unusual, vibrant and full of the deep, but somehow lively, flavors of Sicily, which I adore. If you can get them, the small pale Turkish green peppers work best here. This recipe was kindly passed on to me by Emily Ezekiel, my cooking other half and one of the best cooks I know.

———

Start with the pesto. Char the peppers over an open flame on your stove or under your broiler until the skin is black all over. Remove and place in a bowl with a plate or lid on top and allow to cool.

Put your vegetable stock in a saucepan and place over a low heat to warm.

Heat a wide saucepan over a medium heat, add the olive oil and the onion and fry for about 10 minutes, or until soft and sweet. Add the garlic and cook for a further 2 minutes. Turn the heat up to high, add the rice and a little more oil if needed and toast the grains on all sides for about 5 minutes or until they turn a little translucent. Pour in the white wine and allow to evaporate, stirring as it does. Add a ladleful of the hot stock and stir until it evaporates, then continue this process until all the stock is used. This should take about 15–20 minutes. Keep adding and stirring from time to time while you get on with your pesto.

The peppers should be cool enough to handle now. Use your hands to peel off and discard the charred skin, then tear the peppers into pieces and remove the seeds. Put them into a food processor, add the toasted pistachios (reserving a small amount to top the risotto at the end), garlic, lemon juice, olive oil, basil leaves and half the grated cheese, and blend until you have a smooth, vivid green pesto. Add a little water if it looks too thick.

The risotto is perfectly cooked when the rice is al dente: break a grain of rice with your finger and you should be able to see a tiny fleck of white in the middle. Add the butter and half the remaining cheese, season with salt and pepper to taste and stir through most of the pesto, then put a lid on the risotto and allow it to sit for 5 minutes.

If the risotto looks a little thick, add a little more hot stock or boiling water. Divide into 4 portions, top with the rest of the pesto and the remaining cheese, the reserved basil leaves and chopped pistachios. Eat straightaway.

SERVES 4

FOR THE PESTO
4 green peppers or 6 smaller
    Turkish green peppers
⅔ cup/75 g shelled pistachios,
    toasted and chopped
1 clove of garlic, peeled
the juice of 1 lemon, unwaxed or
    organic
½ cup/120 ml extra virgin
    olive oil
a large bunch of basil leaves
    (2 cups/50 g), plus a small
    handful for the top
⅓ cup/30 g freshly grated
    vegetarian Pecorino or vegan
    Parmesan-style cheese

FOR THE RISOTTO
4¼–6⅓ cups/1–1.5 liters
    vegetable stock
2 tablespoons extra virgin olive oil
1 white onion, finely chopped
2 cloves of garlic, peeled and
    finely chopped
2 cups/400 g arborio or carnaroli
    rice
⅞ cup/200 ml white wine
4 tablespoons/50 g butter or
    vegan butter
sea salt and freshly ground
    pepper

One-pot orzo with beets, thyme & orange

This orzo cooks all in one pan to a satisfying deep purple with the spoonable feeling of a risotto. You can use any color of beet you like here; I love the deep magenta of the red ones, but yellow and pink work well too. I make this orzo with different vegetables as the seasons change. I've added a couple of my favorite variations below.

———

Put the grated beets, pasta, thyme leaves, garlic and vinegar into a medium saucepan with 1 teaspoon of sea salt, the 2 tablespoons of oil and 3½ cups/850 ml water. Crumble in the stock cube or add the powder. Place the pan over a high heat, cover with a lid and bring to the boil, then simmer for 10 minutes until the pasta is cooked and all the water has been absorbed.

Stir it every minute or so to make sure that the pasta doesn't catch on the bottom of the pan. If the orzo looks a little thick (you want it to be the consistency of risotto) add a little more hot water.

Spoon onto warm plates and finish with some orange zest, arugula, a crumbling of feta (if using), some toasted nuts and a good drizzle of oil.

Variations

— Squash/lemon/sage—swap in the same amount of grated squash for the beets, use lemon in place of the orange, and top with crispy sage leaves
— Broccoli/chili/oregano—swap out the beets for 2 pounds/900 g of roughly chopped broccoli and use lemon in place of the orange, oregano instead of thyme, and finish with chopped red chili and lemon zest

SERVES 4

a bunch of beets (around
    1½ pounds/650 g), peeled
    and grated
10½ ounces/300 g orzo pasta
a small bunch of thyme,
    leaves picked
3–4 cloves of garlic,
    finely chopped
1 tablespoon balsamic vinegar
2 tablespoons good olive oil,
    plus more for finishing
½ vegetable stock cube or
    2 teaspoons stock powder

TO SERVE
zest of a small orange or
    clementine, unwaxed or
    organic
4 handfuls of arugula
⅔ cup/3½ ounces/100 g feta
    or vegan feta-style cheese,
    crumbled (optional)
a few handfuls of toasted
    chopped nuts (walnuts,
    almonds or hazelnuts will all
    work well)
a drizzle of olive oil

Lemon, chickpea & green herb stew

SERVES 4–6

coconut or peanut oil
a bunch of scallions,
    thinly sliced
2 cloves of garlic, chopped
a small bunch of cilantro, stalks
    chopped and leaves picked
2 teaspoons ground turmeric
3 x 15-ounce/400 g cans
    chickpeas, drained and rinsed,
    or 2 x 1½-pound/660 g jars
⅞ cup/200 ml hot vegetable
    stock
1 x 13.5-ounce/400 ml can
    unsweetened coconut milk
2 lemons, unwaxed or organic,
    zested and cut in half
2 shallots, peeled, halved and
    very thinly sliced

TO SERVE
a large handful of green herb
    leaves picked and torn (I use
    a mixture of mint, basil and
    cilantro)
a pinch of dried chili flakes
    (optional)

This lemony coconut and herb-topped stew has a freshness I love, but it is hearty and filling at the same time. You add the halved, squeezed lemons to the stew as it cooks, which imparts a great citrusy zing. If you have leftovers, remove the lemon halves before storing; otherwise the flavor will become too intense.

Not all chickpeas are created equal. In the UK we can buy brilliant jarred Spanish chickpeas. If I can't get those I cook my own, but in a fix it is of course fine to use canned chickpeas.

———

Put a large saucepan over a medium heat, then add a little oil, the scallions, garlic and cilantro stalks. Cook for about 5 minutes, or until the scallions are soft and sweet.

Add the turmeric and cook for a couple of minutes to toast and release the oils. Add the chickpeas, stock and coconut milk, the zest and juice of both lemons, and the squeezed lemon halves.

Bring to a boil and simmer over a medium-low heat for 20 minutes, until slightly thickened and a vivid yellow.

In a separate frying pan, heat 3 tablespoons of oil and fry the shallots over a medium-low heat until golden and slightly crisp. Remove with a slotted spoon and drain on a paper towel.

Once the stew is ready, scoop out the lemon halves, stir through most of the herbs and serve topped with the crispy shallots, remaining herbs and chili flakes (if using).

Eggplant curry with basil & tamarind

Eggplant doesn't get enough attention in my kitchen; my husband, John, doesn't like it (I think this is because he has eaten so much badly cooked eggplant). But sometimes I crave it, so this is the pleasing sweet-and-sour curry result of one such craving. It's heady with lime leaf and tamarind spooned onto sticky jasmine rice. My eggplant craving is quelled and, of course, John licks his plate clean. Use Thai basil if you can get it (although normal basil will do). If you can't get lime leaves, add a good squeeze of lime juice at the end.

———

Put a large pot over a medium heat, add a little oil, then fry the eggplants in batches for 3–4 minutes until golden. Set aside.

Back in the same pot, add a little more oil, if needed, followed by the shallots and ginger. Cook over a medium heat for around 10 minutes, until the shallots are soft and sweet.

Add the garlic, lemongrass, lime leaves, chili and ground coriander, and cook for a further 5 minutes. Next, add the chopped tomatoes, fried eggplant, tamarind paste, and coconut milk, then simmer for 25–30 minutes, until the eggplant has almost collapsed and the sauce is thick, adding a little water or stock if needed.

Serve immediately with sticky rice, lots of Thai basil and fresh chili.

SERVES 4

coconut or peanut oil

4 medium eggplants, quartered lengthways

4 shallots, peeled and thinly sliced

a 2-inch/5 cm thumb-sized piece of ginger, peeled and finely chopped

3 cloves of garlic, peeled and finely chopped

1 stick of lemongrass, halved and bashed

2 lime leaves

1 red chili, thinly sliced

1 teaspoon ground coriander

10½ ounces/300 g vine tomatoes, roughly chopped, or 1 x 14.5-ounce/400 g can diced tomatoes

2 tablespoons tamarind paste

1 x 13.5-ounce/400 ml can unsweetened coconut milk

TO SERVE
sticky jasmine rice, cooked according to package instructions

a small bunch of Thai basil, leaves picked

1 red chili, thinly sliced

Cinnamon & cherry tomato koshari

SERVES 6

¾ cup/150 g green/brown lentils
1⅔ pounds/750 g fresh
   cherry tomatoes or
   2 x 14.5-ounce/400 g cans
   cherry tomatoes, drained
4 cloves of garlic
6 shallots, very thinly sliced
5 tablespoons extra virgin
   olive oil
a small bunch of cilantro,
   including stalks
1 teaspoon ground allspice or
   4 allspice berries, bashed
1 stick of cinnamon
1½ cups/300 g long-grain rice,
   rinsed
canola oil
a small bunch of parsley,
   roughly chopped
a small bunch of mint, roughly
   chopped

This bravely spiced rice and lentil dish is more than a sum of its parts and comes (mostly) from the store cupboard. It's topped with a crown of crispy frizzled shallots, which brings a key level of crunch and contrast to what is otherwise soft and comforting. In its pure Egyptian street-food form there is pasta—macaroni, to be precise—and often chickpeas, too. I've just used rice and lentils here for simplicity, but you could add a handful of macaroni to the rice, or a drained can of chickpeas, to make it a little more authentic.

———

First, soak your lentils in 1¼ cups/300 ml of warm water for an hour, then drain and rinse. Preheat the oven to 400°F/200°C.

In a large Dutch oven, put the tomatoes, garlic, a quarter of the sliced shallots and 2 tablespoons of the olive oil. Chop the cilantro stalks, then add those as well, along with the allspice and stick of cinnamon. Roast in the oven for 10 minutes, then remove from the oven and sprinkle on the rice and rinsed lentils. Add 4 cups/900 ml of boiling water, season with salt, cover with the lid and place in the oven for another 25 minutes.

Meanwhile, make the crispy shallots. Fill a saucepan with a 1 inch/3 cm depth of room-temperature canola oil. Put over a high heat and then, once hot, add the remaining shallots. You should see the oil bubble up when you add them. Give them a quick stir so they are all evenly submerged in the oil, then leave to cook for around 4 minutes, keeping an eye on them as they cook. Once they start turning a light golden color, remove them from the oil with a slotted spoon and onto some paper towels, then leave to cool completely.

Remove the rice from the oven and, using an oven mitt, take off the lid and remove the whole garlic cloves. Let the rice stand for 10 minutes and, meanwhile, pop the garlic out of its skin and mash with some sea salt and the remaining 3 tablespoons extra virgin olive oil.

Stir the garlic oil through the rice, followed by the chopped parsley, mint and cilantro leaves. Season with salt and pepper and top with the crispy shallots.

Corn risotto

Corn and risotto are not an obvious pairing. Corn is not that Italian (unless you're talking about polenta), but hear me out. The sweetness of the corn and the salty bite of Parmesan work, and really show each other off. The butteriness of the corn means I end up throwing less butter in too, not that that's the aim, just a nice side note. This risotto is perfect to cook when supplies are low, as the ingredient list is quite short and it requires just a stove top. You can use blanched frozen corn in the winter too. I love stirring a risotto—to me there's nothing more comforting to cook or eat.

———

First, cut the corn kernels from the cobs into a bowl, then chop the shaved cobs into three pieces each.

Pour the vegetable stock into a deep pan, add the chopped cobs and bring to a simmer, then keep warm over a low heat while you make the risotto, as you'll want it to be hot when adding it to the rice.

In a food processor, blitz a quarter of the kernels with a tablespoon of stock until smooth and creamy; set aside to add later.

Meanwhile, heat a little olive oil in a large pan, add the celery, onion and garlic with a pinch of salt and cook over a low heat for 10-15 minutes, until everything is soft and sweet, but not browned. Turn up the heat, add the rice and stir for a couple of minutes to seal the grains, then add the wine and let it evaporate.

Once all the wine has evaporated, turn the heat down to medium-low and start adding the stock a ladleful at a time, allowing each ladleful to be absorbed as you stir it in. When half the stock has been added, stir in the remaining corn kernels, then continue adding the stock until the rice is cooked but still has a little bite to it and the corn is tender. This will take about 30 minutes in total.

Remove the risotto from the heat and stir in the cheese, blitzed corn, butter and some salt and pepper. Pop a lid on top and leave to rest for a minute or two, then serve immediately, topped with a little extra grated Parmesan and the chopped chili.

SERVES 4

3 ears of corn
3½ cups/800 ml vegetable stock
extra virgin olive oil
1 stalk of celery, finely chopped
1 white onion, peeled and
  finely chopped
2 cloves of garlic, peeled and
  finely chopped
1 cup/200 g risotto rice (I use
  carnaroli)
1 cup/250 ml white wine
⅔ cup/60 g grated vegetarian
  Parmesan or vegan Parmesan-
  style cheese, plus extra to serve
1 large knob of butter or more
  olive oil
1 green chili, de-seeded and very
  finely chopped

Ancho chili & peanut mole

SERVES 8,
WITH LEFTOVER MOLE SAUCE

4 dried ancho chilies
   (see note in intro)
1 onion, peeled and quartered
3 cloves of garlic, peeled
3 vine tomatoes
2 tablespoons chipotle paste
2 ounces/60 g dark chocolate
   (minimum 70% cocoa solids)
½ cup/75 g unsalted peanuts
½ cup/75 g almonds
¼ cup/50 g pumpkin seeds
1 teaspoon cumin seeds
½ cup/75 g raisins
3 tablespoons/25 g sesame seeds
3 cups/750 ml vegetable stock

FOR THE ROASTED VEGETABLES
3⅓ pounds/1.5 kg new potatoes
1⅓ pounds/600 g shallots,
   peeled and halved
1 pound/500 g butternut squash,
   peeled and cut into large
   chunks
olive oil
the kernels from 3 ears of corn,
   or canned/frozen kernels
   (about 15 ounces/400 g)

TO SERVE
fresh cilantro
tortillas
the zest and juice of 1 lime,
   unwaxed or organic

This recipe requires a bit of love but creates a rich, rounded, deeply fruity chili sauce that you can use to flavor roasted vegetables, add to beans in tacos or burritos or use for a more traditional mole stew. Homemade flour tortillas work perfectly with the mole, too, and it can be heated up throughout the week as well.

This recipe makes more mole sauce than you will need, so store any extra portions in the fridge or freezer for a quick dinner—ideas on how to use it are on page 48. Whole dried ancho chilies are available from most supermarkets in the spice section. If you can't get your hands on them, you can replace them with a teaspoon of dried chili flakes.

———

Start by removing and discarding the seeds and stems from the dried ancho chilies, then lightly dry-toast them in a Dutch oven, taking care not to burn them. Remove from the pot and soak in a heatproof bowl of just-boiled water for 20 minutes. If you are using dried red chili flakes instead, then just toast but don't soak them.

Wipe the Dutch oven clean with a paper towel. Half fill with water and bring to the boil, then add the onion, garlic and tomatoes with a good pinch of salt. Turn down to a simmer for 10 minutes or until the skin on the tomatoes starts to come away and the onion is soft.

Drain the boiled onion, garlic and tomatoes and the soaked ancho chilies, but reserve the chili water. Put into a food processor and blitz on a high speed with ⅞ cup/200 ml of the reserved chili water and the chipotle paste until really smooth. Add the chocolate, broken into pieces, while the mixture is still warm so that the chocolate melts.

Toast the nuts, pumpkin seeds, cumin seeds and raisins in a pan. You want them to be golden and well toasted, so don't be afraid to take them a little further than you usually would. Add the sesame seeds for the last few minutes to toast, then add everything to the food processor containing the chocolate mix, along with the stock and a good pinch of salt and blitz until it is smooth and silky. Tip the liquid back into the pan and add a bit more stock if you want the texture to be a little looser. →

← For the roasted vegetables, preheat the oven to 425°F/220°C. Put all the vegetables, except the corn, on your largest sheet tray (you might need two if yours are small), cutting any large potatoes in half. Pour over a good glug of olive oil and 8 tablespoons of the mole sauce, season with salt and pepper, then give everything a good mix with your hands so it is all coated in the lovely smoky sauce.

Roast in the oven for 35 minutes, adding the corn halfway through and giving everything a shake, until the shallots are soft and sticky, the potatoes and squash are soft, and the corn is a little crispy.

Gently heat the mole through, then spoon a few spoonfuls of the silky sauce into the bottom of each bowl or plate. Top with the roasted vegetables and charred corn, a little fresh cilantro, tortillas and a squeeze of lime.

Save any leftover sauce and store in the fridge for up to a week, or freeze in portions for later (it will last in the freezer for up to 3 months).

Using your extra mole sauce

— Stir one portion of the sauce into a can of drained beans (black beans or pinto beans are best) and heat through. Serve on warmed tortillas with a tomato salsa and some chili sauce.
— Spoon a portion of the sauce over a tray of vegetables ready to roast in the oven, add a little oil and toss well, and serve in wraps, or with rice (see page 193).
— Use the mole as a sauce for enchiladas or in burritos.
— Stir into fried rice with vegetables for a quick leftovers dinner.

Miso & caramelized banana rice pudding

SERVES 4

3 ripe bananas, peeled
   and mashed
½ cup/100 g soft light brown
   sugar
1½ cups/300 g short grain white
   rice or arborio rice
1 star anise
2 cardamom pods, split open
   with the side of your knife
3½ cups/800 ml oat milk or any
   milk of your choice
1 teaspoon vanilla extract
   or paste
1 teaspoon sweet white miso paste
the juice and zest of a mandarin
   or clementine, unwaxed or
   organic

TO SERVE
⅔ cup/100 g toasted sesame
   seeds

Rice pudding is the Marmite of desserts. I don't think there is a pudding that splits opinion more. School dinners are perhaps to blame. This rice pudding is cooked like a risotto rather than baked (so no dreaded skin), and it is flavored with a rich banana caramel which is hit with a bit of miso. You could leave the miso out if it's too much of a stretch for you, or just use a teaspoon of soy sauce in its place: it adds a salty sweetness—think salted caramel.

———

Put the mashed bananas and soft brown sugar into a medium-sized saucepan over a medium heat and cook for 5–7 minutes, until the sugar has dissolved and caramelized. Keep stirring until thick and glossy. Remove 4 tablespoons of the banana caramel and set aside for later.

Add the rice to the pan and stir through the banana caramel for a couple of minutes. Add the spices, milk and vanilla extract or paste and bring to the boil. Once boiling, place a lid on the saucepan and simmer gently for 25 minutes, stirring frequently so it doesn't stick.

Mix the miso and reserved banana caramel with the juice and half of the zest of the mandarin or clementine and combine until you have a thin, glossy caramel.

Once the rice is cooked, divide it among warm bowls, swirl the miso caramel through each one, and top with toasted sesame seeds and the rest of the zest.

ONE PLANET I

Eating for health & sustainability / The protein question / How not to waste food (& money) / The most wasted foods / How to save energy (& money)

Eating for health & sustainability

Sometimes we make eating more complicated than it needs to be. The section of the Venn diagram where food, health and sustainability intersect, where we would all like to be, can seem impossible to reach. But when it comes to food, common sense is more useful than we realize. I have long been an advocate of a diet of seasonal fruit and veg, nuts and seeds, pulses and legumes, and a healthy scattering of treats. But now, a landmark study by Oxford University has proven that this is the best way to eat, for our health as well as for the planet. While studies like these are really helpful as a guide, it's important to take an interest in the products you're buying, as there is much more to consider. Consider the following questions: Am I eating too much of one thing? Where is this food from? Was it produced responsibly? I'll explore this later on pages 219–227.

Much of the power we have to affect the climate crisis, and our health and well-being, comes from the food choices we make. The study by Oxford University, "On the Multiple Environmental Aspects of Food and Health," found that healthy foods are almost always best for the environment, as well as best for us. The study found that poor diets threaten society by seriously harming people and the planet. Hopefully, this research can help inform better choices.

The researchers assessed the health and environmental impacts of fifteen foods common in Western diets and found fruit, vegetables, beans and whole grains were best for both avoiding disease and protecting the climate and water resources. Conversely, eating red and processed meat excessively causes the most unhealthy emissions and pollution.

There were a small number of foods that bucked the trend, however. Fish is considered by some to be a healthy choice, but it has a bigger environmental footprint on average than plant-based diets. High-sugar foods—such as cookies and sweetened drinks—have a relatively low impact on the planet but are bad for health. So while environmental measures, such as our carbon footprint and water use, are important in considering food choices that are better for environmental health, we need to take a commonsense approach and create a balance of foods that benefit our own health too.

Of all the foods studied, a daily serving of processed red meat was associated with the largest increase in risk of mortality and incidences of coronary heart disease, type II diabetes, and strokes.

A sustainable and unsustainable diet can be made up of the following key areas:

Sustainable

— Eating with a completely or predominantly plant-based approach
— Eating a broad range of products and ingredients to support a diverse diet
— Eating locally and seasonally
— Supporting local communities and farmer-community livelihoods when buying imported foods
— Opting for lower-impact transportation for imported foods (for example, shipping rather than air-freighted food)
— Choosing foods that have been produced sustainably by farmers who protect natural resources and limit their chemical use

Unsustainable
— High intake of meat and dairy
— Eating fish that are overharvested
— Overreliance on a small number of foods
— Relying on imported/air-freighted foods
— Predominantly buying from large, industrial agricultural systems with little protection of workers and support for communities
— Buying from farms that degrade soil and biodiversity, deplete water resources, routinely use chemicals and are intensifying climate change

Ultra-processed foods

Some food and drinks in the study did buck the trend. Soft drinks, an example of ultra-processed foods, are not resource-heavy in terms of planet health, but are extremely detrimental to human health.

Ultra-processed foods are foods that are altered so much that it can be hard to recognize the underlying ingredients. Made from cheap vegetable oils, flours, whey proteins and sugars, they are whipped up into something more appetizing with the help of industrial additives and emulsifiers. Ultra-processed foods (or UPFs) now account for more than half of all the calories eaten in the UK and the U.S., and other countries are catching up fast.

Some UPFs, such as sliced bread or store-bought cakes, may not seem "ultra"-processed to us. And that's why most of us do not get through the day without consuming a UPF.

Here are some examples of UPFs: your morning bowl of cereal or a pot of flavored yogurt; chips, blueberry muffins or vegan hot dogs; a canned diet drink or a protein bar. When eaten on their own, once in a while, these foods are perfectly fine. But evidence now suggests that diets heavy in UPFs can cause overeating and obesity.

"Consumers may blame themselves for overindulging in these foods, but what if it is in the nature of these products to be overeaten?" says food writer Bee Wilson, in an article for *The Guardian* newspaper.

What to take from all this information? I think it's pretty much where I started at the beginning: eating is complicated. I try to eat as wide a range of fruits, vegetables, nuts, seeds, grains, flours, pulses and sweeteners as possible, thus maximizing the variety of flavors, colors and nutrients that my body is exposed to. It's like betting on every horse in the race, and it helps to support smaller farms and organic producers, and helps support biodiversity, too.

Things we can do

I want to make it clear that while I eat healthily almost always, I also feel strongly that eating is one part of our brilliantly fallible humanness. So there is always a place for a trashy chocolate bar or French fries from a fast-food joint.

Despite the trend-bucking exceptions I have mentioned above, the same dietary changes—eating more vegetables, legumes, whole grains—that could help reduce the risk of diet-related diseases could also help us meet crucial sustainability goals.

The protein question

Search #protein on Instagram and, at the time this was written, you are met with 24.3 million posts. Among the six-packs and the weightlifters you find the food: protein-packed flapjacks and pancakes, take-home containers of hard-boiled eggs and edamame beans, shakes and enriched juices, granola and sashimi . . . the list goes on.

We've become a bit obsessed with protein. In some ways it's easy to see why. Protein performs a vital role in every cell in our body. It's needed to build and repair tissue, and is a building block of our muscles, skin and blood. For a long time, meat has been seen as an important source of protein in the Western diet, but for those of us who put vegetables at the center of our plates, how do we know if we are getting enough? This is still one of the questions I get asked the most.

The truth is, on average we eat almost double the protein we need.

The average-sized adult needs 1.5-2 ounces/45-55 g of protein per day. That's about two handful-sized portions of nuts, tofu, meat or fish, per day. But in the UK, most of us consume around 45% to 55% more protein than we need each day, according to the National Diet and Nutrition Survey.

Some research has shown that vegans do require a higher protein intake because of the way our bodies process plant protein. Even then, a daily intake of .36 grams of protein per pound of body weight is recommended. There are, of course, plenty of plant-based protein sources. Pulses, beans, quinoa, nuts, seeds and whole grains are all brilliant ingredients for a diet rich in nutrients, fiber and protein. See the note on complete proteins on page 59.

Scientists believe that the idea of needing additional protein in your diet to build up muscle, either through meat or with supplements such as protein shakes, is a myth. Furthermore, according to the American Heart Association, relying on meat for your protein and eating too much of it has been linked to an increased risk of several diseases.

Even athletes training more than once a day need only twice as much protein as the average adult. Most of us, professional sportspeople or not, are already eating that amount.

Dozens of high-profile athletes, from Venus Williams to Lewis Hamilton, rely on plant-based diets to get the most from their bodies. If it's working for them, then I can't help but feel it can work for us, too.

Another thing to consider is that industrial animal production systems create huge demand for protein crops. Of the total plant protein produced within agriculture, less than half is used for human consumption. (Source: Vaclav Smil, *Feeding the World: A Challenge for the Twenty-first Century* [MIT Press, 2000].)

Soy/Tofu

Unlike other pulses, soybeans are a complete protein, comparable in quality to animal protein, but are lower in fat and contain fiber and iron. Eating just under

1 ounce/25 g of soy protein a day (e.g., edamame, tofu), instead of meat, can help lower cholesterol levels. This is equivalent to a glass of soy milk, a pot of unsweetened soy yogurt or just under 3 ounces/80 g of tofu.

Quinoa

Quinoa is cooked and eaten like a grain, but is actually the seed of a green vegetable related to rhubarb, chard and spinach. It is a complete protein, but it's not the amount that is impressive, it's the type. Unlike cereals, quinoa has all of the essential amino acids you find in animal protein. It is an easy substitute for rice and pasta.

Beans and legumes

Beans and legumes, so all types of fresh, dried or canned beans, lentils and split peas, are fiber-rich nutrient powerhouses and an excellent source of protein. One serving of pulses averages about ⅓ ounce/ 7 g of protein per 3½ ounces/100 g; some, like pinto beans, are much higher. Beans and legumes also keep you feeling fuller for longer because they are so fiber-rich and are high in antioxidants. One serving of pulses a day can help to lower "bad" cholesterol. Four servings (versus less than one) per week can reduce the risk of heart disease.

Nuts and seeds

Nuts are an easy and obvious way to up your protein intake. They contain ½–⅔ ounce/15–20 g of protein per 3½ ounces/100 g, and are high in fiber and protein. Peanuts, which are actually part of the legume family, not a seed like other nuts, have slightly more at ⅞ ounce/25 g per 3½ ounces/100 g. Nuts are quite high in fat, so a handful a day is a good guide.

I eat them as a snack, roasted with maple syrup, chili and rosemary, toss them through salads or make them into pestos and dressings.

Grains

Some whole grains like oats are much higher in protein than you might imagine. Whole-grain breads, rice and pasta have more protein, fiber and iron than white versions. Brown rice with beans, or bread with hummus or nut butter, can give you as much protein as a piece of meat.

Meatless meat

On the whole I veer away from things that are made to look like meat. Sure, on occasion I'll have a vegetarian sausage or a burger that masquerades as meat. But in general, I prefer to celebrate vegetables rather than eat something that's trying to trick me by looking and tasting like meat. I know, though, that for some vegetarians and vegans, it's a different story, and these "burgers" and "sausages" are an easy swap for the meats they used to eat and satisfy a craving for those who miss the taste. I would encourage you to consider the impact of these products on the environment. Some are locally made, and have low-impact ingredients and are a good choice. Others, though, are engineered to eat like meat, and some are flown halfway across the world. Sometimes I think the vegan/plant-based tag can suggest that a certain food is sustainable and low-impact when, in fact, it could have a higher impact than some locally raised beef. I am not encouraging you to eat beef—quite the opposite—but instead am inviting you to look a little deeper at the ingredients in these products, where they are made and how good for you (and the planet) they actually are.

Eggs

If you eat them, eggs are a low-carb, low-calorie and low-cost source of protein. One egg provides about ¼ ounce/6–8 g of protein. Extremely nutritious, eggs are a complete protein and have a rich supply of key vitamins and minerals. Much of the egg's nutrition, including vitamin D, omega-3 fatty acids, B vitamins and choline (which may contribute to mental clarity), is in the yolk.

Protein-rich vegetables

Bean sprouts, peas, sugar snap peas, asparagus, sweet potatoes and Brussels sprouts are all relatively high in protein. Seaweeds like kombu are also naturally high in protein and lots of other nutrients.

Greek yogurt

If you eat dairy, then Greek yogurt is a great option, as it's much higher in protein than normal yogurt. I buy an unsweetened full-fat version and 3½ ounces/100 g contains about ⅓ ounce/10 g of protein, three times the amount of normal yogurt. Most Greek yogurt also contains probiotics, the healthy bacteria that support gut health. And it is a good source of calcium and vitamin D.

Complete proteins

In most diets, different proteins tend to complement each other in their amino-acid pattern, so when two foods providing vegetable protein are eaten at the same time, such as a cereal (let's say bread) and pulses (like baked beans), the amino acids of one protein may compensate for the lack of amino acids in the other. This is known as the complementary action of proteins.

A complete protein contains all nine essential amino acids that our bodies can't produce. Amino acids are organic compounds, considered the "building blocks" of protein, and 20 different ones bond together in a chain to form a protein. Eleven amino acids are produced by our bodies. The other nine—the so-called essential amino acids—we get through food.

Many foods contain some but not all of the essential amino acids, and in various amounts. These are incomplete sources of protein, and they include legumes (e.g., beans, peas, lentils), nuts, seeds, whole grains and vegetables.

Complete proteins include eggs, dairy, whole sources of soy (tofu, edamame, tempeh, miso), plant-based proteins and quinoa.

There are ways of eating incomplete proteins together—matching them up so that by eating them together you get all nine of the amino acids. For instance, chickpeas and tahini (sesame seed paste), as used in hummus, make up a complete protein. But including a wide variety of plant foods such as legumes, lentils, nuts, seeds and whole grains in your diet on a daily basis should allow for you to get the complete protein you need. Casting the net of foods you eat as wide as possible is my approach, so just as I eat a rainbow of fruit and veg, I also aim for a full spectrum of different grains, flours, nuts and seeds.

You can get most of the nutrients you need from eating a varied and balanced vegan diet.

How not to waste food (& money)

Along with eating mostly plants, reducing the amount of food we waste is one of the most impactful things we can do to reduce our food footprint, and will also save us money. At home, we try to run a tight ship, but even with the best intentions, a little food that could have been eaten makes it into the food waste bin.

The facts on food waste make quite sobering reading. In the U.S., according to a study in *The American Journal of Agricultural Economics*, the average household wasted 31.9% of its food. That's a huge amount of food, money and wasted resources, especially when far too many people are still going hungry. Wasting our food is also a moral issue. If global food waste (that's household, farm and retail) were a country, it would be the third biggest emitter of greenhouse gases (after the U.S. and China).

The food we waste is not just the food we throw into the bin. It's also the farmer's effort growing it, the energy and water that it takes to grow, the resources used to transport and store it and the money you spent buying it. There is also the impact on our soil health to consider. Some farmers think we have very few harvests left (see page 216 for more on this), and we don't want to waste harvests by growing food that won't get eaten.

I find the more I engage with how food is grown and who grows it, the less likely I am to waste it. If I know where my food comes from, it's no longer, for example, just an apple; it's a story, it's grown by a human, there is an emotional connection, which means I respect it more and am less likely to waste it. As with many things in the confusing world of sustainability, there seems to be a holistic cycle—the more you engage with the food you eat, the less you will waste, the less negative an impact you will have on the planet and the healthier you will be.

It's encouraging to see that media coverage and activism on industrial and domestic waste has seen reduction and redistribution. Supermarkets have made steps to remove confusing best-before dates, especially on fruit and veg, though there is still a lot of work to be done. And a number of supermarkets have embraced "ugly" or "misfit" veg, previously a huge cause of rejected food. Chefs have been using some out-of-date food, especially dairy and veg, to make it seem less scary.

I have tried to shift how I think about food waste and to view some of the things I usually throw away as ingredients. I freeze veg peelings as I go (to make stock), use up soured dairy (which adds welcome acidity and is actually better in some recipes), roast and salt pumpkin seeds for a snack and use aquafaba (chickpea water) in cakes and vegan mayo.

Storing food to reduce waste

Herbs

I store herbs in glasses filled with a little cold water, as you would flowers, and keep them in the milk/bottle compartment in my fridge. This means I am met with an amazing smell every time I open it, it reminds me to use them and they last longer. You can also chop and freeze herbs in ice-cube trays or reusable bags.

Things you might store in the cupboard that are more suited to the fridge:
My rule of thumb for storing things in the fridge is, unless you're going to use up the following in 6–8 weeks, keep them cold. I keep things in glass jars so I can easily see what's in them.
— Olive oil (or any other oils that are liquid at room temperature); I keep these in the fridge only if I have space
— Nuts, seeds and their flours/butters
— Whole-grain flours
— Maple syrup
— Condiments like harissa, miso, mustard, preserved lemons, pickled chilis, etc. These will often keep way past their use-by dates in the fridge.
Equally, some foods often stored in the fridge last longer in a cool, dark cupboard, such as onions, garlic, bananas, potatoes and basil.

Best-before dates

Sell-by, best-before and use-by dates are confusing and sometimes (let's face it) unnecessary. What do these terms mean?

The **use-by date** is the date after which food is no longer deemed safe to eat by the manufacturer. This is important to remember, as some foods can't be eaten after this date, unless they are frozen beforehand.

The **best-before date** has more to do with quality, and it's the date the manufacturer puts on its product to ensure that you eat it when it's in its optimum condition.

The **sell-by date** is the date by which the shop needs to sell the product. They are for the shop and you can ignore them; they are generally shorter than best-before dates and create a lot of in-store waste.

The Food Standards Authority (FSA) has recommended that sell-by dates should be scrapped and that use-by dates should be extended or kept only on products that really need them—i.e., ignoring them could be dangerous. Until this happens, we need to employ a commonsense approach. With high-risk foods such as dairy or cooked rice, be cautious; we don't want food wasted, but it's not worth risking illness. Check food by looking it over well and smelling it. If a food has small amounts of harmless white/light gray mold, you can usually cut or scrape those bits off and the rest of the item will be fine to eat. Colored mold is NOT okay, and any food with colored mold should be thrown away immediately.

Use technology

olioex.com connects neighbors and local retailers so surplus food can be shared; **rescuingleftovercuisine.org** lets restaurants sell uneaten meals at reduced rates; and **sharewaste.com** helps us recycle kitchen scraps by finding neighbors with a compost bin (or chickens).

Most food banks are desperate for donations too. Check their lists and see if any of your excess food can be donated.

Compost

This one will be obvious to most of you, but composting any food waste that you really can't eat is getting easier. A lot of councils in the UK collect it.

The most wasted foods

These are some of the most wasted foods in the UK, based on information from the WRAP household food and drink waste report. Meat and fish do feature too, but I'm not tackling those in this book; suffice to say, if you eat meat and fish, it's imperative you do not waste it.

Bread (and cakes and pastries)

The best-quality bread is made at a bakery with few ingredients and no preservatives. Bread should last 5 to 7 days, so if you are buying sliced white that lasts a month, think about what's keeping it fresh for so long. Storing your bread in a wooden bread box and/or in a sealed cotton or paper bag will give it the longest life.

Freeze
The simplest and most obvious way to extend the life of your bread. Slice or tear into pieces or blitz into breadcrumbs and store in reuseable bags until needed. This goes for cakes/muffins/pastries too.

Add to soup
Tear stale bread into soup 5 minutes before serving in the style of the Tuscan soup ribollita, adding olive oil to finish. The bread gives a brilliant creaminess. Sounds weird but it's genius: trust me.

Make croutons
These elevate soup or salad (see panzanella opposite). Cut the bread up into cubes or small pieces, toss in a generous amount of olive oil, salt and pepper, then roast in a hot oven at 350°F/180°C for 5-10 minutes until golden and crisp on the outside but still chewy on the inside. Leftover croutons can be kept for up to 5 days in an airtight container.

Make panzanella
A bread salad, traditionally made with tomatoes and olive oil—the bread mops up all the juices. Mix well-salted, chopped fresh tomatoes with a little red wine vinegar, add torn stale bread, then lots of olive oil and basil. A winter version can be made with roasted roots in place of the tomatoes.

French toast
Mix some milk of your choice (with an egg if you like), some spices (either sweet ones like cinnamon/vanilla or savory like cumin/smoked paprika) and salt and pepper. Dip stale bread slices into the mixture, leave for a minute each side to soak up the liquid, then fry in a little oil or butter until golden on both sides. Serve with fruit and maple syrup (sweet), or some wilted spinach and chopped tomatoes (savory).

Breadcrumb toppings
Basically everything is better with a crispy breadcrumb topping: cauliflower gratin, roasted veg, pasta bakes, salads, soups, even some cakes. If the dish is going to be baked, toss your breadcrumbs with salt, pepper, olive oil, herbs and citrus zest, if you like, and scatter over whatever you are baking. If not, make a topping: fry the breadcrumbs in olive oil, then season as above. For a sweet breadcrumb topping, fry in a flavorless oil, then add a splash of honey/maple syrup and a pinch of a spice (like cinnamon) to sweeten.

Refresh

Heat will freshen up your bread, cakes and pastries. Try running a stale loaf or baguette under the tap for a second, then warming it in the oven—works like magic. Toast leftover stale cake or pastries in a pan to refresh them.

Potatoes

Can you eat green potatoes? The chlorophyll that initially turns potatoes green is harmless, but older green potatoes are more likely to contain the potentially harmful toxin solanine. To avoid potatoes turning green, store them in a dark place, in a paper or cloth bag (plastic packaging will make them sweat and deteriorate faster). If they do go green, you can cut away any smaller green patches and safely eat the rest. If the whole potato is green and/or bitter, then it's ready for the compost. If your potato is sprouting, that's not a problem: just cut the sprouts off and use the potato. I do think dirt-covered potatoes last longer; the dirt hides them from the light and therefore stops them from going green. That's not a scientific fact, just my opinion.

Fry-up

There is rarely a leftover cooked potato in our house, but when there is I fry them in oil or butter with any other leftover vegetables we have for what my dad calls "fry-up," also known as bubble and squeak, the best Sunday-night dinner. Egg optional.

Rösti

Grating potatoes past their best gives them new life. For my rösti, I blanch potatoes whole for about 4-8 minutes, until just beginning to soften. I then cool, peel and coarsely grate them, press them into patties or a large pancake and fry in oil or butter until golden.

Potato cakes

Roughly mash or crumble potatoes and mix with a couple of chopped scallions or fried red onion. Add any spices you fancy: cumin, cilantro, mustard seeds are all favorites. Season and add a teaspoon of flour. Shape into cakes, then dust in flour and fry in olive oil until golden on both sides. Be careful when flipping; they can be delicate but will firm up as they cool.

Get-ahead roasted potatoes

If you have a waning bag of potatoes, try this: the process actually seems to make them extra-crunchy. Chop into large pieces, parboil them, shake to rough up the edges a little, then arrange on a sheet tray, cool and freeze until solid. Once they are solid, tip them into a bag and store in the freezer. You can then roast them from frozen in hot oil; they should take about an hour.

Mash for the freezer

A stash of mash (sorry) is highly useful. Make it your usual way, but be generous with the butter/oil you add, as it will improve the consistency when you freeze it. Thaw before reheating in a pan or baking in the oven (which gives a very delicious crispy top).

Milk

As with all shopping, buy the amount you need. Milk, like potatoes, is sold in large (I'd argue too large) quantities. Try a milkman if there is one in your area; buying smaller amounts more regularly will mean less waste. Massively obvious, I know. Most dairy milk is sold by the pint, but plant milks are generally sold in 4¼-cup/1-liter cartons. Making your own small-batch plant milk is the obvious solution here, but if I'm honest I rarely find the time to do that.

Almost any milk can be used here: cow's, oat, almond, hemp, etc. In my house, we don't drink cow's milk. Just make sure the alternative is not the sweetened stuff.

Freeze

Freeze wasted milk (if it's in a plastic container) before it hits its best-before date. I largely ignore this date with milk, as you can smell/taste if it's gone bad, but it's a good marker of when to freeze. If you make smoothies, you can freeze it in ice-cube trays and add them to the smoothie straight from the freezer.

Scones

Scones are better with slightly soured milk; it helps them rise. Make a batch—they are quicker than you think. I'll leave you to use your mum's/gran's/uncle Dave's recipe.

Soup

Putting milk in soup can add richness and leaves you feeling more sated. Use your common sense, though; stick to things which go well with milk like leeks, root veg, squash and European flavors. If it would taste good with cheese, then you are onto something.

Paneer

Paneer is a type of fresh cheese common throughout the Indian subcontinent. Making paneer is a great way to use up too much milk, though it works only with full-fat cow's milk.

Yogurt

Again, this works best with full-fat cow's milk. Making milk kefir is another great use for leftover milk; you will need kefir grains, and there is a lot of information online on how to make it.

White sauce

I have fallen back in love with béchamel. It's a friendly blanket to almost all veg. Cauliflower, leeks, potatoes and squash all do well under this cheesy sauce. Melt about a tablespoon of butter or non-dairy butter in a small saucepan, add a heaped tablespoon of all-purpose flour and cook, stirring all the time, for a couple of minutes so the flour loses its rawness. Slowly add milk or plant milk, mixing in each addition until it thickens.

Sweet things

From custard to pannacotta, rice pudding and ice cream, there are a million sweet recipes which use up a lot of milk.

Bagged and boxed salad greens

Bagged and boxed lettuces are two of the most annoying things when it comes to waste. First, they are expensive. Second, it's hard to store bagged salad without damaging it. And third, they can go from edible to revolting in the blink of an eye. I tend not to buy either unless I know I can use it almost straightaway. I go for sturdier whole lettuces like Little Gem, romaine and radicchio; this tends to work out cheaper too.

If you do buy bagged salad, store it at the top of a salad drawer or in the fridge with nothing on top and eat it quickly once open. Or store as follows: Line a container with a piece of paper towel and place the leaves inside, being careful not to pack them too tightly to avoid bruising. Cover with another sheet, pop the lid on and store in the fridge. The paper and cloth help absorb extra moisture, keeping your greens fresher for longer.

If your salad does wilt, don't throw it away. You can restore a droopy leaf to its original perkiness simply by refreshing it. First, remove any brown or mushy leaves, then refresh the rest in a bowl of cold iced water for 5-20 minutes with a few slices of lemon and a sprinkle of salt. Then lift the leaves out of the water and allow them to drain or spin in a salad spinner before serving or storing as above. If it's past its best but still okay to eat, you can use it as follows.

Freeze

You can freeze bags of salad and use them directly from the freezer for adding to soups or stir-frying. Obviously, they are not good for eating raw once frozen.

Pesto

Rocket/watercress/peppery leaves can be used like basil to make pesto. Once made, it can be kept under oil in the fridge for at least a week, prolonging its life even further.

Soup

All green lettuces/watercress/arugula can be added to soup (blended or chunky); you can even make them the hero of the dish. Transform watercress/arugula by blending with a little cooked potato, hot water and a dash of cream to make a simple watercress soup. Or make a refreshing chilled soup with delicate leaves, like romaine blended with cucumber, herbs, avocado, radishes and yogurt, and topped with olive oil.

Stir-fried

Asian salad leaves such as mizuna and frilly mustard are common in good salad bags and taste incredible: potent, citrusy and full of flavor. These leaves are delicious added to a stir-fry or chopped and sprinkled over the top. I often wilt past-its-best arugula in a little olive oil and serve next to scrambled eggs.

Smoothie

Add leaves to a green smoothie with ingredients like apple, ginger and lemon.

Green pancakes

See the recipe on page 85 and use spinach/green salad leaves instead.

Chopped salad

Chop them with other crunchy veg, like carrot, cucumber and tomato, and finish with a simple lemon and oil dressing.

Fresh veg

Refreshing vegetables. As vegetables get older they lose their water content, which can make them limp. So try refreshing your veg in cold iced water: the vegetables will take on the water and become crunchy and "fresh" again. Store your veg in a bowl of cold iced water and, if you have space, put this in the fridge for extra crispness. If not, out of the fridge works fine too. This works for all salad leaves, leafy greens, carrots, radishes, lettuce, sugar snap peas, beans, snow peas, cabbages and parsnips. This is by no means an exhaustive list, just what I have tried.

There are endless ways to use up your waning fresh veg. I have included a few choose-your-own-adventure recipes/flavor maps at the back of the book to guide you. Put simply though, my favorite ways are:

Soups see pages 316-317
Frittatas see pages 314-315
Dressings see page 313

Cheese

The carbon footprint of cheese is high (only beef and lamb are greater), so if you do buy it, please, please use it.

Storing
Always double-wrap your cheese in waxed paper, parchment or a beeswax wrap and then put it in a glass or plastic container lined with a damp paper towel. Cover and put it in the top of the fridge, where the temperature is the most constant. It'll keep very happily for as long as it takes to eat it.

Cheese trick
I learned this tip from cheese queen Patricia Michelson of La Fromagerie. It's a good trick. Put two sugar cubes in the plastic box (see above) with the cheese, then seal and refrigerate. The sugar helps to regulate the atmosphere inside the box, keeping the cheese fresher. Over time, the sugar will start to melt, though hopefully you'll have used the cheese before then. If not, clean the box, replace the cloth and put the cheese back in with new sugar cubes.

Best-before dates
I largely ignore the best-before dates on cheese. I use my nose, taste buds and instinct to tell if it's okay. If mold forms it can be cut off and if the rest of the cheese still looks and tastes good, it's okay to eat. Cheese rarely goes off. If the flavor gets too intense for you as the cheese ages (blues and soft cheeses can), then use it to cook with or mix with other milder cheeses to temper it.

Parmesan rind
(I use a vegetarian Parmesan.) Your old Parmesan rind might look unpromising, but it's the most concentrated hit of flavor, a secret weapon. Added to vegetable soups (minestrone or ribollita) or stews, it lends a deep umami, lip-smacking, indefinable extra level of savoriness.

Grate and freeze
Very boring but actually very useful to remember, grated or crumbled cheese freezes well and is ready to use immediately. Freeze in small portions so you can use what you need.

There are endless cheese recipes I could suggest here, from cheese on toast to cauliflower gratin or macaroni and cheese. A handful of cheese on top of any bake, tray of roasted veg, gratin, soup or stew will improve it tenfold. I'll leave it in your hands.

Fruit

Grapes
Freeze unused grapes because kids love them frozen, though babies/toddlers should not have them unless they are cut in half—they are a choking hazard. They are also delicious with coffee and dark chocolate after dinner for grown-ups. If anyone is sick, they're also great to cool down and hydrate.

Apples and pears
Grate soft ones into porridge or yogurt, or into cake or flapjack mixtures before baking. Once stewed, apples will last longer in the fridge and can be eaten for breakfast with yogurt, frozen or used in a crumble. To stew, peel (unless you like the peel) and chop your apples, put them in a pan with a splash of maple syrup and a pinch of spice (I use cinnamon and ground cardamom), add a little water and cook until soft.

Bananas

Peel, chop and freeze bananas that are getting older than you like (I am not a fan of black bananas), then store in the freezer to use for smoothies, sweetening cakes or banana bread, which is the spiritual home of all overripe bananas.

Oranges and clementines

Try using these in savory cooking as you might a lemon. Put orange juice in a salad dressing, or cut in half and roast them with vegetables, then squeeze the roasted oranges over the veg for incredible flavor.

Lemons and limes

Lemons and limes are in almost every recipe I make, so I end up with a lot of zested lemons and halves of lime. I slice odds and ends and add to hot water with a sliver of ginger in the morning, and if I see them looking like they really need using up, I slice and freeze them for gin and tonics.

Berries

Buy them when they are cheap and in season and freeze. Then use them for puddings and smoothies, or mash into porridge. My son loves to eat them frozen, too.

Stone fruit

Apricots, peaches, nectarines and plums all make a super-easy and quick purée that will keep for 10 days in the fridge or even longer in the freezer. Roughly chop, add to a pan with a little water and enough sugar to sweeten, then cook for 5-10 minutes, until soft and spoonable. Eat on toast or with yogurt and granola, or use to sandwich a cake.

Pineapple

My favorite way to eat pineapple is to cut it into wedges, then make a mint and lime sugar by pounding lime zest, chopped mint and a little sugar in a pestle and mortar until it smells like a mojito. Scatter the mixture over the pineapple and serve. If you want to be fancy, add a couple of pink peppercorns before bashing.

Leftovers

Not officially part of the top ten, but I know for many people leftover cooked food is a big part of their food waste. These are harder to quantify and predict, but your freezer is your friend here. Unless you know you will be eating the leftovers for lunch or dinner within two days, then freeze them; think of it as a waste insurance policy. Leftover meals can legitimately be the best meals. Here are a few ideas for how to improve/stretch out the common ones.

Cooked veg

Almost any veg (as long as it's not too wildly flavored) can be made into a frittata or omelet. They are the savior of leftovers. See pages 314-315 for a frittata recipe and some ideas.

Soup/Stew

To stretch it further, add a can of drained, cooked pulses, or a couple of handfuls of greens or croutons (see pages 316–317).

Cooked rice

Fried rice is one of our go-to dinners. In fact, I usually cook double the rice so we can have fried rice the night after, say, with a curry. It's a great vehicle for leftover veg too. Fry ginger and garlic until beginning to brown, turn the heat up, add a few chopped scallions or thinly sliced red onion and any roughly chopped slow-to-cook veg and cook for a couple of minutes. Then add

the rice and any quicker cooking veg and stir until the rice is piping hot. Beat 2 eggs in a cup with a splash of soy sauce, clear space in the pan for them, then add and cook until set before stirring into the rice. Serve with more soy sauce. Be careful when reheating rice: it must be piping hot so it's safe to eat. Cooked and cooled rice can be safely frozen. Freeze it as soon as possible after cooking and make sure it is reheated thoroughly at a high temperature before you eat it.

Cooked noodles
Leftover noodles mean quick miso soup dinner to me. Chop all the delicate veg you have—greens, fennel, sugar snap peas, green beans and asparagus all work—then put them in a bowl with some cubed tofu and chopped scallions. Add a small handful of noodles and top with miso soup (mix miso paste with cold water first, then whisk into boiling water to keep the fermented properties of the miso alive).

Cooked pasta
Use pasta instead of potatoes to make a frittata. Plain cooked pasta, or with a simple sauce (tomato is the best), will work.

Eggs

Eggs have a high carbon footprint, so please make sure you use what you buy.

The best egg mayo
Boil all the eggs you need to use for 6 minutes in boiling water, then run under cold water for 2 minutes and peel. Mix a heaped teaspoon of mayo per egg with a few drained capers, a couple of chopped gherkins and a grating of lemon zest as

well as some chopped fresh herbs if you have them. Roughly chop the eggs and mix in.

Baked eggs
Baked eggs can be super flexible. Any leftover sauce can be made into a base for them. Amp up tomato sauce with some olives and capers and then crack in some eggs and finish with feta. You can make a green version too. I even crack eggs into leftover dhal, then bake the lot. Eggs can easily be frozen: whisk the yolks and whites and freeze in 1 or 2 portions if you can.

Fruit juice and smoothies

These are high on the list of wasted goods, along with carbonated soft drinks. They are not something I tend to buy (especially the carbonated soft drinks). I would encourage you to buy cans if you buy soft drinks (cans are infinitely more recyclable than plastic bottles and less likely to be wasted). I freeze fruit juice and smoothies in Popsicle molds for my son, or in ice-cube trays for smoothies. Plain fruit juices like orange or pomegranate can be used in dressings.

Shopping to reduce waste:
What kind of cook are you?

It's been received wisdom for years that a weekly grocery run is the most economical and least wasteful way of shopping. I guess this is a symptom of out-of-town shopping centers and changing lifestyles. But I don't think that's the case for everyone. To reduce your waste I would encourage you to ask yourself the question "What kind of cook am I?" and shop accordingly.

For me, a weekly trip to the grocery store does not work. I am not a planner and I like to decide what to cook on the day I want to eat. Checking exactly what's in my cupboards for that meal, then going out to the shops with my tote and buying specifically for that meal with a few extras to top up the cupboards, breakfast or snacks is the way we waste the least. Granted, I live close to a lot of shops, which I know is not the case for everyone.

When I shop online, I stock up on cans, jars and some (non-refillable) cleaning products and household stuff, then I shop daily for each meal or each couple of meals. It means I am on top of what's in my cupboards and in my fridge and I use what I buy; nothing gets forgotten about. This method may not work for you, though. So I've laid out the kind of cooks I most often come across here.

Having spent a lot of time teaching cooking, in people's homes all over both the UK and the U.S., and observing how different people shop, cook and prep, I think that cooks generally fall into three camps: daily cooks, weekly planners and batch cooks. What kind of cook are you?

DAILY COOKS

Those who decide what
to cook that day

How to waste less
— Do a monthly shop for long-life, store-cupboard goods you know you will use.
— Before you do that monthly shop, do a quick audit (this might be the night before, if you are going to shop on your way home from work) of what's in your cupboards and fridge.
— If your schedule permits, do a daily or every-other-day shop for fresh fruit, veg, dairy, bread, etc.
— Buy loose fruit and veg so you are not left with leftovers from large packages.
— Store any leftovers in the freezer if you will not eat them within 2 days.
— Take a bimonthly look at everything in your cupboard. If things need to be used up, move them to the front of the cupboard, then write a list of those things and stick it on the front of your cupboard so you can keep them in mind when you decide what to cook.
— I find limiting the amount I can buy to one tote bag's worth makes sure I do not keep adding extra things we don't need.

WEEKLY PLANNERS

Those who love to plan or those who are unable to shop frequently

How to waste less
— A weekly grocery run suits planners.
— Before you shop, do a good audit of what's in your cupboards and fridge.
— Write a detailed shopping list based on recipes, with amounts that you can refer back to at the shops to make sure you don't overbuy fresh food.
— Buy loose veg so you are not left with huge leftovers from large bags.
— Avoid being tempted by offers and 2-for-1 deals. If you waste the excess, it's not a good deal; if you know you will use it or can adapt a recipe, then go for it.
— Do not shop when you are hungry.
— If you shop once a week, then it is key to make sure your food is stored carefully—see the suggestions below.
— Make sure you cook the food you buy. If plans change and you don't cook, then double-cook the night after and freeze that meal. Or take into account what food may last until next week and shop accordingly the week after.
— Try to cook the things with a shorter life early in the week and the things that may last longer at the end.
— If you are left with waste, see my suggestions on pages 63–71. Soup is your friend.
— Learn how to make the things that don't last a week or plan to pick those up in the week. If your bread lasts a month, you are buying the wrong bread.

BATCH COOKS

Those who cook a couple of meals to last throughout the week

How to waste less
— Before you shop, do a quick audit of what's in your cupboards and fridge.
— Plan out the number of meals you want to make and be sure you have containers to freeze any excess.
— Write a detailed shopping list and stick to it. How often you write it is up to you. See the notes above and below, depending on whether it's weekly or daily.
— Don't be tempted by offers and other things unless you know exactly how to use them or they can be cooked and stored in the freezer.
— Think about toppings—if you are eating the same things for a few meals, think about varying what you put on top (this can be a good way to use up leftover herbs, breadcrumbs, stray nuts and seeds, etc.).
— If you are unsure if you will eat leftovers, freeze them; don't forget about them in the back of the fridge.

How to save energy (& money)

The energy we use to cook and store our foods at home is not something we often consider when looking at the sustainability of our eating habits. Sure, the growing and transportation of our food has the biggest overall footprint, but the way we cook is something we can each have an impact on, and every bit we can do helps.

The major kitchen food-based activities involve cooling things down (in fridges and freezers) and heating things up (with kettles, ovens and stove tops). The U.S. Department of Energy estimates that cooking accounts for 4.5% of total home energy use, not including energy costs associated with refrigeration, hot water heating, and dish-washing. Added together, as much as 15% of the energy in the average American home is used in the kitchen. So that's a big piece of the pie.

Here are some easy ways I try to save energy in the kitchen.

General
— Most important, make sure you use a green-energy provider. This will mean all your electricity is coming from green sources, not fossil fuels. In the UK, it's easy to switch and there are lots of providers; you may want to try to do the same.
— It's much more energy-efficient, not to mention sociable, to cook for more than one person at a time. Even if it's just me at home, I will cook for 4. Batch cooking is so much more efficient. I always double a soup or stew recipe and keep the remainder in the fridge or freezer for meals later.

— Try to cook in one pot/pan/tray and use one heat source (stove top/oven) when you cook. It's not always possible, but it's a good challenge and it's how I have written most of the recipes in this book.
— Cooking in huge batches by food producers is much more efficient than individual cooking at home. From canned/jarred chickpeas to pre-roasted peppers and ready-made stock, easy, ready-to-use cooking solutions can actually be more energy-efficient, as long as they are packaged in recyclable packaging (cans are highly recyclable).

Stove tops
— Heat water in a kettle, rather than on the stove top (unless you have induction, which boils water very quickly and efficiently). You can transfer it into a pan once it's already boiled. I like this, as it also speeds things up.
— Use only as much water as you need— boiling extra water takes more time and energy and is wasted.
— Pick the right burner and the right pan for the job—a bigger burner will take longer to heat up and a bigger pan will need more water to fill it if you are boiling. Fill your pans—a pan filled only one-fifth of the way is 80% less efficient than a full pan.
— Make sure the pan covers the burner. If there is space around the edge, wasted energy will be escaping.
— Always cover your pans—water will boil faster and you will use 8 times less energy to heat your food.

- Turn off the heat a couple of minutes before your food is fully cooked—particularly if you've got an electric stove top, as they take some time to cool down and will continue to cook. Soups and stews work perfectly like this.
- Steamers are great for cooking several things at once on one heat source.

Ovens

- If you are cooking in your oven, think about what else you could cook while it is turned on. For me, it's a tray of roasted veg for the following day's lunch. Or toasting nuts, seeds or breadcrumbs to top pasta (these will store for up to 2 weeks in a sealed container). Or even making a loaf of bread.
- I have tried to be mindful of when I ask you to preheat the oven in this book, but prep times will differ for everyone so use your common sense. Most modern ovens take 5–10 minutes to preheat, and most recipes ask you to preheat at the start of a recipe, which means the oven is ready and wasting energy long before you need it. This is a new habit for me and I am really surprised how effective it is.
- Think about how you cut your food. Sounds basic, but the smaller you cut it, the quicker it will cook. Of course, sometimes small pieces are not what's needed but it's good to bear in mind.
- Don't open the oven door repeatedly—you'll let out hot air and waste energy. If you can, take a look through the glass door instead.

Fridges and freezers

- Never put hot food directly into the fridge or freezer. It will raise the overall temperature of your fridge and it will have to use more energy to bring the temperature down again. Allow the food to cool on the side before refrigerating it.
- Don't hold the fridge door open for extended periods of time, as it'll have to work harder to lower the temperature afterwards. Keep your fridge at 41 degrees Fahrenheit or less.

Appliances

- Make sure new appliances you buy are energy-efficient—all new appliances have a rating from A+++ to G. The Energy Star website has lots of info on this and can tell you where your appliance sits on the scale.
- If you are considering buying a new stove top, opt for induction as they are more energy-efficient.
- Slow cookers, microwaves and pressure cookers are all super-efficient ways of cooking. I don't own a microwave and would never do proper cooking in one, but if you own one, then it can be an energy-efficient way to heat up food.

Washing up

- Reducing the number of pans you cook in, as I have aimed to do in most of the recipes in this book, will reduce your pile of dishes and will save water, cleaning products and time.
- Using a washing-up bowl in your sink to catch water is a super-easy way to avoid waste.
- Generally, an energy-efficient dishwasher will be more eco-friendly than hand-washing, though there are a number of factors that affect this. If you use a dishwasher, do not rinse with water first (unless you have something particularly stubborn), as then you are using water twice; most modern dishwashers are very efficient at cleaning.

ONE PAN

Carrot & sesame pancakes

SERVES 4

½ a small white cabbage
  (about 12 ounces/350 g)
a small bunch of scallions
1 small carrot, peeled and grated
2 tablespoons toasted
  sesame seeds
a small bunch of cilantro,
  mint or Thai basil, or a
  mixture, roughly chopped
2 tablespoons kimchi, roughly
  chopped (optional)

FOR THE BATTER
2⅓ cups/200 g chickpea flour
1 tablespoon rice flour
  or cornflour
2 teaspoons white miso paste
2 cloves of garlic, crushed or
  finely chopped
a small thumb-sized piece
  of ginger, peeled and
  finely chopped
1 tablespoon tamari or soy sauce
coconut or vegetable oil, for
  frying

FOR THE DIPPING SAUCE
2 tablespoons tamari or soy sauce
the zest and juice of 1 lime,
  unwaxed or organic
1 tablespoon chili oil (depending
  on the heat of your chili oil)

TO SERVE
tōgarashi seasoning

There used to be a Korean vendor at the market near my house who made these pancakes every Sunday. The vendor disappeared or moved to another market, so I resolved to make them myself. These vegetable-packed pancakes are made with rice and chickpea flour, miso and ginger and have a killer dipping sauce. I tend to make them as larger pancakes so everyone gets one each, but you could make them smaller too if you prefer.

———

Using a food processor fitted with a slicer attachment, a mandoline or just your knife, shred your cabbage and scallions. Tip the lot into a large mixing bowl with the grated carrot and the toasted sesame seeds, most of the chopped herbs (reserving a few for later) and the chopped kimchi, if using.

Put all the batter ingredients, except the oil, in a food processor with 1¼ cups/300ml of cold water, with the blade attachment fitted, and pulse until the batter is combined, or beat together in a mixing bowl. Pour over the top of the vegetables and mix well. Let your batter rest for 30 minutes, if you can, but if you haven't got time, don't worry.

Mix the dipping sauce ingredients together with 1 tablespoon of cold water in a small bowl.

Put a small, heavy-bottomed frying pan (about 8 inches/20 cm) over a medium-high heat, add a little coconut or vegetable oil to the pan, and a ladleful of batter. This recipe makes 6–8 pancakes, and each should be about ¼ inch thick. Use the back of a spoon to spread it out to the edges if needed. Cook each pancake for 2–3 minutes—until golden underneath and there are bubbles on the top—then flip. The pancakes should be golden brown and the vegetables should be just cooked but still keep some bite.

Serve topped with a little tōgarashi seasoning and the remaining herbs and dipping sauce on the side.

Fava bean &
green herb shakshuka

SERVES 4–6

3 pounds/1.5 kg fava beans in
    their pods, or 14 ounces/400 g
    podded beans (fresh or frozen)
olive oil
a bunch of scallions, sliced
2 cloves of garlic, peeled and
    finely chopped
1 tablespoon sweet smoked
    paprika
1 tablespoon cumin seeds
1 teaspoon coriander seeds
a good pinch of dried chili flakes
2 x 14.5-ounce/400 g cans diced
    tomatoes
a bunch of cilantro,
    roughly chopped
a small bunch of dill,
    roughly chopped
7 ounces/200 g firm tofu or
    4-6 organic eggs

TO SERVE
1 lemon, unwaxed or organic
⅔ cup/150 ml plain yogurt of
    your choice
4-6 flatbreads

I love ful medames, an Arabic stew made from dried fava beans. This is a fresher version that uses fresh or frozen fava beans. Add a few crushed boiled new potatoes if you want it to be really substantial. This can be made with eggs or tofu for vegans. If you are using eggs, the number you need depends on how many you're feeding. Peas also work well here in place of the fava beans.

———

If you have the patience, cover the podded fava beans in boiling water, drain, and when cool enough to handle, pop the little green fava beans out of their casings. If not, it will still taste great.

Add a good glug of olive oil to a deep, 10-inch/25 cm ovenproof frying pan. Add the scallions, garlic and a good pinch of salt and sauté for 5 minutes, until soft and sweet. Add the spices and chili flakes, cook for another couple of minutes, then stir in the tomatoes. Cook for 10 minutes until the tomatoes are sweet and the sauce is a thick, deep red.

Heat the oven to 400°F/200°C. Add half the cilantro, half the dill and most of the fava beans. Stir and cook for another couple of minutes.

Now either crumble over the tofu and season well with salt and pepper or make four to six little wells in the sauce and break in the eggs. Put the pan in the oven and bake for 10 minutes for runny yolks and a little longer for set yolks or if using tofu.

Grate the zest of the lemon and reserve for later. Squeeze half the lemon juice into the yogurt, season and mix well.

Take the pan out of the oven using an oven mitt, sprinkle with the rest of the fava beans, herbs and the zest of the lemon, then serve in the middle of the table with the yogurt and flatbreads.

Pan-roasted cauliflower with saffron butter

Cooking vegetables like this (pan roasting) happens a lot in restaurant kitchens, but it's a good thing to do at home too. You get the vegetables going in the pan, building up a bit of color and texture, then blast them in the oven to cook through; they get some direct heat and char from the stove top, then some more mellow even heat from the oven. I love adding vinegar when I am cooking vegetables, and it's balanced here by the sweetness of the cauliflower, saffron and pine nuts. This recipe is inspired by the brilliant cook Lola DeMille.

———

Preheat the oven to 425°F/220°C. Mix the mint and/or parsley and yogurt in a small bowl. Season with salt and pepper, stir in a splash of olive oil, then set aside.

Heat a large ovenproof frying pan over a medium heat, add a good glug of olive oil, then add the cauliflower in a single layer (you may need to cook it in a few batches). Once all your cauliflower is browned on both sides (this will take about 10 minutes), put the lot back into the pan and bake in the oven for about 10 minutes, until the stalks are soft and the florets crisp.

Remove the pan from the oven using an oven mitt, then put it back on the stove top over a medium heat, add the vinegar and saffron or turmeric, then reduce the vinegar for about 2 minutes. Take off the heat, add the butter, toss the cauliflower in it to create a thick and glossy sauce, then stir through most of the parsley and/or cilantro.

Spoon the yogurt into a shallow serving bowl and use the back of a spoon to swirl it over the bottom, then tumble the buttery cauliflower in. Finish with the last bit of parsley, the pine nuts and some sumac, and serve with flatbreads.

SERVES 4

FOR THE YOGURT
a small bunch of mint and/or
    parsley, finely chopped
6 tablespoons thick Greek yogurt
    or yogurt of your choice
a drizzle of good olive oil

FOR THE CAULIFLOWER
olive oil
1 large cauliflower (about
    2 pounds/800 g), florets
    separated and stalks finely
    sliced
¼ cup/60 ml white wine vinegar
a good pinch of saffron
    strands (or ½ teaspoon
    ground turmeric)
3-4 tablespoons/50 g butter or
    vegan butter, cubed
a small bunch of parsley and/or
    cilantro, roughly chopped

TO SERVE
1 cup/150 g pine nuts, toasted
a good pinch of sumac or
    Aleppo chili
4 flatbreads

Green chickpea pancakes

I love these pancakes. I eat them straight out of the pan like traditional pancakes, topped with a fried egg, some flash-fried vegetables and cheese. Or I keep them in the fridge, then heat them up gently in a pan to use like wraps or instead of chapatis for dipping into curries. I've included some topping ideas, and variations on the spinach, below.

—

Put all the ingredients, except the oil, into a blender and season well with salt and pepper. Blend on high until the mixture is a thin, smooth pancake batter. You can add a splash more milk if your batter feels too thick.

Heat 1 teaspoon of oil in a roughly 10-inch/24 cm nonstick frying pan over a medium heat. Add a small ladle of the batter to the pan. Working quickly, swirl the pan around so the batter covers the base, and cook for a couple of minutes, then flip over and cook on the other side for another 30 seconds.

Repeat for the rest of the batter, adding a little more of the oil each time. Stack on a plate with a layer of parchment paper in between each one and keep warm in a low oven. Top with your favorite sweet or savory combinations; there are lots of suggestions below.

These pancakes can be made ahead of time and stored covered in the fridge for up to 4 days. They can also be frozen, separated by sheets of parchment paper, for up to 2 months; allow to defrost for 30 minutes at room temperature before using.

Pancake-topping ideas

— Chopped sun-dried tomatoes, toasted pine nuts, basil, Parmesan
— Peas, mint, lemon, date salad and ricotta or vegan-style ricotta
— Roasted tomatoes, whipped ricotta, wilted spinach, toasted almonds
— Grated carrots sautéed with cumin seeds, chopped fresh cilantro, yogurt, mango chutney
— Roasted squash, dukkah spice, feta
— Thick Greek yogurt or plant yogurt, chopped pistachios, toasted sesame seeds, fennel seeds, honey

SERVES 4 (MAKES 8 PANCAKES)

2¼ cups/250 g chickpea flour
1½ cups/350 ml oat milk
½ cup/50 g spinach, washed
a small bunch of parsley
the zest of 1 lemon, unwaxed or
    organic
coconut oil or olive oil for frying

SWAP THE SPINACH FOR
1 medium beet, peeled
    and grated (add 1 teaspoon
    fennel seeds)
1 medium carrot, grated
    (add 1 teaspoon cumin or
    caraway seeds)

Asparagus & greens frittata

SERVES 4

8 organic eggs or
   2 cups/200 g chickpea flour
2–4 tablespoons olive oil
2 cloves of garlic, peeled and
   finely chopped
a small bunch of scallions,
   thinly sliced
2 x 9-ounce/250 g bunches of
   asparagus, woody bottoms
   snapped off and discarded,
   spears sliced into ¾-inch/2 cm
   pieces
3 big handfuls of greens—
   spinach, sorrel, watercress,
   ramps, nettles
   (about 5–6 ounces/150 g)
the zest of 1 lemon, unwaxed or
   organic
½ cup/100 g ricotta or vegan
   ricotta (I like the Tofutti brand)
1 tablespoon nigella seeds

FOR THE SALSA
a small bunch of parsley
1 red chili
juice of ½ the lemon (from above)
1 teaspoon harissa
½ teaspoon maple syrup
   or honey
1 tablespoon olive oil

Frittatas are one of the dishes that often get thrown together with leftovers in my house. This one, though, was more deliberate, and worthy of a meal and a shopping trip in itself. I love frittatas, but I don't always want to eat eggs, so I have come up with a vegan version using chickpea (gram) flour. I have kept the egg option in too, for those who prefer it. Use any springtime greens; this could be spinach or kale or even ramps or nettles if you can pick or buy some near you. If you are using ramp leaves, just don't add the garlic cloves. When asparagus is out of season I make this with blanched broccoli or cauliflower in its place.

———

If you are using eggs, turn the broiler on high. If you are using chickpea flour, heat the oven to 400°F/200°C. You will need a 10-inch/25 cm ovenproof frying pan.

For the vegan (chickpea flour) version, pour 1¾ cups/400 ml of warm water into a large mixing bowl. Sift the chickpea flour into the bowl too, whisking as you go to prevent any lumps forming. Add half a teaspoon of salt to the bowl and season with black pepper. Whisk again to combine, then cover the bowl and set aside for 1 hour.

For both versions—prepare the veg. Heat 2 tablespoons of oil in the pan. When warm, add the garlic and all but a small handful of the scallions, and let them sizzle and soften. After 2–3 minutes, add the asparagus spears and cook for a further 3–4 minutes, until they have lost their rawness but are still crisp.

Add the greens (use tongs to protect your fingers if you are using nettles), allow everything to wilt for 2 minutes or so, season well, add the lemon zest and keep on a low heat.

If you are using eggs, beat the eggs in a bowl and season well. Pour the eggs into the pan on top of the greens. Let the eggs cook for a minute, to set a little, then use a rubber spatula to pull them away from the sides of the pan, allowing the raw egg to run into the gaps. Let that set for 10 seconds or so, then repeat a few times. You are creating little layers of egg, which will make a lighter frittata. Once the eggs are mostly set but still a bit runny on top, scatter on the ricotta, then put the frittata under the broiler to brown. This should take between 5 and 10 minutes, depending on the heat and proximity to the pan of your broiler. →

← If you are using chickpea flour, pour the remaining 2 tablespoons of oil into the batter and whisk to combine. Pour this batter over the asparagus and greens, then scatter over the ricotta and bake in the preheated oven for 25 minutes.

While this is cooking, make your salsa. Roughly chop the parsley with the rest of the scallions and the chili (discard the seeds if you prefer things milder), then transfer to a bowl and add the lemon juice, harissa, maple syrup or honey and the tablespoon of olive oil. Taste and adjust, adding salt, more lemon or chili as needed.

Use an oven mitt to remove the pan from the oven, then loosen the frittata by running a spatula around the edges. Turn out the frittata by flipping the pan over onto a large plate. Then turn the frittata back over onto another plate so the pretty brown top is showing and sprinkle with the nigella seeds. Cut it into slices and eat warm or cold, with the salsa and some lemon-dressed salad leaves.

Seasonal variations

— **Summer**—peas
— **Autumn**—leftover roasted root vegetables
— **Winter**—purple-sprouting broccoli and winter greens

Crispy tofu & broccoli pad Thai

SERVES 4

FOR THE TOFU AND BROCCOLI

9 ounces/250 g flat wide rice
noodles

9 ounces/250 g block of firm tofu

9 ounces/250 g purple-sprouting
broccoli

neutral oil for frying (I like
odorless coconut oil or another
neutral-flavored oil
for cooking)

2 tablespoons soy or
tamari sauce

3 cloves of garlic, peeled and
finely chopped

a ¾-inch/2 cm piece of ginger,
peeled and grated

6 scallions, thinly sliced

2 organic eggs (optional)

4 ounces/115 g bean sprouts

FOR THE SAUCE

4 tablespoons tamarind paste

1 tablespoon vegetarian
fish sauce

2 tablespoons rice vinegar

3 tablespoons maple syrup

4 tablespoons light soy sauce

TO SERVE

⅔ cup/100 g roasted unsalted
peanuts, roughly chopped

2 red chilies, finely chopped

1 small handful of Thai basil
leaves, shredded

1 small handful of mint leaves,
shredded

a handful of crispy shallots
(see page 200)

2 limes, unwaxed or organic

I am a sucker for a pad Thai. I know it's predictable, but I can't seem to bypass it on a menu. This version brings together all the things I love about it: crispy tofu, lots of greens, a tamarind-heavy sauce, roasted peanuts and crispy onions, as in my mind, a pad Thai is pointless without them.

———

Soak the rice noodles in cold water for at least 10 minutes, until softened. Lay the tofu between 2 sheets of paper towel on a plate or clean surface. Place a small plate over the top and a jar or weight on the plate to press down. Leave the tofu like this to dry out for half an hour.

Mix all the sauce ingredients in a small bowl with 4 tablespoons of cold water. Set aside. Cut the broccoli into florets and thinly slice the stalks, keeping them separate.

Slice the tofu into ⅜-inch/1 cm-thick pieces about half the length of your little finger. In a large nonstick frying pan or wok, heat 3 tablespoons of oil over a medium-high heat, then fry the pieces of tofu for 6–8 minutes, turning them every minute, until golden all over. Add the soy sauce and stir for another 30 seconds (be careful here, as the sauce may spit). Lift the tofu out of the pan with a slotted spoon onto a plate. Keep warm in a low oven.

When cool enough, wipe the pan out with paper towel and add a couple more tablespoons of oil. Heat over a medium heat. Add the garlic and ginger to the pan and cook for 2 minutes. Then add the broccoli stalks, drained noodles and 6 tablespoons of water and cook for 3–4 minutes, until the broccoli stems are tender and the noodles are beginning to cook and crisp up. Add the broccoli florets, sauce and most of the scallions along with 2 more tablespoons of water. Stir and cook for another 3–4 minutes until the noodles are soft enough to eat.

If you are using eggs, push the noodles to the side of the wok and add a little more oil, then the eggs. Pierce the yolks and, when starting to set on the bottom, scramble, then mix into the noodles.

Take the pan off the heat and fold through the bean sprouts, then spoon the noodles among four warm plates. Sprinkle over the peanuts and the rest of the scallions. Scatter over the chilies, herbs and crispy shallots. Squeeze over the juice of a lime, and serve immediately, with wedges of the other lime.

Zucchini & Halloumi fritters with chili & mint jam

MAKES 16 (SERVES 4)

FOR THE CHILI JAM
6 red chilies, thinly sliced
6 tablespoons red wine vinegar
5 tablespoons superfine sugar
a small bunch of mint, leaves
   picked and finely chopped

FOR THE FRITTERS
¾ cup/100 g rice flour
1 cup/100 g all-purpose or white
   spelt flour
1 teaspoon baking powder
a pinch of dried oregano
the zest and juice of
   a lemon, unwaxed or organic
3 medium zucchini
   (about 14 ounces/400 g)
7-ounce/200 g block of Halloumi
   or vegan Halloumi-style
   cheese (sometimes called
   "Mediterranean-style")
olive oil, for frying

TO SERVE
plain natural or vegan yogurt
lemon-dressed leaves or
   tomatoes

I use both rice flour and all-purpose flour here, which I think together are key to the crispness of these fritters. If you don't have two flours, then all-purpose, spelt or rice by themselves would work fine. If you are vegan, you can use a vegan Mediterranean-style cheese (vegan Halloumi) or 2 more zucchini instead.

———

Put all the chili jam ingredients into a nonstick frying pan (you will use this for your fritters too) and bring to a simmer for 6–8 minutes, until the liquid has thickened and the chilies are soft and sticky. The chili jam should be thin, like a dipping sauce, rather than a thick jam. You may need to add a little water here, and warm it through again if you reduce it too much.

While the jam is cooking, mix the flours, baking powder, oregano, and lemon zest and juice in a large bowl. Grate in the zucchini and Halloumi and mix well. Season well with black pepper. You might need to add a little water here to make the batter spoonable—this will depend on how much moisture your zucchini have released.

Once the jam is ready, spoon it into a bowl and rinse out your frying pan. Place over a medium heat and add a generous drizzle of olive oil. Next add the batter—about 2 tablespoons for each fritter—and fry for a couple of minutes, until the edges are well set, then flip and cook for another couple of minutes. Keep going until all your batter is used up— keep the cooked fritters warm in a low oven.

Serve 3 or 4 fritters per person with a spoonful of the chili jam, yogurt and some lemon-dressed leaves or tomatoes, depending on the season. Leftover fritters keep well in the fridge for up to 3 days—reheat in a 350°F/180°C oven for about 10 minutes.

Blackened corn salad with pickled chili peppers & herbs

I use one of my all-time favorite ingredients here, pickled chili peppers, which add an instant pop of heat, acidity and sweetness: a great foil for the smoky corn. I buy the jarred Peppadew ones from the supermarket, or make them myself. To make your own, heat 7 tablespoons/100 ml white wine vinegar with a tablespoon of sugar until dissolved and add four sliced red chili peppers. Leave to pickle in the liquid for at least an hour.

————

If using fresh corn, use a sharp knife to slice the kernels from the cob. If using frozen, cook in boiling water and allow to cool.

Put the shallots into a small bowl, squeeze over the lime juice, add a pinch of salt and massage a few times with your hands.

Heat about 1 tablespoon of oil in your largest frying pan over a medium-high heat. Add the corn kernels and a good pinch of salt, then cook, undisturbed, until well charred underneath—this will take about 3 minutes. Toss and cook again until the corn is charred all over—another 3–4 minutes.

Once the shallots have sat for a little while, add the pickled chili peppers, 3 tablespoons of olive oil and the yogurt. Season and mix.

Put the charred corn in a large bowl with half the cilantro, pour over the shallot dressing and toss together, adding more salt if needed. Finish with the rest of the cilantro.

Serving suggestions

— With crumbled feta and flatbreads
— On top of a baked sweet potato with more yogurt or sour cream
— In corn tacos with some warm cinnamon-spiked black beans
— On top of sourdough toast with a poached egg

SERVES 4

4 ears of corn, or about
   1 pound/450 g frozen corn
2 small shallots, peeled and
   very thinly sliced
juice of 2 limes, unwaxed or
   organic
extra virgin olive oil
4 pickled red chili peppers
   (store-bought, or make
   your own—see note in intro)
4 tablespoons Greek or
   vegan yogurt
a large bunch of cilantro,
   roughly chopped

Crispy potato, cornmeal & cheese pancake

SERVES 2–4

1¼ pounds/500 g cooked
  potatoes, peeled and roughly
  chopped
1 onion, thinly sliced
extra virgin olive oil
3½ ounces/100 g sharp Cheddar
  or vegan Cheddar-style cheese,
  grated
3 tablespoons medium-grind
  cornmeal

TO SERVE
a bunch of greens (about
  ½ pound/200 g)—e.g., spring
  greens, cavolo nero, kale,
  destemmed and torn into
  bite-sized pieces
a small bunch of parsley
a small bunch of cilantro
1 lemon, unwaxed or organic

A crispy potato and sharp Cheddar pancake with the pleasing crunch of cornmeal, topped with greens and lemony herbs. I make this using leftover cooked potatoes, but it's good enough to cook them for. These quantities will make enough to serve four as a light meal and two as a hearty one.

———

If you need to cook your potatoes, peel, then boil them in well-salted water for about 20 minutes, or until soft. Drain and leave to steam-dry.

Meanwhile, cook the onion in an 8-inch/22 cm nonstick frying pan with a little olive oil over a medium heat until it is soft and sweet, but not brown. This should take about 8–10 minutes.

Put the potatoes into a bowl and use a spoon to mash them a little: you want some texture, but no large pieces. Add the cooked onion, cheese and cornmeal, and season well with salt and pepper.

Heat some olive oil over a high heat in the pan. Once it's sizzling, press the potato mixture into the pan to form one big pancake (it should look like a Spanish tortilla). Turn down the heat to medium and cook for 10–15 minutes, until the pancake has a deep golden crust underneath.

To turn, use a kitchen towel to protect your hand, then cover the pan with a plate, tip the pan upside down so that the pancake is on the plate cooked side up, then slide it back into the pan to cook the other side for another 10–15 minutes until golden. If it falls apart a bit, don't worry— as it cooks it will come together.

Once the pancake is cooked, flash-fry your greens in a little olive oil, salt and pepper. Dress your herbs in olive oil and lemon juice with a good pinch of salt. Pile the greens and herbs onto slices of pancake.

Crispy white beans with kale, lemon & Parmesan

A simple dinner we eat a lot, usually with a green salad and, if I am hungry, a slice of bread, toasted and rubbed with a little garlic and drizzled with olive oil. It's a well-loved favorite from my *Guardian* column. You need your biggest pan here so you have as much surface area as possible to get the beans crispy. If you don't have a big one, you can crisp up the beans in batches.

——

Heat most of the olive oil in a large frying pan over a high heat. Add the beans in a single layer. Stir to coat the beans in the oil, then let them sit long enough to brown on one side—about 3–4 minutes—before turning them to brown the other side for about the same length of time. Once all the beans are golden and a bit crunchy on the outside, transfer them all to a plate lined with paper towels. Put the pan back on the heat.

Add the tomatoes and allow them to cook for a few minutes, or until they begin to burst.

Add a little more oil to the pan and allow it to heat a little. Add the kale and a pinch of salt, then cook for a couple of minutes, turning all the time until it is tender and the edges have crisped.

Add the walnuts and garlic and stir around the pan for a minute, then stir in a good grating of nutmeg and the lemon juice and zest. Carefully stir in the crispy beans. Remove from the heat. Serve with grated Parmesan if you like, and some bread for a hearty meal.

SERVES 4

3 tablespoons olive oil
2 x 15-ounce/400 g cans white
    beans, drained and rinsed
14 ounces/400 g vine or cherry
    tomatoes
7 ounces/200 g kale, stems
    removed, roughly torn
½ cup/50 g walnuts, toasted and
    roughly chopped
2 cloves of garlic, thinly sliced
a few gratings of a whole nutmeg
the zest and juice of 1 lemon,
    unwaxed or organic
¼ cup/20 g vegetarian Parmesan
    or vegan Parmesan-style
    cheese, for grating on top
    (optional)
bread, to serve (optional)

Cashew pakoras with green dipping sauce

Pakoras, flavor-packed fritters commonly made from vegetables, are a popular snack and side dish in Indian cuisine. These pakoras are crisp-edged, highly spiced and everything I want to eat with friends. I like to eat these with the lemon and cardamom dhal on page 16 or the biryani on page 275. They are also great wrapped in a chapati with the green sauce and some crunchy shredded veg.

———

Measure the cashews into a small heatproof bowl and cover with double the volume of hot water. Set aside.

Next, make the green dipping sauce. Toast the mustard and cumin seeds in a dry deep frying pan until the cumin smells fragrant and the mustard seeds start to pop. Remove from the heat and tip into a blender with the rest of the green dipping sauce ingredients. Blend until smooth (adding up to 2 tablespoons of cold water to loosen if you need—it should be like thick yogurt), stir in the toasted spices, then taste and add salt, lime or honey to balance. Cover and set aside.

Mix the onion, chili powder, curry leaves, chili, ginger, garlic, fennel and cumin seeds in a large mixing bowl and give it a really good stir. Season generously with salt and black pepper and leave to one side. Drain the cashews well and add to the bowl.

Add a good 1-inch/3 cm depth of oil to the frying pan and heat gently over a low-medium heat. Add the baking soda, chickpea flour and ghee to the mixing bowl along with ¼ cup/60 ml of cold water and mix until it comes together in a chunky batter.

Test to see if the oil is ready by dropping a little of the mixture into the hot oil. If it sizzles and rises to the top, it is ready. Add tablespoons of the mixture to the hot oil, a few at a time so as not to overcrowd the pan. Fry for a couple of minutes on each side, using a slotted spoon to turn them over. Drain the cooked pakora on paper towels and continue until all the mixture has been used.

Season with a pinch of salt while warm and serve with the dipping sauce and some lime-dressed salad leaves if you like.

MAKES 12 PAKORAS

FOR THE PAKORAS
¾ cup/100 g cashews
1 red onion, thinly sliced
1 teaspoon chili powder
1 handful of fresh curry leaves
1 green chili, thinly sliced
1 thumb-sized piece of ginger,
    finely grated
3 cloves of garlic, finely grated
1 heaping teaspoon fennel seeds
1 heaping teaspoon cumin seeds
peanut or vegetable oil for
    shallow frying
½ teaspoon baking soda
¾ cup/80 g chickpea flour
2 tablespoons ghee, softened

FOR THE GREEN DIPPING SAUCE
1 teaspoon black mustard seeds
1 teaspoon cumin seeds
a bunch of cilantro,
    stalks and leaves
½ a bunch of mint, leaves picked,
    stalks discarded
1 thumb-sized piece of ginger,
    peeled and roughly chopped
1 clove of garlic, peeled
1 green chili
juice of 1 lime, unwaxed or
    organic
1 teaspoon honey or agave syrup
1 tablespoon coconut oil

TO SERVE
lime-dressed salad leaves
    (optional)

Sticky squash & pistachio flatbreads

There is a corner shop about 100 paces from my house, but I still find myself making these when we run out of bread. They are pleasingly simple and work brilliantly in a frying pan or on a barbecue. Here I top them with a quick spiced squash. Zucchini would work in the summer. You can use a vegan cheese instead of the feta or, if you'd rather not, add a squeeze of lemon over the flatbread to balance the acidity.

———

Put all the flatbread ingredients into the bowl of a food processor with a good pinch of salt and pulse until the mixture forms a ball. If you don't have a food processor, this can be done in a bowl using a fork and your hands to bring everything together to a wet dough. Put to one side to rise a little for 10–15 minutes. Don't expect it to rise like normal dough, but it may puff up a bit.

Heat a large frying pan over a medium heat. Once hot, add a little olive oil, then the onion and a good pinch of salt, and cook for 3–4 minutes, until beginning to brown. Add the grated squash and the ras el hanout and cook for a further 10 minutes, until the squash is tender. If it gets dry, adding a splash of water will loosen things up. While the squash is cooking, roughly chop the pistachios and the cilantro.

Now roll out your flatbreads. Dust a clean work surface and rolling pin generously with flour, then divide the dough into two equal pieces. Using your hands, pat and flatten out the dough, then use the rolling pin to roll each piece into a disc roughly 8 inches/20 cm in diameter and ⅛ inch/2–3 mm thick.

Once the squash is cooked, carefully taste a little, adding more salt if needed. Drizzle in the pomegranate molasses and stir around the pan, then tip the lot into a bowl.

Put the frying pan back on the high heat, no need to clean it, and once it is nice and hot, cook each flatbread for 1–2 minutes on each side, turning it with tongs, until puffed up and golden in places.

Once the flatbreads are cooked, spoon some yogurt over each one, top with the squash and then the pistachios, cilantro, crumbled feta, chili (if using) and pomegranate seeds.

SERVES 2

FOR THE FLATBREADS
¾ cup/100 g all-purpose flour, plus extra for dusting
½ teaspoon baking powder
1 teaspoon cumin seeds
scant ½ cup/100 ml plain yogurt of your choice, plus extra to serve

FOR THE FILLING
olive oil
1 small or ½ a medium red onion, thinly sliced
9-ounce/250 g piece of butternut squash, grated
1 teaspoon ras el hanout
½ cup/50 g pistachios, shelled
a small bunch of cilantro
1 teaspoon pomegranate molasses, plus extra for drizzling
½ cup/50 g feta or vegan feta-style cheese
a pinch of urfa chili flakes/ pul biber (optional)
the seeds of ½ a pomegranate

Spiced eggplant with Halloumi

SERVES 4

2 medium eggplants
1⅓ pounds/600 g tomatoes
a pinch of cumin seeds
a pinch of smoked paprika
olive oil
2 cloves of garlic, peeled and
  finely chopped
1 tablespoon tomato purée
1 tablespoon red wine vinegar
½ teaspoon sugar

TO SERVE

7-ounce/200 g block of Halloumi
  or vegan Halloumi-style
  cheese (sometimes called
  "Mediterranean-style"), sliced
  lengthways into ⅜-inch/1 cm-
  thick slices
extra virgin olive oil
a small bunch of mint, parsley or
  both, leaves picked
warm flatbreads (see page 103)

This recipe is based on zaalouk, which I am told is half-dip, half-salad, and is Morocco's answer to baba ghanoush. I eat it topped with grilled Halloumi (not in any way traditional, but delicious), with some flatbreads and a good green salad. It would also be brilliant as part of a spread when you have people over.

———

Blacken the eggplants all over, either under a hot broiler on a foil-lined tray or by turning them with tongs over a gas burner or hot barbecue. Make sure they char completely. On a gas stove top it will take 4–5 minutes on each side, so about 20 minutes in total. They need to be softened all the way through. Leave them to cool so that the skin comes away from the flesh.

For an authentic finish, peel the tomatoes (I sometimes skip this step if I am in a hurry): score a cross in the base of the fruit, place them in a heatproof bowl, then cover them with just-boiled water. Leave for 30 seconds to a minute, then drain and cool slightly before peeling off the skin. Chop finely.

Heat the spices in a dry frying pan until fragrant. Add a glug of oil and the tomatoes and garlic, season well and fry for a few minutes, until the tomatoes start to break down. Stir in the tomato purée, vinegar and sugar, then squeeze the flesh from the charred eggplant into the tomatoes. Simmer for 20–30 minutes, until thickened slightly. Transfer to a bowl, then give the pan a quick wash.

If you are serving it with Halloumi, heat the frying pan over a high heat. Cook the Halloumi for 2 minutes on each side, until melting and golden brown. Serve it on top of the warm dip. Drizzle with extra virgin olive oil, add the herbs and scoop it all up with warm flatbreads.

Golden rösti with ancho chili chutney

SERVES 4

FOR THE RÖSTI

1¾ pounds/800 g medium-sized
  waxy potatoes, peeled
sea salt and freshly ground
  pepper
a small bunch of thyme,
  leaves picked
2–3 tablespoons/30 g butter or
  vegan butter

TO SERVE

a handful of pan-fried kale
a small bunch of cilantro, stalks
  chopped and leaves picked
2 scallions, thinly sliced
a grating of manchego or
  vegan cheese (optional)

FOR THE ANCHO CHILI CHUTNEY

1 teaspoon cumin seeds
1 dried ancho chili
olive oil
1 red onion, finely chopped
2 cloves of garlic, finely chopped
1 thumb-sized piece of ginger,
  grated
1¼ pounds/500 g ripe cherry
  tomatoes
¼ cup/50 g superfine sugar
⅔ cup/150 ml red wine vinegar
juice of 1 lime, unwaxed or
  organic

For his birthday most years, I ask John what he'd like for breakfast. The answer is usually rösti. We lived in the Alps for a winter, where we both fell in love with it. I worked in a bar, John worked up the mountain. We weren't together then; we lived in a one-bed studio flat with four friends. There was a small stove and our cooking options were as limited as our budget, so we ate a lot of those röstis from a package, with chili sauce. This is a long way from that vac-packed version. I serve it with a punchy tomato and ancho chili chutney and sometimes an egg.

———

Coarsely grate the potatoes, then season with salt and pepper. Place the grated potatoes into a clean kitchen towel, gather it up and twist the towel to squeeze as much moisture as possible out of your potatoes. Add thyme. Heat half the butter in the frying pan until melted and bubbling, then add the grated potato. Flatten the grated potatoes onto the pan slightly to make a pancake. Allow to cook for a couple of minutes without touching, then gently give the pan a shake so the butter coats the bottom evenly and the rösti comes loose.

Continue to cook over a medium-low heat for about 10 minutes, until the bottom looks golden and crisp. To turn the rösti over, place a plate that fits just inside the pan on top, cover your hand with a kitchen towel to protect it, then turn the pan upside down with confidence so the crispy bottom is now facing up on the plate. Add the second half of the butter to the pan. Now carefully slide the rösti back into the pan so the other side can crisp up. Cook for another 10 minutes, then slide it back onto the plate or a chopping board to serve.

Cut into quarters and then serve each quarter with a dollop of chutney, the kale, cilantro leaves and stalks, scallions, cheese, salt and pepper.

Homemade ancho chili chutney

Put the cumin and chili in a dry frying pan and toast for a couple of minutes, then crush in a pestle and mortar. Put the frying pan back on the heat, add a little olive oil and fry the onion, garlic and ginger until soft. Add the tomatoes, the spices, the sugar and the red wine vinegar. Bring to the boil, then simmer for 25 minutes, squashing the tomatoes with the back of a spoon as they soften, until the chutney is sweet and sticky. Take the pan off the heat and squeeze in the lime juice.

Mapo tofu

SERVES 4

1¼ cups/500 g plain tofu

4 baby leeks, washed, or
    scallions, green parts only

4 tablespoons vegetable or
    peanut oil

2½ tablespoons Sichuan chili
    bean paste or good chili oil

3 tablespoons good black
    bean sauce, or 1 tablespoon
    fermented black beans,
    drained and rinsed

a small thumb-sized piece of
    ginger, peeled and finely
    chopped

2 cloves of garlic, finely chopped

¼ teaspoon ground white pepper

2 teaspoons cornstarch mixed
    with 2 tablespoons cold water

¼–½ teaspoon ground roasted
    Sichuan pepper

TO SERVE

rice (see page 193)

pan-fried greens

This dish is up there as one of my favorite things to eat. Clean white tofu bathed in a slick of delicious chili and black beans. It's hard to find the Sichuan chili paste and the fermented black beans traditionally used here, so this version uses good black bean sauce and chili oil. When buying the black bean sauce, look for something dark, with lots of black beans, and not the thick light brown stuff supermarkets stock. Try flybyjing.com for ingredients. This method is inspired by the undisputed queen of Sichuan food writing, Fuchsia Dunlop.

———

Cut the tofu into ¾-inch/2 cm cubes and leave to steep in very hot, lightly salted water in a heatproof mixing bowl while you prepare the other ingredients. Slice the baby leeks or scallions at an angle.

Heat a wok or large frying pan over a high heat. Pour in the vegetable oil and swirl it around. Reduce the heat to medium, add the chili paste or chili oil and stir-fry until it's a rich red color and smells delicious. Add the black bean sauce or fermented beans and stir-fry for a few seconds, then add the ginger and garlic and cook for a few seconds more.

Drain the tofu, using a slotted spoon, gently shaking off any excess water, and put it carefully in the wok. Press the tofu gently with the back of your spoon to mix it into the sauce without breaking it up. You need to be really delicate here.

Add ½ cup/120 ml of hot water, the white pepper and salt to taste and mix gently, again using the back of your spoon so you don't break up the tofu. Bring to the boil, then simmer for a few minutes to allow the tofu to take on all the flavors.

Add the leeks or scallions and carefully nudge them into the sauce. When they are just tender, add a little of the cornstarch and water mixture and stir gently as the liquid thickens. Add the cornstarch mixture once or twice more in this way, until the sauce clings to the seasonings and tofu (don't add more than you need).

Put the tofu and sauce into deep bowls. Sprinkle with the ground roasted Sichuan pepper and serve with plenty of steamed rice and some pan-fried greens.

Green olive & herb Welsh cakes

I grew up eating Welsh cakes. My dad is from a massive Welsh family (11 brothers and sisters), so Welsh cakes were a permanent fixture and are still my dad's favorite. I make the traditional raisin-studded ones a lot, but I've been meaning to try a savory version for years, and I finally got around to it. This green-olive-and-caper version is my favorite; the cakes come together as quickly as pancakes, but are much more satisfying. Add some chutney and a quick salad and they are a great easy dinner.

———

Heat the oil in a 10-inch/25 cm nonstick frying pan and add the leeks or scallions along with a pinch of salt. Cook over a medium-low heat for 8 minutes, until soft and translucent. Tip the scallions or leeks into a mixing bowl. Wipe out the pan with a paper towel and remove from the heat.

Sift the flour and baking soda into the bowl with the scallions. Use your hands to rub in the butter until the mixture resembles breadcrumbs. Add the olives, capers, herbs and (if using) cheese to the bowl. Season well with salt and pepper and mix to combine. Add an extra pinch of salt if you are leaving out the cheese.

Stir in the egg or yogurt and add a splash of milk, if needed, to form a dough—you want to be able to roll out the dough, or shape it with your hands, so don't let it get too sticky.

Lightly flour a clean work surface and roll the dough out to ½-inch/1.5 cm thickness or use your hands to make golf-ball-sized rounds and press down. Use a 2-inch/5 cm round cutter to cut out 12 little circles, gathering the dough scraps back together until all the dough has been used up.

Heat the frying pan over a low-medium heat and cook the Welsh cakes in the dry pan in batches of four. This should give you plenty of room to flip the cakes over and will ensure they cook evenly. Cook for 6-8 minutes each side, until deep golden but not burnt.

Serve warm, with tomato chutney and some lemon-dressed leaves and a little more cheese if you like.

SERVES 4
(MAKES 12 LITTLE WELSH CAKES)

1 tablespoon olive oil
a small leek, washed, or a bunch of scallions, thinly sliced
scant 2 cups/200 g all-purpose or white spelt flour, plus extra for dusting
1 teaspoon baking soda
½ cup/100 g cold unsalted butter or vegan butter, cubed
¼ cup/50 g green olives, pitted and roughly chopped
2 tablespoons baby capers, drained
a small bunch of dill, leaves roughly chopped
a small bunch of parsley, leaves roughly chopped
¾ cup/80 g Cheddar or vegan Cheddar-style cheese (optional), grated
1 organic egg, beaten, or 3 tablespoons soy yogurt
2 tablespoons of milk of your choice

TO SERVE
tomato chutney, store-bought or see recipe on page 106
lemon-dressed leaves (optional)
more Cheddar (optional)

Pimentón burgers

1 cup/120 g walnuts

olive oil

1 small red onion, finely chopped

1 red chili, finely chopped

1 teaspoon ground cumin

1 tablespoon sweet smoked
  paprika (pimentón)

1 x 15-ounce/400 g can white
  beans, rinsed, drained and
  patted dry

⅔ cup/75 g sun-dried tomatoes,
  drained and roughly chopped
  (keep the oil)

4 dried apricots, roughly chopped

½ cup/75 g cooked rice
  (or another cooked grain)

¼ cup/30 g fresh breadcrumbs
  (or you could use fine porridge
  oats)

FOR THE SALSA

2 roasted red peppers

7 ounces/200 g datterini or
  cherry tomatoes

⅓ cup/50 g green olives, pitted

a splash of sherry vinegar

2 tablespoons olive oil

TO SERVE

4 burger buns, chargrilled

mayonnaise, or vegan mayonnaise

a little more sweet smoked
  paprika

Manchego or vegan cheese,
  thinly sliced

1 handful watercress

This is a veggie (actually vegan) burger that puts all others in the shade. I don't want a veggie burger that tastes and looks like meat. Making something what it's not is not my thing. I want food to taste of what's in it. This burger is all plump white beans, walnuts, sun-dried tomatoes and a proud hit of smoked paprika topped with a quick red pepper salsa. I like to serve all the toppings in little bowls with a basket of toasted buns, and then a plate of crisp-edged burgers, and get everyone to make their own.

———

Put the walnuts into a hot dry frying pan and toast over a medium heat for 5–7 minutes, stirring often, until golden. Tip into a bowl to cool. Return the pan to the heat. Add a little oil, the onion and chili. Cook for 10 minutes, or until soft and sweet. Remove from the heat and set aside.

In a blender, blitz the cooled walnuts with the cumin and paprika. Add half a teaspoon each of salt and black pepper to the blender until the mix resembles fine breadcrumbs. Mash the beans in a bowl with a fork. Add the sun-dried tomatoes, apricots, rice, onion and chili mixture, walnut mixture and breadcrumbs and mix well to a moldable dough. If it seems dry, add a little oil from the tomatoes.

Line a tray with parchment paper. Squeeze together a quarter of the mixture, put it on the tray and flatten slightly into a burger shape. Repeat until you have four burgers. Brush each with a little oil. Chill in the fridge for 15 minutes or until you need to cook them. You can freeze them at this point too; they keep in the freezer for up to 3 months.

Heat a frying pan until hot. Add a little oil and fry the burgers for about 3–4 minutes on each side, not moving them until a crust has formed. The burgers are quite fragile, so be gentle with them. Alternatively, you could bake them in the oven at 425°F/220°C for 10 minutes.

Meanwhile, make your salsa. Chop the peppers, tomatoes and olives together on a board, then add to a bowl with a good pinch of salt, the vinegar and oil. Taste and add more salt, vinegar and oil as needed.

To assemble the burgers, spread both halves of each bun with a little mayonnaise. Sprinkle with smoked paprika and add the salsa to the bottom half of the bun. Put the burger on top, then a couple of slices of Manchego, a big pinch of watercress and the second half of the bun.

Quick chickpea braise
with kale & harissa

SERVES 4

olive oil

1 red onion, peeled and
  thinly sliced

2 cloves of garlic, peeled and
  thinly sliced

2 big handfuls of kale (about
  7 ounces/200 g), leaves
  roughly chopped, stems
  shredded

1 heaped teaspoon ground
  turmeric

1 preserved lemon

1 x 14.5-ounce/400 g can diced
  tomatoes

2 x 15-ounce/400 g cans
  chickpeas or a
  1½-pound/660 g jar

a bunch of flat-leaf parsley,
  roughly chopped

TO SERVE

4 tablespoons plain yogurt
  of your choice

1 tablespoon harissa

tahini, for drizzling

4 flatbreads

This is a meal in a pan, a pan full of all the things I want to eat on a
cold weeknight, and there is little more comforting than that. Most
greens would work here in place of the kale. Jarred chickpeas are
my choice—always. If you don't have preserved lemons, the zest of
a lemon, unwaxed or organic, will do fine.

———

Put a little oil in a large frying pan, add the onion and cook over a medium
heat for 5 minutes.

Once the onions have had 5 minutes, add the garlic, kale stems (leaves
go in later) and turmeric to the pan and cook for a couple of minutes.

While that happens, cut the preserved lemon in half, remove and discard
the flesh, then finely chop the rind. Add this to the pan along with the
tomatoes and the chickpeas, including their liquid. If you are using jarred
chickpeas you might want to add another ⅔ cup/150 ml water here, as
there will be less liquid than if you are using 2 cans.

Cook for about 10 minutes, until the tomatoes have thickened and
reduced. Add the reserved kale leaves and cook for a few minutes, until
wilted. Taste and season with salt and pepper as needed (the jarred
chickpeas are usually already well seasoned, so be sure to taste first).
Stir in most of the parsley.

Ripple the yogurt and harissa together in a bowl and serve with the braise,
a drizzle of tahini, the last of the parsley and some warm flatbreads.

Arepas with black beans & salsa verde

These are what we ate the day after we got married. One of the amazing people who cooked our wedding feast, Bea Rodriguez (@bmangobajito), is from Venezuela and she made the most perfect arepas—feather light but hearty enough to soak up a few wines from the night before. While we ate this for breakfast, these arepas could be eaten for any meal. Happy, happy food. Thank you, Bea, for sharing this recipe with me.

———

First, pickle the onions. Add the red onion to a small bowl with the juice of a lime and a pinch of sea salt, then massage together with your hands so they start to become a bright pink color. Put to one side to lightly pickle.

To prepare the dough, place the cornmeal, sea salt, oil and 1⅔–2 cups/ 400–450 ml of boiling water into a bowl. Allow to sit for about a minute to let the water absorb into the cornmeal a little. Then carefully mix the dough with your hands until combined. You want it to come together a bit like Play-Doh. It shouldn't be crumbly. Let the dough rest for 5 minutes or up to 30 if you have time.

To make the black beans, add a little olive oil to a medium frying pan and, once hot, add the cumin seeds, cilantro stalks and paprika for 1 minute. Then add the black beans with the liquid from the can and simmer for 10 minutes. Turn the heat off and then add the chopped green chili and cilantro leaves.

For the salsa verde, put ¼ cup/1 ounce/30 g of the feta and half the cilantro leaves into a food processor with the rest of the ingredients and blitz until you have a deep green, slightly creamy salsa. Season to taste, then set aside for serving.

Once your dough has rested (it should clean the bowl and be easy to work with), pull off golf-ball-sized pieces and form 3-inch × ⅜-inch/8 cm × 1 cm-thick patties (you should be able to make 10). Heat a little oil in a large frying pan, and once hot, add the arepas and put the lid on, cooking on a medium heat for 7 minutes on each side until they are golden brown on both sides. Place in a warm oven while you continue to fry the rest of the arepas.

Finish the black beans with the chopped green chili and the rest of the cilantro leaves. Serve the arepas while they are warm, split open and fill with a spoonful of the black beans, some salsa, radishes, pickled red onions, a squeeze of lime juice and a crumble of the remaining feta.

SERVES 4–6 (MAKES ABOUT 10 AREPAS)

2 cups/300 g fine cornmeal (I use the P.A.N. brand)
1 heaping teaspoon sea salt
1 tablespoon olive oil

FOR THE BLACK BEANS;
olive oil
1 teaspoon cumin seeds
a large bunch of cilantro, stalks and leaves chopped
1 teaspoon smoked paprika
2 x 15-ounce/400 g cans of black beans (or 3 cups/ 1¼ pounds/500 g home-cooked beans)
1 green chili, finely chopped

FOR THE PICKLED RED ONIONS;
1 red onion, halved and very thinly sliced
juice of 1 lime
pinch of flaky sea salt

FOR THE MEXICAN SALSA VERDE:
5.5 ounces/150 g block of feta or vegan-style feta cheese
small bunch of cilantro, leaves picked
3–4 tablespoons olive oil
zest and juice of 1 lime
1 green chili

TO SERVE
cilantro leaves
a small bunch of radishes, thinly sliced
a couple of limes for squeezing over
crumbled feta

ONE VEG

One vegetable—
easy recipes for favorite veg

There are vegetables that all of us gravitate toward when we shop. We know how to handle them and we know that our families will (probably) eat them; they are easy. They are old friends. It's these favorite vegetables that we tend to love and buy, and so are most likely to be wasted. I do, of course, encourage you to spread the net as far and wide as you can with the vegetables you eat. That way you will be getting a wider range of flavors, textures and nutrients, as well as supporting crop biodiversity. The reality is, though, we (myself included) are some way away from eating monk's beard one night and sea kale the next.

Over this chapter, I have gathered the top vegetables that we buy in UK supermarkets and written ten loose recipes for each. If you find yourself with too many red peppers, or a generous amount of runner beans in your veg box, here are some ideas. The intention of all my books is to instill cooks with confidence beyond recipes, to help them be intelligent, adaptable cooks who enjoy making dinner with leftovers or odds and ends, as much as a recipe you have carefully shopped for. These recipes are versatile, they can be halved or doubled, and I majorly encourage you to swap and change the ingredients based on what you have and what you love. These recipes are yours once the book is opened and you start cooking.

So, here are some rough ideas on how to substitute ingredients. I like to think of foods as families, whether that's by flavor, texture or how they cook. If you are swapping out an ingredient, if you stick within the same "family" you should be pretty safe. For example, butternut squash could be swapped for any other root vegetable in a curry. Dill in a salad could be swapped with any other soft green herb—something that is a flavor match like tarragon would work best, but mint or basil would work too. If you have no fresh chili for a stew, then look to smoked paprika, chipotle paste, even chili sauce. Use your senses to guide you: Is it the flavor, texture or how it cooks you need to replicate? And go from there. This way less is wasted—and we don't go to the store to buy just one thing and end up with a bag full of things we didn't really need.

↑ PURPLE-SPROUTING BROCCOLI ↗ TENDERSTEM BROCCOLI

Broccoli

TYPES Calabrese is regular broccoli. Purple-sprouting has thinner purple florets and long stalks, with lots of leaves. Tenderstem are longer-stemmed, with sparser florets and (you guessed it) tender stems. I lean toward purple-sprouting when it is in season.

SEASON Some types are available all year. Purple-sprouting is available from January to May. Calabrese runs from roughly May to November.

PREP Calabrese (normal) broccoli: cut the florets into bite-sized pieces, thinly slice the stalks. Purple-sprouting and Tenderstem: cut down the stalks lengthways to allow them to cook at the same time as the florets.

COOKING Steam or blanch for 3–4 minutes in salted water. Roast for 30 minutes at 400°F/200°C with a good pinch of salt and 2 tablespoons of olive oil, stirring halfway.

GOES WITH garlic, tahini, almonds, peanuts, lime, lemon, peanut butter, blue cheese, spinach and other greens, olive oil, mustard, capers, ginger, soy, olives, feta, chili.

Ten simple broccoli ideas

Fiery broccoli (serves 2)

Trim **10 ounces/300 g of broccoli**, cut into florets and slice stalks in half lengthways thinly. Heat **2 tablespoons of oil** in a frying pan, add **4 peeled and sliced cloves of garlic** and cook for 4–5 minutes until golden, then remove with a slotted spoon. Add the broccoli and stalks to the frying pan and sauté for 8–10 minutes, until tender and charred in parts. Season well with **salt** and sprinkle over **½–1 teaspoon of dried chili flakes**, depending on your love of chili heat. Finish with the fried garlic.

Charred broccoli & tahini (serves 2)

Cut a **10-ounce/300 g head of broccoli** in quarters and steam or boil for 6 minutes or until tender. Drain. Heat a griddle pan over a high heat, and char the broccoli on all sides until blackened and cooked through. While the broccoli is cooking, mix **2 tablespoons of tahini** with **1 teaspoon of maple syrup**, the **juice of half a lemon** and some **salt**. Drizzle over the cooked broccoli and top with **toasted nuts** or **seeds**.

Quick broccoli gratin (serves 2)

Steam or boil **10 ounces/300 g of trimmed broccoli** until tender, about 3–4 minutes. Mix **⅞ cup/200 ml of crème fraîche** (or **vegan crème fraîche**) with **¾ cup/75 g of grated Cheddar** and **¼ cup/25 g of grated Parmesan** (or **1 cup/100 g of vegan cheese**) and **2 tablespoons of grainy mustard**. Add a little **water** if the sauce seems very thick. Put the broccoli into a baking dish, cover with the sauce, grate over a little more cheese, then bake at 400°F/200°C for 25 minutes, until golden and bubbling.

Broccoli & sesame noodles (serves 2)

Blanch **10 ounces/300 g of broccoli** for 3–4 minutes until tender. Drain. Cook **2 nests of egg noodles**. While they are cooking, peel **a thumb-sized piece of ginger** and **2 cloves of garlic** and finely grate both into a large bowl. Mix **2 tablespoons of soy sauce**, **3 tablespoons of rice wine vinegar**, **1 teaspoon of toasted sesame oil** and **a pinch of ground black pepper** into the ginger and garlic. Drain the noodles and toss with the broccoli and the dressing and **2 tablespoons of toasted sesame seeds**. Top with **a fried egg** if you like, and **some chili sauce** or **oil**.

Orecchiette with chili & broccoli (serves 2)

Boil **10 ounces/300 g of broccoli** until almost soft and mashable (about 12 minutes). Scoop out with a slotted spoon, keeping the cooking water for the pasta. Heat **6 tablespoons of olive oil** over a low-medium heat, then add **1 finely chopped chili**, **2 peeled and sliced cloves of garlic** and **half a teaspoon of fennel seeds**. Cook until the garlic is crisp, then scoop everything out of the pan and keep to one side. Add the broccoli to the same frying pan and cook until broken down, almost creamy. Cook **7 ounces/200 g of orecchiette** in the reserved broccoli water until al dente, then scoop into the pan with the broccoli, adding a little pasta water if needed. Toss with ½ cup/50 g grated Parmesan (or vegan Parmesan) and the fried chili and garlic.

Broccoli pesto (serves 2)

Blitz **10 ounces/300 g of cooked broccoli** with **1 peeled and roughly chopped clove of garlic**, a handful (⅓ cup/50 g) of toasted almonds, ¼ cup/25 g of grated Parmesan (use a dairy-free one if you're vegan, or 1 tablespoon of nutritional yeast), **a good pinch of sea salt**, and **the juice of half a lemon** in a food processor. Drizzle in ¼ **cup/60 ml of extra virgin olive oil** until you have a textured pesto. Serve with pasta, in sandwiches, on top of baked sweet potatoes or tossed through roasted vegetables.

Broccoli, peanut & lime sauté (serves 2)

Steam or blanch **9 ounces/250 g of broccoli** in boiling water until just tender—about 3–4 minutes, depending on its thickness. In a large frying pan, toast **2 tablespoons of unsalted peanuts**. Drain the broccoli, add to the pan with the nuts and toss. Add **4 tablespoons of lime juice** or **ponzu** and **1 teaspoon of honey** and toss again. Take off the heat and serve with **fluffy white rice or noodles** and **chili oil**.

Broccoli miso salad (serves 2)

Blanch a trimmed and chopped **10 ounces/300 g head of broccoli** and drain. Once cool, add to a bowl with **2 tablespoons of toasted sunflower seeds**, **a handful of chopped olives**, **2 large handfuls of arugula**, **1 drained 15-ounce/400 g can of chickpeas** and **a couple of stalks of celery** (or half a head of fennel), thinly sliced. Make a dressing by mixing together **1 tablespoon of white miso paste**, **1 tablespoon of mirin**, **1 tablespoon of rice wine vinegar** and **2 tablespoons of olive oil**. Toss the broccoli salad with the dressing and serve.

Green broccoli soup (serves 2)

Cook **1 chopped onion in olive oil** in a frying pan until soft and sweet. Add **1 clove of garlic** and **a pinch of salt** and cook for another 2 minutes. Add **2 chopped heads of broccoli** and **2¾ cups/660 ml of water**. Simmer for 8–10 minutes, until tender. Add **1½ cups/200 g of frozen peas** and bring back to a simmer and cook for a couple of minutes until the peas are cooked. Turn off the heat, add **7 ounces/200 g spinach** and **¾ cup/100 g more frozen peas** and allow to wilt. Season and blend. Top with **chopped nuts**, **toasted seeds** or **croutons** for texture.

Rice, black sesame & broccoli (serves 2)

Cook and drain ⅔ **cup/125 g of basmati rice**. Slice **4 scallions**, and cut **7 ounces/200 g of broccoli** into very small ⅜-inch/1 cm pieces. Fry the scallions and broccoli in a little **peanut** or **coconut oil** until bright green. Add **half a teaspoon of Chinese five-spice powder** and **a tablespoon of black sesame seeds**. Fold the rice into the broccoli and serve with **soy sauce** and **sesame oil**.

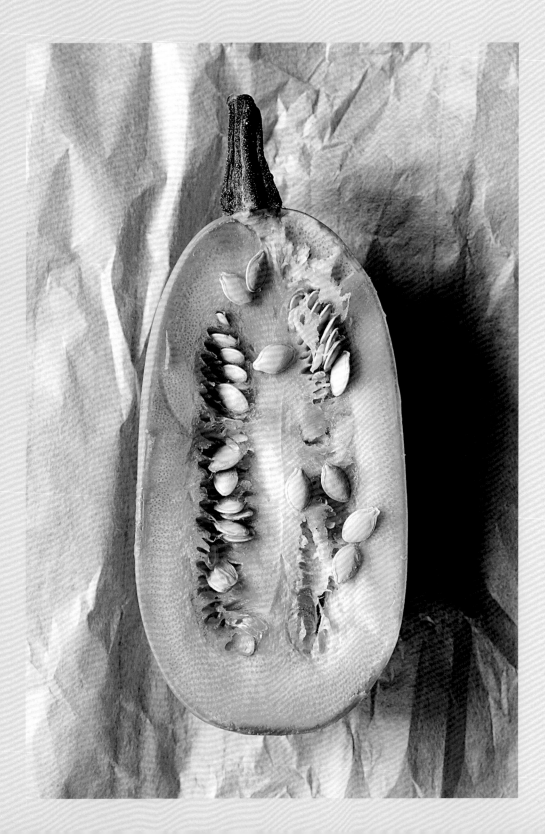

Squash & pumpkins

TYPES The most common squash is <u>butternut,</u> which is cheap and reliable, but I would encourage you to seek out others too—<u>Crown Prince</u> and <u>onion</u> are my favorites. Others I love: <u>spaghetti</u> (though this is cooked slightly differently), <u>acorn</u>, <u>delicata</u>, <u>kabocha</u>, <u>pumpkin</u> and <u>turban</u>.

SEASON <u>Autumn/winter</u>. When stored in a cool, dry place, most varieties keep for months.

PREP Most can be cooked without peeling. Or scooped out of their skin once cooked, which saves on prep time. Take care preparing squash—its thick skin makes it easy to lose control when cutting. Try to cut a flat base for your squash before cutting it in half for more stability.

COOKING I favor <u>roasted</u> squash—cut into wedges; dress with salt, pepper and olive oil; and roast at 350°F/180°C under foil until tender, then remove the foil to let it crisp.

GOES WITH sage, almonds, rosemary, thyme, chili, citrus, butter, apple, blue cheese, bitter leaves, chestnuts, garlic, cinnamon, fennel, ginger, goat cheese, lemongrass, coconut, nutmeg, mushroom.

Ten simple squash ideas

Slow-roasted squash (serves 4)
Cut a **medium butternut or other squash** in half. De-seed, then use a knife to make small incisions in the flesh without cutting through the skin. Sprinkle with **sea salt**, **freshly ground black pepper** and **a pinch of dried red chili flakes**, drizzle with **olive oil** and scatter over a **hardy herb or spice of your choice**, rubbing it all into the incisions. Roast for 2 hours at 350°F/180°C.

Winter-spiced roasted squash (serves 4)
Cut **a whole squash** into 1¼-inch/3 cm pieces, keeping the skin on if you wish. Put onto a sheet tray with **a pinch of sea salt** and **black pepper**, **a teaspoon of crushed fennel seeds**, **a teaspoon of crushed coriander seeds**, **a small cinnamon stick** crumbled, and **a pinch of dried chili flakes**. Roast at 350°F/180°C for 1 hour until soft inside and golden outside.

Squash stew (serves 4)
Finely chop **1 onion**, **1 carrot** and **2 cloves of garlic** and cook in a glug of **olive oil** in a large frying pan until soft, then add the leaves from **a few sprigs of thyme or rosemary**. Next, add **a teaspoon of fennel seeds** and **a teaspoon of cumin seeds**. Then add **1 chopped squash** (no need to peel), cover in **hot vegetable stock (about 4¼–6⅓ cups/1–1.5 liters)** and season well with **sea salt** and **freshly ground black pepper**. Cook for 30–40 minutes until the squash is tender. If you like you can add a drained **15-ounce/400 g can of white beans** for the last 10 minutes. Keep as it is or blitz into a smooth soup. Serve with **chili oil** and **yogurt**.

Squash & chickpea pancake (serves 2)
Mix **1¼ cups/150 g of chickpea flour**, **a generous pinch each of salt** and **freshly ground black pepper** in a bowl. Whisk in scant **1 cup/230 ml of milk** (use dairy-free if you're vegan) and **2 tablespoons of extra virgin olive oil** and let the mixture rest for a few minutes. Grate **a 7-ounce/200 g piece of peeled squash** and mix in. Add all the batter to a hot oiled frying pan and allow it to cook for 4–5 minutes, until the pancake is set around the edges and starting to brown and crisp. Place a plate on top of the pancake, then cover your hand with a tea towel and flip the pancake onto the plate. Slide the pancake off the plate back into the pan and cook on the other side for 4–5 minutes. Serve with **lemon-spiked yogurt** and **salad leaves**.

Squash, sage & hazelnut pasta (serves 4)
Heat some **olive oil** in a large saucepan, add **a handful of sage leaves**, roughly chopped, and **2 pounds/1 kg of squash**, peeled and cut into ¾-inch/2 cm pieces, along with **a small finely chopped onion** and **2 sliced cloves of garlic**. Cook until the onion is soft. Then add **2 cups/500 ml of hot vegetable stock** and simmer for another 15 minutes until the squash is soft. Blend until smooth. Cook **1 pound/500 g of pasta** until al dente, then toss with the squash purée and a little of the cooking water, some **Pecorino or feta cheese** (use a dairy-free one if you're vegan) and finish with some **toasted hazelnuts**, good **extra virgin olive oil** and crispy fried **sage leaves**.

Whole roasted squash soup (serves 4–6)

Roast **a whole squash** as in the slow-roasted squash recipe, with **2 quartered onions**, **a whole head of garlic**, **a few sprigs of rosemary** and **a good pinch of dried chili**. Once the squash has had its time, discard the rosemary sprigs and squeeze the garlic from its papery skins into the tray. Blitz in a food processor with **10½ cups/2.5 liters of hot vegetable stock** until you have a thick soup. Top with **extra virgin olive oil** or **yogurt** and some **chili oil**.

Ribboned raw squash salad (serves 4 as a side)

Pare a peeled **1-pound/500 g piece of squash** into thin ribbons with a Y-shaped peeler or mandoline. Place in a mixing bowl with **the zest and juice of 1 lime** and **a pinch of sea salt**, then toss to coat. Next, roughly chop **a small bunch of mint** and toss it through the squash. Serve as a salad or with **rice** and **pan-fried tofu** for a more substantial dinner.

Cheat's squash katsu curry (serves 2)

Fry **2 finely chopped onions** and **a finely chopped large carrot** in **peanut oil** for 10 minutes until soft. Slice **1 pound/500 g of butternut squash** into thin rounds. Add **2 teaspoons of curry powder** and **1 teaspoon of ground turmeric** to the onions and stir. Add **2 cups/500 ml hot vegetable stock** and the squash and cook for 15 minutes until tender. Blitz half the squash and put back into the pan and allow to cook for another 5 minutes. Top with **crispy breadcrumbs** and **lime zest**. Serve with **rice**.

Squash & feta fritters (serves 2–3)

Fry **2 sliced cloves of garlic** in **olive oil** until they sizzle, add **10 ounces/300 g of peeled, grated squash** and cook for 3–4 minutes. Beat **7 ounces/200 g crumbled feta cheese** (use a dairy-free one if you're vegan) with **4 tablespoons of all-purpose flour**, **sea salt** and **freshly ground black pepper** and **a small bunch of chopped parsley**. Add **¼ cup/60 ml of milk** (cow's, oat or soy), the grated squash and garlic and mix until you have a thick batter. Shallow-fry tablespoonfuls in **peanut oil** until golden and crisp. Serve with **natural yogurt** (vegan if you like) for dipping and **lemon-dressed salad**.

Squash caponata (serves 4)

Tip **2 x 14.5-ounce/400 g cans of diced tomatoes** into a large, high-sided sheet tray, then squish the tomatoes between your fingers to break them up. Add **2 pounds/1 kg of squash**, peeled, de-seeded and chopped into ¾-inch/2 cm chunks; **3 red onions**, cut into quarters; **4 peeled and bashed cloves of garlic**; **4 tablespoons balsamic vinegar**; **3 tablespoons olive oil**; and **some salt** and **pepper**. Roast for 35 minutes in the oven at 475°F/240°C, until everything is charred, sticky and soft. Add **⅓ cup/50 g pitted black olives**, **3 tablespoons capers** and **¼ cup/50 g raisins**; give everything a good mix, mashing slightly with a fork; and return to the oven for 15 minutes. Remove from the oven, and while the mix is still piping hot, add **another tablespoon of vinegar**, toss through a **large handful of chopped parsley** and serve.

Peas

TYPES <u>Peas in their pods</u>, <u>marrowfat peas</u>, <u>sugar snap peas</u>, <u>snow peas</u>, <u>petits pois</u>—fresh or frozen.

SEASON <u>Spring through autumn</u> for all types of peas. Fresh peas in their pods will be sweetest at the start of the season, so eat them raw. I tend to cook them later in the season. The rest of the year I eat frozen peas, which I adore.

PREP Fresh peas need podding. The pods can be frozen and kept to make a great stock or soup. Eat fresh peas as quickly as possible, as their sugars start to turn to starch as soon as they have been picked.

COOKING <u>Fresh</u>: Steam or blanch for 3-4 minutes in boiling salted water or eat raw. <u>Frozen</u>: Steam or blanch for 3-4 minutes in boiling salted water. <u>Snow peas and sugar snap peas</u>: I prefer to eat these raw in salads or very swiftly added at the end of cooking, to keep their crunch.

GOES WITH mint, lemon, Parmesan, chili, Cheddar, dill, asparagus, horseradish, onion, potato, leek, rosemary, thyme, basil, mozzarella, eggs, feta, coconut, paneer, potato, lime.

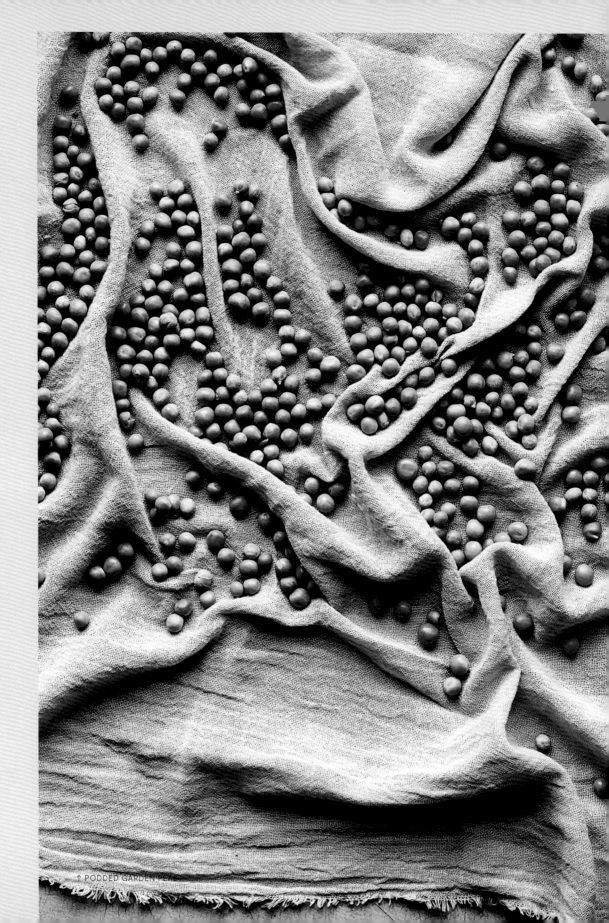

↑ PODDED GARDEN PEAS

Ten simple pea ideas

Pea & coconut soup (serves 4)
In a large saucepan, fry a **finely chopped bunch of scallions** in **a little oil** until soft. Add **5 cups/750 g of frozen or fresh peas**, **a 13.5-ounce/400 ml can of unsweetened coconut milk** and **3 cups/750 ml of hot vegetable stock**. Bring to a simmer and cook for 5 minutes. Take off the heat and blitz in a blender (or using an immersion blender) until smooth. Finish with **a squeeze of lemon juice** and top with **mint or basil leaves**.

Pea, potato & lemon traybake (serves 4)
Cut up about **2 pounds/1 kg of starchy potatoes** and put into a tray with **2 quartered lemons** (skin and all), **4 unpeeled cloves of garlic**, **a few sprigs of thyme**, **a pinch of dried chili flakes** and some **sea salt** and **freshly ground black pepper**. Break **a 7-ounce/200 g block of feta** (use a dairy-free one if you're vegan) into large chunks and add to the tray. Drizzle with **olive oil** and toss everything together. Roast at 400°F/200°C for 45 minutes, until the feta and potatoes are golden. Next, scatter over **1 cup/150 g of cooked frozen or raw fresh peas**. Roast for another 5 minutes. To serve, discard lemons and squeeze the soft garlic out of its skins into the tray. Finish with **a handful of chopped soft herbs** (parsley, mint, basil, dill, tarragon, chives all work).

Mushy garden peas with olive oil & herbs (serves 2 as a side)
Boil **2 cups/300 g of frozen peas** for 3 minutes. In a blender, blitz **a small bunch of parsley** with **a couple of sprigs of mint**, **¼ cup/60 ml of olive oil** and **2 tablespoons/30 ml of white wine vinegar**. Add the drained peas and pulse until you have a vivid green paste. Season well with **sea salt** and **freshly ground black pepper**. The texture should be somewhere between dressing and sauce. You may prefer it thicker, like a mash, in which case you should go carefully with the quantity of olive oil.

Peas on toast (serves 2)
Blanch **1 cup/150 g of frozen peas**. If using fresh, then keep them raw if they are sweet, or blanch for a couple of minutes if they are less sweet. Drain and leave to cool a little (if blanching), then put in a food processor with the leaves from **a couple of sprigs of mint**, **half a roughly chopped red chili** or **a pinch of dried chili flakes**, the **zest and juice of half a lemon**, then pulse until you have a rough-textured pea paste. Serve on **toast** topped with **grated Parmesan** (I use a vegetarian or vegan one), **crumbled feta** or even **soft-boiled eggs**.

Pea & pine nut pasta (serves 4)
Boil **1½ cups/250 g of frozen or fresh peas** in salted water until tender, then remove from the pan with a slotted spoon. Put the pan back on the heat and cook **7 ounces/200 g of pasta of your choice** until al dente. Toast **⅓ cup/50 g of pine nuts**, then put them into a food processor with **3 tablespoons of olive oil**, **the juice of half a lemon**, **half a clove of garlic**, **a pinch of salt** and a third of the peas. Blitz until you have a pea pesto. Toss with the

drained pasta and the rest of the peas, finish with **a squeeze more lemon juice**, **pea shoots** or **arugula** and a good grating of **Parmesan** (vegetarian or vegan).

Crispy pea salad (serves 2)

Put 1½ **cups/250 g of frozen peas** into a heatproof bowl, cover with boiling water and leave to stand. Toast **2 handfuls of breadcrumbs** in a pan with **olive oil** until golden and crisp. Drain the peas and dress with **1 tablespoon of red wine vinegar**, **2 tablespoons of olive oil** and some **lemon zest**. Add some **chopped** or **dried red chili** and at the last minute the breadcrumbs. Serve with some **crumbled feta** or **a fried egg**.

Pea & white bean fritters (serves 4)

Drain **1 x 15-ounce/400 g can of white beans** and tip into a food processor with 1⅓ **cups/200 g of blanched frozen or fresh peas**. Pulse to mash a little. Tip into a bowl with **4 sliced scallions**, 1⅓ **cups/200 g more peas**, the **zest and juice of half a lemon** and **a few sprigs of chopped mint or parsley**. Season well with **sea salt** and **freshly ground black pepper** and mix. Fry tablespoons of the mixture in **a little olive oil,** then serve with **lemony yogurt** and **green salad**.

Risi e bisi (serves 4)

Cook **a finely chopped onion** in **a little olive oil and butter** in a large frying pan until soft. Add 1¼ **cups/250 g of risotto rice** and cook and stir for a couple of minutes to seal the rice. Add a few ladlefuls of **hot vegetable stock** (with pea pods added if you have them). Stir until each ladleful is absorbed, then add more, ladle by ladle, until the rice is tender and the risotto is thick and soupy. When the rice is al dente (about 12 minutes), add **2 cups/300 g of podded fresh or blanched frozen peas**. Season well and finish with a **knob of butter** and **grated Parmesan** (I use a vegan or vegetarian one). Add some **chopped mint or parsley** to finish.

Quick buttery masala peas (serves 4)

In a frying pan, melt **1 heaping tablespoon of butter, ghee or coconut oil** and add 3⅓ **cups/500 g of cooked peas**. Turn the heat to high and let the peas absorb the butter, then tip into a bowl. Put your pan back on the heat and add **another tablespoon of butter, a tablespoon of grated ginger** and **1 chopped green chili**. Allow to sizzle, then add **a teaspoon of chili powder**. Stir in the peas, **a good pinch of salt** and **a teaspoon of garam masala**; turn off the heat, then add **the juice of half a lemon**. Serve with **rice** and **mango chutney.**

Paneer & peas (serves 4)

Chop **1 pound/500 g of hard paneer** into ¾-inch/2 cm pieces and fry in **vegetable or coconut oil** for around 4 minutes, until golden and crisp, then take out of the pan. Put the pan back on the heat, add **2 cloves of sliced garlic** and **2 chopped tomatoes** and cook for 5 minutes, then add **1 teaspoon each of ground turmeric, ground cumin** and **chili powder**. Add 1⅓ **cups/200 g of cooked drained peas**, return the paneer to the pan and warm it all through. Serve with **chapatis** or **rice** and **chutney**.

Potatoes

TYPES There are more types of potatoes than I have space for here, but some of my favorites are: Yukon Gold, fingerling, russet, Red Norland, Anja, Pink Fir Apple, Désirée, Vivaldi and sweet potatoes.

IDEAL FOR Mash: Désirée. Salad: new, fingerlings, Red Norlands. Roast: russet. Bake: Yukon Gold.

SEASON Most potatoes are available year-round, thanks to the fact they store well. The main crop is harvested in mid-September. In spring, look for Red Norlands and fingerlings, but most white varieties are available year-round.

PREP Scrub away the dirt and peel if required.

COOKING I cook potatoes in boiling water for speed; many people prefer to start with cold, but having tried both ways, I can't taste a difference.

GOES WITH salt, garlic, butter, lemon, olive oil, tomato, capers, spinach, cabbage, celery, chili, horseradish, mint, thyme, rosemary, nutmeg, onion, parsley, soft herbs, peanuts, saffron, truffle, cheese, watercress, turmeric, mustard seeds, cauliflower, peas, other roots.

Ten simple potato ideas

Lemon & potato boulangère (serves 4)

Scrub and thinly slice **2 pounds/1 kg of waxy potatoes**. Slice **2 lemons**, unwaxed or organic, thinly, keeping the rinds on. Butter a shallow ovenproof dish. Next, lay some of the potatoes in a row at the end of the dish, propped up a little, then add a row of lemon slices. Repeat until the dish is full, shuffling the potatoes down as you go if you need to. Season well with **salt** and **pepper** and scatter over **1 teaspoon of bashed fennel seeds**. Dot the top with a **few small knobs of butter** or **vegan butter**. Cover with foil and bake at 425°F/220°C for 30 minutes. Take the foil off and bake for a further 30–40 minutes, until browned and the lemons are sticky.

My perfect crispy roasted potatoes (serves 4–6)

Peel, chop into chunks and then parboil **3 pounds/1.5 kg of Maris Piper** or **starchy potatoes** in their skins in salty water for 15 minutes. Drain well. Roughly shake to give craggy edges. Add **5 tablespoons of olive oil** to a sheet tray, then add the potatoes, **salt** and **pepper** and the crushed skin-on cloves from a **whole head of garlic**. Roast at 400°F/200°C for 1 hour. Take the tray out, squash the potatoes with the back of a spoon or a masher, and add strips of **lemon** or **orange peel, rosemary, thyme, sage** or **spices** (e.g., cumin, coriander, fennel seeds or dried chili flakes) with the garlic to flavor. Put back in the oven for 25 minutes.

Perfect potato salad (serves 4)

Scrub and boil **1²⁄₃ pounds/750 g of new potatoes** in salted water for 20–25 minutes, until cooked. Meanwhile, chop **2 tablespoons of gherkins** and **2 tablespoons of drained capers** with a **big bunch of parsley**. Add this to a bowl with **1 tablespoon of Dijon mustard**, **1 tablespoon of white wine vinegar, a teaspoon of honey** or agave and **4 tablespoons of good extra virgin olive oil**. Drain the potatoes and steam dry, then mix with the dressing while warm and serve.

Potato, thyme & onion flatbread (serves 2)

Fry **1 sliced onion** in **olive oil** for 10 minutes, until soft and sweet. Blanch **4 thinly sliced new potatoes** for 3 minutes, until they have lost their rawness. Drain the potatoes well, then toss with **leaves from 4 sprigs of thyme** and some **salt, pepper,** and **olive oil**. Lay **2 store-bought flatbreads** on a sheet tray, spread with **crème fraîche** (or **oat crème fraîche**), top with the onions and potatoes, then finish with a **grating of Parmesan** (or **vegan cheese**). Cook in the oven for 8–10 minutes at 400°F/200°C, until everything has melted together.

Easy gratin (serves 4)

Peel and slice **1²⁄₃ pounds/750 g of waxy potatoes** as thinly as you can (I use a mandoline). Put into a bowl and toss with **2 grated cloves of garlic**, a good **pinch of sea salt** and a **grinding of black pepper** and **⅞ cup/200 ml of heavy cream, oat cream** or **vegetable stock**. Add the leaves from **a few sprigs of thyme**. Toss together, then pour into a snug baking dish and bake in the oven at 400°F/200°C for 45 minutes, until the top is golden and the sides bubble.

Masala dosa potatoes (serves 2 for a meal, 4 as a side)

Boil and mash **2 large starchy potatoes**, seasoning well with **salt**, or use **1¼ cups/300 g of leftover mashed potatoes**. Fry **1 chopped onion** in a splash of **oil** over a medium heat until soft and sweet. Add **1 teaspoon of black mustard seeds** and let them pop, then add **1 teaspoon of ground turmeric** and **5 curry leaves** (leave these out if you want) and fry for another minute. Add the mashed potato to the onions and then stir in **2 cups/50 g of spinach** until wilted. Season and serve with **curry, dosas** or some **simple green veg**.

Aloo gobi (serves 4)

In a large pan, blanch **14 ounces/400 g of chopped or whole new potatoes** for 6 minutes, then add **1 large cauliflower** cut into florets for another 4 minutes (so the total cooking time is 10 minutes). Meanwhile, fry a **grated thumb-sized piece of ginger, 2 chopped green chilies** and **4 sliced cloves of garlic**. Add **1 teaspoon each of ground coriander** and **ground turmeric** to the frying pan, cook for 1 minute, then add a **1 x 13.5-ounce/400 ml can of unsweetened coconut milk**. Drain the vegetables well and add to the sauce. Cook for 10 minutes to bring everything together. Season and finish with **the juice of 1 lemon**. Serve with **chapatis, rice** and **yogurt**. This goes well with other curries.

New potato & leek hash (serves 4)

Cook **2 shredded leeks** in **butter** or **oil** until soft. Cut **14 ounces/400 g of new potatoes** into ⅜-inch/1 cm pieces and boil or steam for 10 minutes until cooked through. Drain well, then add to the leeks and fry until golden. Season well. Once golden, scatter over **3 tablespoons/25 g of crumbly cheese (or vegan cheese)** and allow to melt. Squeeze over **the juice of half a lemon** and top with **chopped soft herbs**. Nice served with an **egg**, if that's your thing.

Harissa roasted potatoes with kale (serves 4)

Scrub **1⅔ pounds/750 g of new potatoes** and parboil for 8 minutes in salted water. Put the drained potatoes on a sheet tray and crush a little with a potato masher. Mix **1 tablespoon of harissa** with **1 tablespoon of white miso paste** and **the juice of 1 lemon**. Pour over the potatoes and mix. Roast in the oven for 25 minutes at 400°F/200°C, until golden and crisp, add **7 ounces/200 g of torn kale** to the tray and toss with a little **olive oil**, then roast for a further 10 minutes until the kale is crisp.

Brown butter new potatoes (serves 4–6)

Bring a large pan of salted water to the boil, add **2 pounds/1 kg of scrubbed whole new potatoes** and **2 bay leaves**, bring back to the boil and simmer for 10–12 minutes, until the potatoes are just cooked. Drain, put the bay leaves to one side for later, and leave the potatoes to steam dry in a strainer. Heat the oven to 400°F/200°C. Put the potato pan back on the heat, add **½ cup/100 g of salted butter** and heat gently until the butter melts, turns a nutty-brown color and smells toasty. Take the pan off the heat and throw the potatoes and bay back in and toss well in the butter. Heat a sheet tray in the oven, tip the potatoes in and season with **salt and pepper**. Roast for 30–35 minutes until golden and crisp, turning and basting halfway through.

Five things to do
with baked potatoes

Wash and dry **2 starchy potatoes (Maris Piper or King Edward)**, weighing about
10–14 ounces/300–400 g each, then prick, rub with **oil** and **salt,** and bake at 425°F/220°C
for 1 hour.

Toppings for 2 potatoes:

1. Capers and gherkins: Chop **6 gherkins** with **half a bunch of parsley** and **2 tablespoons
capers,** put into a bowl and mix with **the zest of 1 lemon** and **1 tablespoon crème fraîche or
Greek yogurt** (use **dairy-free crème fraîche** or **yogurt** if you're vegan), **salt** and **pepper.** Mash
into the potatoes and top with **arugula.**

2. Homemade chili beans: Simmer **1 can of white beans** until tender for 30–60 minutes.
Add leaves from a **sprig of thyme, a pinch of chili powder** and **sea salt.** Top your potatoes
with the beans, some **grated Cheddar** and **chili sauce.**

3. Quick lemony slaw: Finely chop **half a cabbage** with **half a bunch of parsley** and
1 apple. Grate **1 carrot.** Thinly slice **1 red onion** and massage it with **the juice of half a lemon**
and a **pinch of salt.** Mix the lot with **1 tablespoon natural or coconut yogurt** and the **juice of
the other half of the lemon.** Pile onto the potatoes.

4. Leeks with mustard and cheese: Cook **1 shredded leek** in oil until soft, add
a **small head of shredded greens** and wilt, then add the leaves from **2 sprigs of thyme.**
Stir in **1 tablespoon whole-grain mustard** and **2 tablespoons grated Cheddar.** Top your
potatoes with the cheesy leeks.

5. Spiced lemony greens: Cook **1 tablespoon mustard seeds** with **a handful of curry
leaves** in **ghee** or **coconut oil** until the seeds pop. Add **a handful of spinach** and
4 chopped scallions. Cook for a few minutes. Add the **zest of a lemon,** then pile
onto the potatoes.

Cauliflower

TYPES Cauliflower comes in white, yellow, orange, and purple. The natural purple is from an antioxidant called anthocyanin and the orange from a higher level of beta-carotene. The futuristic-looking Romanesco is also a cauliflower. Pick a clean white (or colored) cauliflower, with no brown spots and with perky leaves. Florets should be tightly packed.

SEASON Year-round but best in early summer and mid-autumn.

PREP The leaves of a cauliflower are delicious. Roast them as below, or crisp them up in a pan to top a soup. Or you can save them to cook as a green in their own right.

COOKING To roast: Cut into small florets and roast, tossed in oil and salt, with the leaves for 30 minutes, turning halfway. To steam or boil: Place in a steamer or a pan of boiling salted water and cook at a simmer for 5–8 minutes, until just tender.

GOES WITH butter, mustard, horseradish, garlic, parsley, cumin, coriander, saffron, caraway, curry, capers, broccoli, chili, chocolate, nutmeg, coconut milk, potato, walnut, green olives.

Ten simple cauliflower ideas

Cauliflower cheese orecchiette (serves 2)

Break a **medium cauliflower** into florets and fry in a little **olive oil** or **butter** until golden. Meanwhile, boil **7 ounces/200 g of orecchiette** in salted water for about 9 minutes. Add **2 sliced cloves of garlic** to the cauliflower pan and cook until the edges brown, then add **⅞ cup/200 ml of crème fraîche** (use a dairy-free one if you're vegan), **1 teaspoon of whole-grain mustard** and **1½ cups/150 g of grated Parmesan** (or **vegan Parmesan-style cheese**). Add the drained pasta and a little of the cooking water and toss to coat. Serve with lots of **black pepper**.

Roasted cauliflower, lemon & capers (serves 4)

Place florets from **a whole large (2 pounds/1 kg) cauliflower** onto a sheet tray with **sea salt**, **freshly ground black pepper**, **olive oil** and **the juice and zest of 1 lemon**. Toss, then roast in the oven at 350°F/180°C for 25 minutes. Add **capers** and **parsley** to the tray, toss again and roast for another 20 minutes. Serve as a warm salad.

Crispy lemon & cashew cauliflower rice (serves 4)

Put your largest frying pan over a high heat (two smaller ones will work). Peel and thinly slice **1 red onion**, and add to the pan with **a teaspoon of oil**. Cook for 5 minutes, or until soft, stirring from time to time. Meanwhile, chop **a medium (1⅓ pounds/600 g) cauliflower** into big chunks, put the chunks into a food processor and pulse until you have a rice-like texture, then add to the onion. Finely chop **2 cloves of garlic** and **a thumb-sized piece of ginger**, add to the onion and cauliflower with **1 tablespoon of mustard seeds** and cook for 2 minutes to toast the seeds. Serve, topped with **toasted cashews** and **lemon zest**, as you might rice next to a curry.

Caper & cauliflower fritters (serves 4/makes 12 fritters)

Bring **1¼ cups/300 ml of milk** (dairy or unsweetened oat) to the boil in a large saucepan, break **a medium (1⅓ pounds/600 g) cauliflower** into florets, add to the milk and cook for 7 minutes. Strain, reserving the milk, then mash and season the cauliflower, adding a little of the strained milk to loosen. Stir in **a handful of chopped parsley**, **1 beaten egg** and **2 tablespoons of all-purpose flour**. Shape into 12 small patties. Gently fry in batches for 3 minutes on each side, until golden. Fry **3 tablespoons of drained baby capers** until crisp. Serve the fritters with the capers and a **lemony salad**.

Whole roasted tandoori cauliflower (serves 4–6)

Break off leaves from **1 large (1¾ pounds/800 g) cauliflower** and reserve. Fill a large pan (big enough to hold the whole cauliflower) with salted water, bring to the boil, then blanch the cauliflower for 10 minutes. Drain and cool slightly. Mix scant **½ cup/100 ml of natural yogurt of your choice** with **1 teaspoon garam masala**, **a teaspoon each of bashed cumin and coriander seeds** and **a good pinch of sea salt**. Rub the cauliflower with the spiced yogurt and put in a roasting pan. Roast for 40 minutes at 400°F/200°C, adding the reserved leaves, drizzled with

a little oil, around the cauliflower for the last 20 minutes. The cauliflower is ready when you can push a knife easily into the center. Serve with **rice**, **cilantro leaves** and **mango chutney**.

Cauliflower ceviche (serves 2)

Very finely slice **half a medium cauliflower (10 ounces/300 g)** and add it to a bowl with **the juice of 2 limes** and the **zest of 1**, a teaspoon of toasted **cumin seeds** and **a chopped green chili**. Leave for at least 15 minutes to take on the flavors. Serve in **corn tacos** with **quick tomato salsa**.

Flash-roasted spiced cauliflower (serves 4–6)

Break **a whole large (2 pounds/1 kg) cauliflower** into smallish florets, toss in a large sheet tray with **a teaspoon of dried chili flakes, a teaspoon of fennel seeds, half a teaspoon each of ground coriander and ground turmeric** and some **oil, salt and pepper**. Put into a very hot oven (450°F/220°C). After 15 minutes, toss together and roast for another 15 minutes until the lot is deep brown and crisp. Serve topped with **chopped cilantro and parsley**.

Cauliflower, herb & sunflower seed salad (serves 4)

Whisk together ⅔ **cup/150 ml plain yogurt of your choice** with **4 tablespoons good olive oil, 1 finely chopped clove of garlic, the juice of half a lemon, 1 tablespoon white wine vinegar, a teaspoon of honey, salt,** and **pepper** to taste. This is your dressing. Get a large salad bowl and put in **a medium (1⅓ pounds/600 g) cauliflower** broken into small florets; **a bunch of scallions**, finely chopped; a drained and rinsed **15-ounce/400 g can chickpeas**; **a handful of radishes,** thinly sliced; **1 chopped green chili**; and **2 handfuls of toasted sunflower seeds**. Toss with the yogurt dressing and finish with lots of **chopped dill** and **parsley**.

Cauliflower cheese gratin (serves 4)

Bring **1 cup/250 ml of cream** (you can use oat), **4 tablespoons of butter** or **vegan butter** and **2 sliced cloves of garlic** to a simmer in a small pot over a medium heat. Season with **salt and pepper** and remove from the heat. Slice **a large (2 pounds/1 kg) cauliflower** into ¾-inch/2 cm slices (it may break up a bit). Place the smallest bits of cauliflower in a baking dish, add a layer of very thinly sliced onion (**1 small onion** in total), then a layer of grated Cheddar (2⅔ **cups/300 g cheese** in total), then more cauliflower, onion and cheese, until it is all used. Pour over the cream, cover with foil and bake in the oven at 400°F/200°C for 20–25 minutes. Remove the foil and bake for another 15–20 minutes, until brown on top. Take out of the oven and let cool slightly before serving.

Golden cauliflower steaks (serves 4)

Preheat the oven to 450°F/220°C and place a sheet tray in the oven to heat up for 10 minutes (you may need two if your tray is small). Cut the root off the bottom of **1 large (2 pounds/1 kg) cauliflower** or 2 smaller ones so it sits flat on the chopping board, then cut it into ¾-inch/2 cm-thick steaks. Season the side of each steak with **salt and pepper** and drizzle with **olive oil**. Put on the hot sheet tray and place in the oven for about 20 minutes, turning halfway, until golden on both sides. Serve with **mustard** or **salsa verde** and **greens** or **vinaigrette-dressed salad**.

Tomatoes

TYPES From cherry to vine, there are more tomatoes available than ever before. In the summer, Datterini, San Marzano, Bull's Heart and heritage tomatoes of all kinds are what we eat.

SEASON Tomatoes are available year-round, depending on where you live. Varieties grown in California are in season from May to November, while those grown in Florida are available in the winter months. Good quality canned tomatoes are also a practical option.

PREP Use a serrated knife, which will cut cleanly through the tomato skins. The vines can be used in stocks and tomato soups. They are edible and you can blitz them into the soup, adding a lovely green verdant flavor.

COOKING Use raw in salads or gently pickled, or cooked slowly in sauces.

GOES WITH basil, lemon, chili, olives, dill, capers, mint, cheese, fennel seeds, sage, eggplant, peppers, cucumber, cinnamon, chocolate, peanut, cilantro, ginger, lime, potato, thyme, vanilla, egg, watermelon, cloves.

↑ MIXED HERITAGE & CHERRY TOMATOES

Ten simple tomato ideas

Oven-baked tomato sauce (serves 4)

Add **2 sliced red onions** to a sheet tray with **2 pounds/1 kg halved ripe vine tomatoes or 2 x 14.5-ounce/400 g cans of diced tomatoes**. Add **1 teaspoon hot smoked paprika**, drizzle over enough **olive oil** to coat, then roast in an oven preheated to 450°F/220°C for 45 minutes. Tip into a blender with **1 chopped chili** and blitz. Taste and season with **salt** and **pepper**. Keep in a sealed container in the fridge for up to 5 days.

Tomato cassoulet (serves 4)

Heat a glug of **olive oil** in an ovenproof pan. Add **1 roughly chopped leek**, **1 chopped clove of garlic**, **1 chopped red chili** and a **⅜-inch/1 cm piece of ginger**, peeled and roughly chopped, and cook until soft. Add a **14.5-ounce/400 g can of diced tomatoes**, **4 tablespoons unsweetened coconut milk** and a **15-ounce/400 g can of navy beans**, drained, and season and simmer for a few minutes. Scatter over **1 pound/500 g chopped cherry tomatoes**, **a torn bunch of basil** and **4 torn slices of sourdough bread**. Drizzle all over with **olive oil**, then cook in an oven preheated to 400°F/200°C for 30 minutes.

Easy tomato salad (serves 4)

Slice **2 pounds/1 kg mixed ripe tomatoes** into irregular pieces (some halved, some sliced into wedges and some into rounds). Toss them in a strainer with a **pinch of salt**. Set the strainer above a bowl, season again with **salt** and **pepper** and leave for 15 minutes to draw the juices out and concentrate the flavor. Transfer the tomatoes to a bowl and toss with **1 tablespoon of red wine vinegar**, **3 tablespoons of extra virgin olive oil**, **1 grated clove of garlic**, and **1 chopped and de-seeded red chili**. Stir and serve.

Tomato spoon salad (serves 4 as a side)

Thinly slice **1 red onion** and put into a bowl with **the juice of half a lemon** and **a good pinch of salt**. Massage with your hands, then leave to pickle. Roughly chop **5 ripe vine tomatoes**, then roughly chop the leaves from **a bunch of mint** and **a bunch of cilantro**. Put them into a bowl with **1 tablespoon sumac**, **1 teaspoon harissa** and **2 tablespoons pomegranate molasses**. Add the pickled tomatoes and toss, then drizzle with **extra virgin olive oil** and more **lemon juice** until everything tastes great. Serve on **flatbreads** or as a side.

Ultimate tomato sandwich (serves 2)

Cut **1 pound/500 g mixed tomatoes** into ½-inch/1.5 cm-thick slices. Season with **salt** and **pepper** and set aside. Blitz **2 roasted red peppers from a jar** and **1 peeled clove of garlic** in a food processor, then fold through **1 cup/250 g mayonnaise** (use a vegan one if you like). Cover and set aside. Get a frying pan hot and add **4 tablespoons of olive oil**. Drain **2 tablespoons of capers** and pat dry with a paper towel before transferring to the hot oil in the pan. Fry until crisp, then drain on a plate lined with paper towels. Slice **2 large pieces of focaccia** in half horizontally, then divide the pepper aïoli among the bread. Top with the tomatoes, capers and some **peppery salad leaves**.

Tomato rice (serves 4–6)

Quarter **2 vine tomatoes** and scoop out the seeds, reserving for later. Roughly chop the flesh. Add **another 8 vine tomatoes** to a blender with the reserved seeds, blitz to a purée, then pass through a sieve, pressing the mixture through. Heat an ovenproof saucepan over a medium-low heat and add **olive oil, 1 finely chopped onion and 2 finely chopped cloves of garlic**. Once golden, add **a pinch of saffron**, **half a teaspoon smoked paprika**, **salt and pepper** and cook for a couple of minutes. Stir in the diced tomato, **1 bay leaf** and **more olive oil**. Cook for 5 minutes, then add **1¾ cups/350 g paella rice** and **4 cups/1 liter of the tomato juice** (use water if short) and cook for 20 minutes without stirring. Pour over **⅞ cup/200 ml more liquid** (tomato juice or water) and transfer to an oven heated to 375°F/190°C for 15 minutes. Add **chopped parsley** to serve.

Roasted tomato soup (serves 4)

Cut **2 pounds/1 kg ripe vine tomatoes** in half. Place cut side up on a baking sheet, season with **salt** and **pepper**, and add **1 bay leaf**, **a few sprigs of thyme**, **a handful of tarragon** and **3 unpeeled cloves of garlic**. Drizzle with **extra virgin olive oil**. Roast at 375°F/190°C for 1 hour. Discard the bay leaf. Squeeze the garlic from the skins and tip everything into a blender with **4 cups/1 liter of hot vegetable stock** and blitz. Taste and season with **salt, pepper** and **red wine vinegar**. Serve hot.

Tomatoes & tahini (serves 2)

Roughly chop **12 ounces/350 g mixed tomatoes** and toss in a strainer over a plate or bowl with **1 teaspoon flaky sea salt** and **1 tablespoon red wine vinegar**. Set aside to marinate for at least 10 minutes. Transfer to a bowl, season with **black pepper, 3 tablespoons extra virgin olive oil** and **a handful each of chopped parsley leaves** and **torn basil**. Leave to marinate for a further 30 minutes, then serve with **4 tablespoons capers** stirred through and **5 tablespoons/80 g smooth tahini** drizzled over.

Tomato confit (makes 3 x 1¼-cup/300 ml jars)

Halve **2 pounds/1 kg plum tomatoes** and place cut side up in a snug roasting dish with **2 thinly sliced cloves of garlic, a handful of torn basil** and **2 bay leaves**. Pour over **⅔ cup/150 ml extra virgin olive oil**. Roast in an oven heated to 250°F/120°C for 2 hours, until completely soft. Transfer the tomatoes and all the juices from the tray to sterilized jars and top with a layer of **extra virgin olive oil**. Screw on sterilized lids and keep in a cool place for up to a month. Once opened, keep in the fridge for up to a week.

Kachumber (serves 4 as a side)

Toast **half a teaspoon cumin seeds** in a hot, dry frying pan, then set aside to cool. Roughly chop **1 pound/500 g mixed tomatoes** and mix with the cumin seeds, **zest and juice of a lime**, **a finely chopped bunch of cilantro** and **1 finely diced red onion**. Drizzle with **extra virgin olive oil**, season well with **salt** and **pepper** and toss before serving.

↑ GREEN PADRÓN PEPPER ↗ ROASTED RED PEPPER

Peppers

TYPES Part of the Capsicum family, which includes chilies, with a huge variety of shape, size, flavor and heat. Green peppers are unripe red ones, and yellow and orange are the stage in between. Bell peppers are the stout, sweet ones; Romano the long red ones; Turkish peppers are long, pale and green. Chili peppers come in countless shapes and sizes.

SEASON Summer is pepper season. But peppers from California are available most of the year, or from Mexico all year-round. Jarred roasted red peppers are an essential store-cupboard ingredient for me. Spanish are best.

PREP Remove the seeds and the pith but leave the stalks when cooking, as this will help the peppers hold their shape.

COOKING I love roasted peppers cooked until black and charred in places. This intensifies the sugars in the peppers and softens their flesh.

GOES WITH basil, capers, grains, tomatoes, smoked paprika, crispy bread, sherry vinegar, mint, lemon, pine nuts, feta, goat cheese, chilies, white beans, breadcrumbs, potato, roasted red onions, sweet potato.

Ten simple pepper ideas

Piedmont peppers (a take on the classic popularized by Delia Smith) (serves 4)

Cut **4 red bell peppers** in half. Remove the seeds but leave the stems. Cut a cross in the base of **6 ripe tomatoes**, blanch for 30 seconds in boiling water, then leave to cool before slipping off the skins. Quarter the tomatoes and divide among the cut pepper halves. Divide **3 tablespoons drained capers** among the peppers, along with **2 thinly sliced cloves of garlic**. Pour **2 teaspoons/10 ml olive oil** into each pepper half and season with **black pepper**. Cook in an oven heated to 400°F/200°C for 40 minutes before serving with **a handful of basil** torn over.

Perfect charred peppers (makes 4)

Char **4 red peppers** directly over the flame of a gas stove, under a broiler on high or on the ridges of a searingly hot griddle pan, using metal tongs to turn them as they brown. Turn every 2 minutes until they are black and wrinkled all over. Put the peppers into a bowl and cover with a plate until cool. Use your fingers to peel away the black pepper skin and discard. Roughly chop and stir through cooked **grains** or **chopped tomatoes** for a simple salsa.

Red pepper bisque (serves 4)

Soak ¾ **cup/100 g red lentils** in water for at least an hour, or overnight. Drain. Cut **4 peppers** in half, rub all over with **olive oil**, then bake, cut side down, in an oven heated to 400°F/200°C for 35 minutes. Once cooked, place in a bowl and cover with a plate until cool. Meanwhile, melt **a little more oil** in a large saucepan and stir in **2 thinly sliced white onions**, **a pinch of salt**, **3 grated cloves of garlic**, **2 teaspoons each ground cumin and ground coriander** and **1 teaspoon hot smoked paprika**. When fragrant, add **1 x 14.5-ounce/400 g can whole tomatoes**, **6⅓ cups/1.5 liters hot vegetable stock**, the lentils and ½ **cup/50 g chopped sun-dried tomatoes**. Finally, remove the pepper skins, tip the peppers into a blender with everything else, and blitz until smooth. Season with **salt**, **pepper** and **sherry vinegar**.

Slow-roasted peppers with garlic (serves 4)

Cut **1 pound/500 g mixed peppers** in half and remove the seeds. Toss with **8 peeled cloves of garlic**, **2 sprigs of oregano**, **2 bay leaves**, ½ **cup/120 ml extra virgin olive oil** and **salt** in a shallow baking dish. Bake in an oven heated to 350°F/180°C for 90 minutes, stirring a couple of times. Remove from the oven, and after 5 minutes add **1 tablespoon sherry vinegar** and toss to combine.

Actually nice stuffed peppers (serves 4)

Halve and de-seed **4 red Romano peppers**, brush with **olive oil** and bake in an oven heated to 400°F/200°C for 15 minutes. Meanwhile, mix **1 heaping cup/200 g cooked quinoa or couscous** with **2 handfuls each of chopped mint**, **parsley** and **dill**, **20 chopped pitted green olives**, ¼ **cup/30 g toasted pine nuts** and **2 tablespoons/20 g sultanas**. Scoop the quinoa mixture into the peppers and crumble over ½ **cup/50 g feta** (use a dairy-free one if you're vegan). Bake for another 30 minutes, until the peppers are soft and the filling is golden and crisp in places.

Roasted pepper stew (serves 4)

Char **3 red peppers** (see Perfect charred peppers, opposite) and cover. Halve **1 pound/500 g cherry tomatoes** and mix with **2 handfuls of pitted Kalamata olives**, **2 tablespoons capers**, **zest of a lemon** and **1 tablespoon extra virgin olive oil**. Peel the peppers, slice into ⅜-inch/1 cm-thick strips and add to the tomatoes. Heat **2 tablespoons olive oil** in a pan and fry **9 ounces/250 g sliced Halloumi** on each side until golden. Remove the Halloumi, tip the pepper and tomato mixture into the pan and heat through before adding the Halloumi and **2 handfuls of mixed soft herbs** (**mint**, **basil** and **parsley**).

Flash-roasted green peppers & roasted feta/vegan feta (serves 4)

Preheat the oven to 450°F/220°C and place a sheet tray in the oven to heat up. Put **8 Turkish green peppers** on the tray with **4 quartered red onions**, **4 quartered Little Gem lettuces**, **a bunch of radishes** and **a bunch of scallions**. Drizzle with **olive oil**, add **1 teaspoon Turkish chili flakes** and **salt**. Roast for 25 minutes. Grate the **zest of a lemon** over a **7-ounce/200 g block of feta**, add **a few sprigs of thyme** and roast in a separate tray for 20 minutes. When the veg is golden, squeeze over the juice from **half a lemon**, drizzle with **more olive oil**, scatter over **chopped herbs (mint, parsley** or **dill**). Crumble the feta over the top.

Muhammara dip (serves 4)

Roast a heaping ½ **cup/75 g shelled walnuts** and **1 teaspoon cumin seeds** in a hot oven for 6 minutes. Tip into a food processor with an **8-ounce/220 g jar of roasted red peppers**, **1 cup/100 g breadcrumbs**, **2 tablespoons tomato purée**, **2 tablespoons pomegranate molasses**, **1 teaspoon of Turkish chili flakes** and **the juice of half a lemon**. With the motor running, slowly pour in **4 tablespoons of olive oil** and process until smooth. Taste and adjust the seasoning.

Ratatouille (serves 4)

Grate **4 medium zucchini** onto a sheet tray with **salt**, **pepper** and **olive oil**. Grill for 20 minutes, stirring until charred. Heat some **olive oil** in a frying pan, add **1 thinly sliced red onion** and **half a bunch of thyme**, and cook until brown. Add to the zucchini, with an **8-ounce/220 g jar of roasted red peppers** (drained), **1 finely chopped red pepper**, **1 pound/500 g chopped cherry tomatoes** and **2 sliced cloves of garlic**. Continue to grill for 15 minutes. Fry a **15-ounce/400 g can of chickpeas** (drained) in **olive oil** until crisp, season with **lemon zest**, **salt** and **pepper**, and scatter over the tray to serve.

Easy romesco (makes about 2 cups/500 g)

Roast ⅔ **cup/100 g blanched almonds** and ⅓ **cup/50 g blanched hazelnuts** on a sheet tray in an oven at 400°F/200°C for 12–15 minutes. Heat a glug of **olive oil** in a frying pan and fry **2 torn slices of stale white bread** until crispy. Add **2 finely chopped cloves of garlic** and **1 teaspoon sweet smoked paprika**, cook until the edges turn golden, then remove from the heat. Blitz the bread, nuts and **an 8-ounce/220 g jar of roasted red peppers** (drained) in a food processor until a chunky paste forms. Transfer to a bowl, add **2 tablespoons sherry vinegar**, **a pinch of chili flakes**, **a pinch of saffron** soaked in **1 tablespoon of water** and **1 tablespoon of tomato purée**. Taste and adjust the seasoning.

Carrots

TYPES Carrots come in <u>orange</u>, <u>yellow, black, white</u> and <u>purple</u>. Purple was in fact the original color—the story goes that they were bred to be orange to honor the Dutch royal family. I buy organic if I can, as I think organic carrots do taste much better.

SEASON Carrots are around in the U.S. <u>year-round</u>, but are best in the <u>summer</u> and <u>fall</u>. In the UK, farmers start putting their crop "to bed" for the winter with a thick layer of straw to protect them from frost. The sweetest crop comes in the summer, which is when I love to eat them raw.

PREP Carrots don't always need to be peeled. Keeping the peel on reduces waste and boosts nutrients (many are stored right under the skin).

COOKING Scrub, chop and <u>steam</u> for 8 minutes until tender. <u>Roast</u> for 30-45 minutes at 400°F/200°C.

GOES WITH butter, orange, tarragon, thyme, dill, fennel, cardamom, apple, celery, cinnamon, lemon, coconut, cumin, hazelnuts, almonds, onion, parsley, peanut, rutabaga, mustard seeds, raisins, coriander seeds, and cilantro.

Ten simple carrot ideas

Cumin-roasted carrots (serves 4)

Cut **8 medium carrots** into irregular ¾-inch/2 cm pieces. Toss with **1 teaspoon cumin seeds**, **1 bay leaf** and **the juice and zest of 1 orange**. Drizzle with **olive oil** to coat and season with **salt** and **pepper**. Roast in an oven heated to 400°F/200°C for 40 minutes, tossing two or three times during the cooking time.

Carrot & coriander seed soup (serves 4)

Toast **2 teaspoons of coriander seeds** in a dry frying pan until fragrant, then bash in a mortar with a pestle. Heat **2 tablespoons of olive oil** in a deep saucepan, then add **1 finely chopped red onion** and cook until soft and translucent. Stir in **1⅔ pounds/750 g carrots**, scrubbed and cut into irregular ¾-inch/2 cm pieces. Pour over **3½ cups/800 ml of hot vegetable stock** and season with **salt** and **pepper**. Cook for 25 minutes, until the carrots are tender. Transfer to a blender and blitz with the coriander seeds and **the juice and zest of half a lemon** until smooth. Divide among warm bowls and top with dollops of **yogurt**.

Carrot dip (serves 4)

Place a **14-ounce/400 g bunch of baby carrots** in a sheet tray with **1 tablespoon cumin seeds** and **1 tablespoon coriander seeds**. Drizzle with **olive oil**, season with **salt** and **pepper** and cover the tray with foil. Place in the center of an oven heated to 450°F/220°C for 30 minutes. Lift away the foil, squeeze over **the juice of half a lemon**, then return to the oven for 10 minutes until the carrots are tender and charred in places. Crush with a fork, add more oil or lemon if needed, then transfer to a bowl to serve.

Roasted carrot & grain salad (serves 4)

Toss **1 pound/500 g carrots** (halved lengthways), **2 thinly sliced bulbs of fennel** and **2 red onions**, sliced into 8 wedges, on a sheet tray with **olive oil**, **salt** and **pepper**. Roast in an oven heated to 400°F/200°C for 35 minutes, until soft and charred in places. Make a dressing with **a handful of chopped mixed herbs** (I like **parsley**, **dill** and **mint**), **1 teaspoon maple syrup**, **3 teaspoons harissa**, **3 tablespoons extra virgin olive oil** and **the juice and zest of a lemon**. Fold the carrots, fennel, onion and dressing through **1 cup/200 g cooked grains** (I like millet) and serve with **1½ cups/200 g toasted almonds** on top.

Carrot dhal (serves 4)

Heat **2 tablespoons coconut oil** in a saucepan. Add **2 grated cloves of garlic**, **1 grated red onion** and **1 thumb-sized piece of grated ginger**. Cook for 10 minutes until softened. Grind **1 teaspoon cumin seeds** and **1 teaspoon coriander seeds** in a pestle and mortar and add to the pan to toast. Stir in **1 teaspoon black mustard seeds**, **1 teaspoon ground turmeric**, **1 teaspoon ground cinnamon**, **1 cup/200 g red lentils**, **1 x 13.5-ounce/400 ml can unsweetened coconut milk**, **2½ cups/600 ml hot vegetable stock** and **6 medium carrots**, peeled and grated. Cook for 25 minutes until the lentils have softened, then stir in **the juice of a lemon** and **a handful of greens**. Season and serve.

Carrot socca (serves 2)

Whisk **1¼ cups/150 g chickpea flour** with **scant 1 cup/230 ml milk** (use whichever you prefer: cow's, oat, almond) in a bowl until smooth. Mix in **salt**, **pepper** and **2 tablespoons extra virgin olive oil**. Cover. Scrub and grate **2 medium carrots**, then stir into the batter. Heat **a teaspoon of oil** in a pan and pour the batter into the pan. Cook for 5 minutes, or until the underside is golden, before inverting onto a plate and sliding the other side of the pancake back into the pan to cook for 5 more minutes. Top with **peppery leaves**, **crumbled feta** (use dairy-free if you're vegan) and **a squeeze of lemon juice**. Slice into wedges and serve.

Carrot curry (serves 4)

Finely chop **1 red onion**. Add to a pan with **a tablespoon of hot oil** and fry until soft and golden. Stir in **2 grated cloves of garlic**, **1 finely chopped red chili** and **a grated thumb-sized piece of ginger**. Peel and slice 1⅓ **pounds/600 g carrots** into ¼-inch/6 mm-thick rounds and add to the pan with **1 teaspoon each of toasted fennel seeds and black mustard seeds**, stalks from **a bunch of cilantro**, **1 x 14.5-ounce/400 g can of diced tomatoes**, **1 x 13.5-ounce/400 ml can of unsweetened coconut milk** and **2 tablespoons tamarind paste**. Simmer with a lid on for 25 minutes, until the carrots are tender. Top with **toasted coconut flakes**, **cilantro leaves** and **the zest and juice of a lime**.

Quick carrot-fry with ginger & mustard seeds (serves 4 as a side)

Heat **2 tablespoons coconut oil** in a wide frying pan over a medium-high heat. When the oil is hot, add **1 thumb-sized piece of ginger**, grated, **1 teaspoon black mustard seeds** and **10 fresh curry leaves**. Fry for a minute, then add **1 pound/500 g peeled and grated carrots**. Cook for 8 minutes, stirring all the time, until the carrot is charred in places. Stir in **the juice of half a lemon** and **1 teaspoon honey** or **agave**. Season and serve.

Carrot marmalade (makes 1 x 1½-cup/330 ml jar)

Bash **1 tablespoon of coriander seeds** in a mortar with a pestle. Add to a bowl with **1 pound/500 g grated carrots**, **1 thumb-sized piece of grated ginger**, **1 cup/200 g superfine sugar** and **the zest of 1 lemon and 1 orange**. Cover and place in the fridge for at least 2 hours or overnight. After this time, add **the juice of the lemon and orange** to a saucepan with **2 tablespoons honey**, **7 tablespoons/100 ml white wine vinegar** and **1 teaspoon salt**. Stir until the salt has dissolved and tip in the carrot mixture. Simmer until the carrots are tender, then turn the heat up and boil until almost all the liquid has evaporated. Transfer to a sterilized jar. Store in the fridge. Once opened, eat within a month.

Raw rainbow carrot salad (serves 2)

Peel **1 pound/500 g mixed carrots** into strips and toss in a bowl with **a handful each of chopped basil and mint**, **the juice of a lemon**, **1 chopped green chili**, **1 teaspoon maple syrup** and **a handful of toasted seeds**. Serve with roasted **feta** (you can use a vegan one), cooked **grains** or good **bread** and **tomato spoon salad** (see page 146).

↑ GREEN (FRENCH, FINE OR BOBBY) BEANS

Beans

TYPES I've grouped green/French beans (also known as bobby, dwarf or fine beans) with runner beans and fava beans here, as to me, they sit in the same flavor family.

SEASON July to the end of September.

PREP Green: Cut away the stringy top; the other end is good to eat. Runners: Peel the seams of the runner beans if they are tough. Slice off the stalky top before cooking. Fava: Pod fresh ones. I double-pod them, taking the little beans out of the pale inner (sometimes bitter) pod. But you don't need to.

COOKING Green/runners: Blanch for 4 minutes in salted boiling water. Roast for 15-18 minutes at 400°F/200°C. Fava: Blanch for 4 minutes in salted boiling water. Eat raw when small and sweet.

GOES WITH lemon, new potatoes, parsley, Dijon mustard, basil, mint, tomato, onion, garlic, mustard seeds, orange, feta cheese, Parmesan, olive oil, eggs, olives, capers, Cheddar, walnut, almond, hazelnut, dill.

Ten simple bean ideas

Feta & dill green beans (serves 4 as a side)

Trim and halve **a bunch of scallions** lengthways, then chop into ¾-inch/2 cm pieces. Heat a splash of **olive oil** in a large frying pan. Stir in the scallions and **a pinch of salt**. Cook over a medium-high heat for 8–10 minutes, until soft and golden. Add **14 ounces/400 g trimmed green beans** to the pan and continue to cook for a couple of minutes, until the beans are just cooked. Stir in **a bunch of chopped dill** and serve with **1 cup/100 g crumbled feta** (use a vegan one, if you like).

Kind of Niçoise (serves 4)

Cook **1 pound/500 g new potatoes** in salted, boiling water until tender. Add **10 ounces/300 g halved green or runner beans** for the last 3 minutes. Drain. In a separate pan, **soft boil 4 eggs** for 6 minutes (leave these out for a vegan version). Make a dressing with **3 teaspoons Dijon mustard, 2 teaspoons whole-grain mustard, 4 tablespoons olive oil, 3 tablespoons white wine vinegar** and **1 teaspoon honey/maple syrup**. Crush the potatoes roughly, then toss them and the beans with the dressing and **2 tablespoons capers, ⅔ cup/100 g pitted Kalamata olives, half a roughly chopped cucumber, 10 ounces/300 g roughly chopped tomatoes**, and **a few chopped sprigs of dill** or **parsley**. Peel and quarter the eggs (if using) and dot over the salad.

Roasted green beans with quick vinaigrette (serves 4 as a side)

Trim **14 ounces/400 g green beans** and toss in enough **olive oil** to coat. Season with **salt** and roast in an oven heated to 450°F/220°C for 15–18 minutes until tender and catching at the edges. While the beans are roasting, whisk **2 tablespoons of extra virgin olive oil** with **1 teaspoon good white wine vinegar, 1 teaspoon Dijon mustard, half a teaspoon of maple syrup** and **a pinch of salt**. Blanch, peel and finely chop **a ripe tomato**, discarding the white pith and seeds. Toss the beans with the vinaigrette, tomato and **a handful of chopped parsley**.

Turkish-style green beans (serves 4)

Cut **14 ounces/400 g de-stringed runner beans** into thin strips lengthways. Heat **⅔ cup/160 ml extra virgin olive oil** in a deep pan, then cook **1 finely chopped onion** in the oil with **a pinch of salt** until soft and translucent. Add **2 finely chopped cloves of garlic** and cook until fragrant. Stir in the runner beans, **1 x 14.5-ounce/400 g can diced tomatoes, 1 tablespoon red wine vinegar**, and **2 teaspoons dried oregano** and cook over a low heat for 15 minutes. Stir in **15 roughly chopped, pitted green olives** and **1 x 15-ounce/400 g can of white beans**, drained. Dress with **lemon juice, a bunch of chopped dill** and **7 ounces/200 g crumbled feta** (use a vegan one, if you like) and serve with **flatbreads** at room temperature.

Fava bean & pistachio pesto (makes 1 x 1¼-cup/330 ml jar)

Blanch **9 ounces/250 g podded fava beans** and **2 peeled cloves of garlic** in boiling water for a couple of minutes. Drain. Place the beans, garlic and **1 large bunch of basil**, the leaves from **1 large bunch of parsley** and **½ cup/50 g toasted pistachios** in the bowl of a food processor. Pulse a few times to break down, then, while the motor is running, slowly pour in **½ cup/125 ml extra virgin olive oil** to make a coarse pesto. Taste and season with **lemon juice** and **salt**, if needed.

Citrus green-bean salad (serves 4)

Cook **6 peeled cloves of garlic** in a pan of salted boiling water for 10 minutes. Drain and bash in a mortar with **¼ cup/30 g toasted walnuts, a large pinch of salt** and **1 teaspoon of parsley, dill** or **chives** until a paste forms. Add **4 tablespoons of olive oil** and mix to combine. Cook **14 ounces/400 g green beans** in boiling water for 2 minutes until just tender but with lots of bite. Drain and toss with the walnut mixture, **1 small head of shredded endive** or **radicchio**, the segments of **a grapefruit** or **large orange** and **¼ cup/30 g more toasted walnuts**. Serve with good **bread**.

Green beans & paneer/tofu (serves 4)

Heat **2 tablespoons coconut oil** in a deep pan. Fry **1 finely chopped onion** and **3 chopped cloves of garlic** in the oil until soft. Stir in **1 tablespoon cumin seeds, 1 teaspoon ground turmeric, 1 teaspoon chili powder, 1 heaping teaspoon ground coriander** and toast over a low heat. Turn the heat up and add **4 roughly chopped tomatoes** and **a chopped thumb-sized piece of ginger**. Cook for 3 minutes, then add **1 pound/500 g trimmed green beans**, **the juice of a lemon** and **1 tablespoon maple syrup** with **½ cup/120 ml water**. Once the beans are tender, stir through **1 chopped red chili** and **7 ounces/200 g paneer or firm tofu**, cut into ¾-inch/2 cm pieces. Serve with **chopped cilantro** and **flatbreads**.

Green bean curry (serves 4)

Soak **1 cup/50 g unsweetened shredded coconut** in cold water. Blitz **1 onion, 2 green chilies, 1 peeled thumb-sized piece of ginger** and **2 cloves of garlic** with **2 tablespoons water** in a food processor. Cook the mixture in a pan with **a tablespoon of oil** until fragrant. Add **1 teaspoon ground turmeric** and **2 teaspoons ground coriander seeds**. Pour in a **13.5-ounce/400 ml can of unsweetened coconut milk**, the drained shredded coconut, **a pinch of salt** and **14 ounces/400 g potatoes**, chopped into bite-sized pieces. Cook for 25 minutes, until the potatoes are tender. Add **14 ounces/400 g runner beans**, sliced into ¾-inch/2 cm pieces, and cook until they are tender too. Add **lemon juice** to taste and scatter with **fried curry leaves** and **mustard seeds**.

Green beans & yogurt (serves 2 as a side)

Heat a griddle pan until searingly hot over a high heat. Cook **14 ounces/400 g trimmed runner beans** on the griddle in batches until charred on each side and soft. Cut **2 lemons** in half and char these too while the pan is hot. When cool, mix the **juice from the lemons** with **4 tablespoons extra virgin olive oil, scant 1 cup/200 ml Greek yogurt** and **salt** and **pepper** to taste. Serve the charred beans with the yogurt and **1 teaspoon toasted coriander seeds**, roughly crushed, on top.

Fava bean panzanella (serves 4 as a side)

Tear **2 slices of stale sourdough bread** into chunks, drizzle with **extra virgin olive oil** and season. Toast in an oven heated to 400°F/200°C for 10 minutes, until crisp and golden all over. Blanch **4 ounces/115 g podded fava beans** in boiling water for a couple of minutes. Drain and toss the beans with **7 ounces/200 g halved cherry tomatoes, a handful of chopped mint, 4 sliced radishes**, the bread, and **3 tablespoons olive oil** and **1 tablespoon red wine vinegar**.

Greens

TYPES Greens are a big family of vegetables but most can be used in roughly the same ways as the seasons change. Favorites are <u>curly kale</u>, <u>spring greens</u>, <u>cavolo nero</u>, <u>rainbow</u> and <u>Swiss chard</u>, <u>spinach</u>, <u>collard greens</u>, <u>sprout tops</u> and the girl band of greens: <u>kalettes</u>.

SEASON <u>Available year-round</u>, some at their best in <u>winter</u> and others in <u>spring</u> when other leafy vegetables are in sparse supply.

PREP <u>Wash and dry well</u>. <u>Trim</u> any tough ends from the leaves and finely chop the stalks if you want to eat them (which you should; they are delicious).

COOKING <u>Blanch</u> in boiling salted water for a few minutes until bright green. <u>Steam</u> for 3-6 minutes until tender. Cook stalks for a few minutes longer than the leaves to make sure they are tender. <u>Roast</u> at 400°F/200°C for 10-20 minutes (depending on the green).

GOES WITH chili, citrus, toasted nuts and seeds, soft green herbs, feta cheese, olives, eggs, pasta, potatoes, onions, leeks, good olive oil, capers, mustard, coconut, tomato, yogurt.

Ten simple greens ideas

Easy chard pasta (serves 2)
Cook **7 ounces/200 g pasta** according to the package instructions. Meanwhile, separate the leaves and stalks of **5 ounces/150 g chard**. Finely chop the stalks and fry in a pan with **a glug of olive oil** for 3 minutes. Add **a finely chopped clove of garlic** and **the zest of a lemon** and cook for a minute more. Tear the leaves and add these to the pan with a few tablespoons of water from the pasta pan and cook until wilted. Mix **½ cup/100 g ricotta** (use a dairy-free one if you're vegan) with **salt**, **pepper** and **the juice of half the zested lemon**. Drain the pasta and reserve a mugful of the pasta water. Toss the pasta with the chard, reserved water and **ricotta**. Serve with **nutmeg** grated over.

Kale pesto (serves 4)
Heat **4 tablespoons extra virgin olive oil** in a frying pan. Fry **2 peeled and smashed cloves of garlic** until beginning to color at the edges. Transfer to a food processor with **1 pound/500 g shredded kale, a pinch of dried chili flakes** and **½ cup/75 g toasted almonds**. Pulse a few times, then, with the motor running, slowly pour in **5 tablespoons/75 ml extra virgin olive oil**. Season with **salt** and **pepper** and **lemon juice**. Serve over **pasta** or on toast with **lemony white beans**.

Greens on toast (serves 2)
Separate the leaves from the stalks of **1 small bunch of cavolo nero**. Finely chop the stalks and roughly tear the leaves. Heat **1 tablespoon of oil** in a frying pan and add **1 chopped red chili** and the stalks. Fry over a medium heat until tender, then add the leaves and fry for 5 minutes until wilted. Squeeze over **the juice of a lemon**, season and serve on **slices of toasted sourdough** with **grilled tomatoes** or **a dollop of yogurt**.

Kale chips (makes enough for 4)
Tear **7 ounces/200 g washed curly kale** into large chip-sized pieces and discard the stalks. In a bowl, whisk together **1 teaspoon miso paste, 1 tablespoon soy sauce, 1 tablespoon olive oil, 1 tablespoon maple syrup, the juice of a lime** and **3 tablespoons sesame seeds**. Transfer the kale to a large mixing bowl, then pour over the miso mixture. Massage together with your hands. Lay the dressed kale on two large baking sheets lined with parchment paper, ensuring the kale is spaced out in an even layer. Bake the kale in an oven heated to 250°F/120°C for 30 minutes. Turn the oven off. Remove the sheets, loosen the kale with a spatula and return to the oven for 30 minutes to crisp up. Keep in an airtight container for up to a week.

Greens fritters (serves 2)
Shred **12 ounces/350 g leftover cooked greens** (Brussels sprouts, kale, spring greens and chard all work well). Mix in a bowl with **12 ounces/350 g leftover cooked potato** or **mashed potato, 1 finely chopped clove of garlic** and **the zest of a lemon**. Crumble in **½ cup/50 g feta** (use a dairy-free one if you're vegan) and stir in **½ cup/50 g breadcrumbs**. Heat a splash of **olive oil** in a large frying pan and fry tablespoons of the mixture, pressing down to form little patties. Fry for 3–4 minutes on each side, until golden. Serve with **wedges of lemon** for squeezing over and **peppery salad leaves**.

Easy greens (serves 4 as a side, or use to stir through pasta for 4)

Heat **3 tablespoons of olive oil** in a frying pan with a lid. Fry **2 thinly sliced cloves of garlic** and **1 finely chopped red chili** for 2 minutes. Stir in **7 ounces/200 g shredded greens**. Season and cook over a medium heat with the lid on for 4 minutes, until the leaves are wilted. Squeeze over **the juice of half a lemon**, taste and add **salt**, **pepper** and more **lemon juice** if you like.

Simple ribollita (serves 6)

Heat **2 tablespoons of olive oil** in a deep pan and fry **2 finely chopped red onions**, **3 finely chopped cloves of garlic, 1 finely chopped carrot**, and **6 finely chopped stalks of celery** over a medium-low heat for 30 minutes until caramelized. Add **a bunch of chopped parsley, 1 peeled, chopped potato** and a **14.5-ounce/400 g can of plum tomatoes**. Cook for 15 minutes, until the tomato juice has been absorbed. Add a **15-ounce/400 g can of white beans** and their liquid, **14 ounces/400 g roughly chopped kale** and **8½ cups/2 liters vegetable stock** and season. Simmer gently for 30 minutes. Top with **4 slices of stale bread**, like a lid, **drizzle with extra virgin olive oil** and allow to sit for 10 minutes before serving.

Green quinoa (serves 4)

Place **half a lemon** in a pan with **1½ cups/250 g quinoa**. Cover with **2½ cups/600 ml vegetable stock** and simmer for 15 minutes with the lid on. Just before the 15 minutes is up, lay **9 ounces/250 g roughly chopped purple-sprouting broccoli** and **a handful of frozen peas** on top to steam for a few minutes. Fry **1 sliced leek** in **olive oil** with **a pinch of salt** until soft. Drain the quinoa, squeeze over the lemon, then toss in a bowl with **3 handfuls of shredded spinach, a small bunch of chopped mint, a bunch of chopped basil, 2 tablespoons toasted sesame seeds, 2 tablespoons of toasted pumpkin seeds** and the leeks. Taste and adjust with **salt**, **pepper** and **lemon juice**.

Greens traybake (serves 4)

Toss **7 ounces/200 g purple-sprouting broccoli** in a sheet tray with **2 tablespoons of olive oil, a pinch of dried chili flakes** and **1 tablespoon soy sauce**. Place in an oven at 400°F/200°C for 15 minutes. On a separate tray, toss **3½ ounces/100 g curly kale** with a drained **1⅓-pound/600 g jar of white beans or cannellini beans**. Add **the zest of a lemon** and **1 teaspoon of crushed coriander seeds** and return to the oven for 15 minutes so the broccoli cooks for 30 minutes in total. Meanwhile, whisk **4 tablespoons light tahini, 1 tablespoon soy sauce, 1 teaspoon maple syrup** and **the juice of half a lemon** together in a bowl. Pour in a little water to loosen so the tahini mixture is thick but pourable. Combine the two trays, drizzle over the tahini and scatter over a few **chopped mint leaves**. Serve as is or with **rice noodles**.

Go-to green smoothie (serves 1)

In a blender, combine **1 small peeled banana, 2 apples**, cored and chopped, **2 large handfuls of kale, the juice of half a lemon, 1 tablespoon hemp seeds, ¼ teaspoon ground cinnamon**, and **1 cup/250 ml milk** of your choice. Blend until smooth.

QUICK

Pine & Crane peanut cucumber noodles

SERVES 4

1 medium cucumber
5 ounces/150 g sugar snap peas
9 ounces/250 g dried egg or rice noodles

FOR THE PEANUT SAUCE
5 tablespoons smooth peanut butter
2 tablespoons tahini
2 tablespoons dark soy sauce
2 teaspoons sesame oil
4 teaspoons honey or maple syrup
5 teaspoons rice wine vinegar
2-4 tablespoons chili oil (depending on the heat of your chili oil)
2 cloves of garlic, very finely chopped

TO SERVE
a small bunch of scallions, thinly sliced
a large bunch of cilantro, leaves picked
4 tablespoons toasted and crushed unsalted peanuts
a little chili oil

I ate a bowl of noodles in LA a few winters ago, in a little neighborhood restaurant called Pine & Crane, and they were everything I wanted them to be. This is my version, full of chili-spiked peanut sauce with the freshness of cucumber, sugar snaps and cilantro. Pea shoots would work here, too. Be mindful of the heat of your chili oil when making the sauce. Taste a little first and add and taste as you go until it's right for you.

———

Halve the cucumber lengthways, scoop out the watery middle and keep for later. Cut the cucumber flesh into long, thin matchsticks or use a Y-shaped peeler to make ribbons. Cut the sugar snap peas down the middle so you can see the little peas inside.

Cook the noodles in a large pot of boiling water for a minute or so less than it says on the package, so they still have some bite. Drain and rinse quickly under hot water to separate, then put into a serving bowl.

While the noodles are cooking, make the sauce. Put the watery middle from the cucumber into a small food processor or bowl with the peanut butter, tahini, soy sauce, sesame oil, honey or maple syrup and vinegar. Blitz or whisk until smooth, then stir through the chili oil and chopped garlic. Add a little water if the sauce seems thick; you want it to be the consistency of a creamy salad dressing.

Pour the peanut sauce on top of the cooked noodles and toss together. Add the cucumber and sugar snap peas, and toss again, then top with the scallions, cilantro and crushed peanuts. If you like, finish with a little extra chili oil.

Kale, lemon & crunchy breadcrumb Caesar

I make this salad most weeks in the colder months. It's a salad that feels okay to eat when it's cold. Punchy winter flavors and heaps of texture. It is loosely based on the kale salad from Joshua McFadden's brilliant veg-centered book *Six Seasons*, which claims to be the recipe that started the trend for using kale as a salad leaf. I use cavolo nero, sometimes known as Tuscan kale here and Lacinato kale in North America, but curly kale would work really well too. Leftovers can be warmed in a pan (the leaves go brilliantly crunchy) and eaten with a poached egg or tossed through buttered spaghetti.

This is a great way to use up leftover bread; I find breadcrumbs are so useful for adding texture to salads and on top of soups and stews. Here the crumbs are fried until super crunchy and golden. When they hit the dressing they soften a little but still hold their bite.

———

Roll the leaves of the cavolo nero or kale up like a cigar and shred them as thinly as you can.

Bash the garlic in a pestle and mortar with a little salt until you have a smooth paste (or chop it very finely on a board and then mash to a paste with the side of the knife), then transfer to a bowl. Add the cheese, about 3 tablespoons of oil, the lemon zest and juice, the chili and a good grind of black pepper.

Pour the dressing over the shredded leaves and toss well to coat. Taste, and adjust the flavor, adding more lemon, pepper, salt or chili as needed. Leave the salad to sit for about 10 minutes, so the leaves can soften.

If you are using eggs, bring a saucepan of salted water to the boil, add the eggs, and cook for 6 minutes. Drain and run under cold water, then slightly crack the shells against a hard surface and leave them in cold water. Once cool, peel and cut in half.

Toss the breadcrumbs with a little olive oil, salt and pepper and toast until crisp and golden in a dry pan or in an oven heated to 350°F/180°C.

Top the leaves with the eggs, if using, toasted breadcrumbs and a final grating of cheese, if you wish. Serve with the toasted sourdough.

SERVES 4

a bunch of cavolo nero or kale (10 ounces/300 g), stalks removed
½ small clove of garlic, peeled
¾ cup/75 g grated Pecorino or vegetarian Parmesan or vegan Parmesan-style cheese, plus extra for grating
extra virgin olive oil
the zest and juice of 1 lemon, unwaxed or organic
a pinch of dried chili flakes
4 organic eggs (optional)
1½ cups/150 g breadcrumbs

TO SERVE
4 slices of toasted sourdough

Broccoli on toast

We have reached peak avocado on toast. While I will always love it, the time has come for something else. The last time I was visiting my sister in LA, I went to Kismet, a small restaurant on the city's east side famed for its Californication of Middle Eastern food. The dish du jour? Broccoli toast. I was skeptical. Broccoli, I thought, lacks the creaminess needed to be a good toast topping. I was wrong. Teamed with a tahini layer and some spice, it was all I could have asked for. Here is my version.

Good toast and leafy-stemmed broccoli are key here, although standard (calabrese) broccoli will work if you slice it thinly enough. If you are using your broiler rather than a griddle pan, be sure to turn the broccoli regularly: the result will be charred, crisped leaves that soften when they cool.

———

Boil a large pan of generously salted water and blanch the broccoli for 3–4 minutes, until it has lost its rawness but still holds its shape. Drain and set aside.

Mix the yogurt with the tahini, a good squeeze of lemon juice, some salt and pepper, and a drizzle of olive oil. Taste, and balance with more lemon, salt and pepper as necessary.

Heat a griddle pan over a high heat, or the broiler on its high setting, and, once hot, char the broccoli on all sides, until the edges are crispy. Once you are happy with the broccoli, take it off the heat, then char the bread on both sides, using the same griddle or broiler. Add a glug of oil and half the za'atar to the broccoli and mix to coat.

Spread the hot toast with a little olive oil and the tahini yogurt, then top with the warm, charred broccoli, the toasted seeds and the rest of the za'atar.

SERVES 4

14 ounces/400 g stemmed
  broccoli, purple-sprouting or
  Tenderstem
4 tablespoons Greek yogurt
  or yogurt of your choice
2 tablespoons tahini
1 lemon, unwaxed or organic
extra virgin olive oil
4 slices of sourdough
1 tablespoon za'atar

TO SERVE
⅓ cup/50 g toasted sunflower
  seeds

Asparagus & lemon sauté
with maple seeds

SERVES 4

2 tablespoons sesame seeds

2 tablespoons pumpkin seeds

3 tablespoons maple syrup

a good pinch of dried chili flakes

the zest and juice of a lemon,
    unwaxed or organic

2 × 14-ounce/400 g bunches of
    asparagus

1 teaspoon sesame oil

2 heads of greens or
    7 ounces/200 g sugar
    snap peas

4 nests of egg or rice noodles,
    cooked

FOR THE SAUCE

1 tablespoon maple syrup

1 teaspoon sesame oil

2 tablespoons soy sauce

2 tablespoons rice vinegar

a pinch of dried chili flakes

This recipe was a happy accident when I ordered ten bunches of asparagus from the greengrocer instead of two. It's one to make in prime asparagus season. I also make it in winter with purple-sprouting broccoli.

——

For the brittle, toast both types of seeds in a dry frying pan until they start to give off their aroma. Once toasted, add 3 tablespoons of maple syrup, a good pinch of salt and the chili flakes and cook for another minute, until the syrup begins to bubble up around the seeds and thicken (but not darken). Take off the heat and transfer to a plate lined with parchment paper, sprinkle over the lemon zest and leave to set.

Mix the sauce ingredients together in a bowl with a tablespoon of water and put to one side.

Cut off the asparagus tips and set aside, then cut the stalks into 2-inch/5 cm pieces on the diagonal up to the last 1¼ inches/3 cm from the base. Discard these end pieces or keep in the freezer for vegetable stock.

Wipe out the frying pan with a paper towel and put it back on a high heat. Once it's very hot, add the teaspoon of sesame oil, the asparagus tips and stalks and the greens or sugar snaps and cook for 3–4 minutes, until the edges char and the asparagus softens slightly. Pour in the sauce and add the noodles and cook for a further minute.

Roughly chop the brittle and serve the noodles with the maple seed brittle on top, and quarters of the lemon for squeezing over.

Seasonal variations

— Spring—asparagus or podded fava beans
— Summer—zucchini or runner beans
— Autumn—kale or peeled, thinly sliced squash
— Winter—purple-sprouting broccoli or frozen green veg

Japanese sweet corn fritters with two dips

SERVES 4 (MAKES 12–14 FRITTERS)

FOR THE DIPPING SAUCE
1 red chili, finely chopped
½ cup/125 ml rice vinegar
¼ cup/60 ml ponzu (or a mix of
    lime juice and soy sauce)
¼ cup/60 ml honey or maple
    syrup
1 clove of garlic, peeled
    and crushed

FOR THE FRITTERS
½ cup/60 g all-purpose flour
⅓ cup/50 g rice flour
¼ teaspoon baking powder
1 teaspoon ground coriander
½ teaspoon ground cumin
the juice of a lime, unwaxed or
    organic
½ cup/125 ml water or oat milk
a small bunch of cilantro
4 scallions
the kernels from 2–3 ears of corn
    or 12 ounces/350 g cooked
    frozen corn
1 teaspoon yuzu kosho or the
    zest of 2 limes, unwaxed or
    organic
flavorless oil for frying
    (I use canola)

TO SERVE
lime-dressed salad
tōgarashi seasoning
lime wedges (optional)

I love these little sweet corn fritters. Here they take on a flavor inspired loosely by Japanese ingredients, but they also work well for brunch next to a punchy salsa. Leftovers can be warmed up and are a great addition to a bowl of salad or even in a sandwich or wrap, with some chili chutney, cucumber and crunchy leaves. The flavorful Japanese condiment yuzu kosho is often overlooked and underused outside of Japan. It's a fermented paste of chilies, yuzu lime juice and lots of salt (so go easy adding extra). It packs a serious punch on flavor and it sits quietly in the fridge until you need it. Tōgarashi, or shichimi tōgarashi, is a Japanese blend of six or seven different spices and seeds; recipes vary, but it usually has seaweed, sesame seeds (white or black), citrus zest and some chili.

———

First, make the ponzu dipping sauce. Put the chili in a small saucepan with the other ingredients and place the pan over a medium-high heat for about 2 minutes until the honey dissolves, then turn it up to a boil and let it bubble away for 5 minutes, until it is thickened and syrupy. This will not be a thick chili sauce but more of a thin dipping sauce.

For the fritters, put the flours, baking powder, half a teaspoon of salt, ground coriander and cumin into a big mixing bowl, then add the lime juice (having reserved the zest first) and water or milk and beat until smooth.

Finely chop the cilantro and thinly slice the scallions. Add these to the bowl along with the corn and the yuzu kosho or lime zest and mix well. Season with a little salt if you used lime zest; if you used yuzu kosho there is no need, as it is already salty.

Heat a large frying pan over a medium-high heat. Pour in enough oil just to coat the bottom of the pan. Spoon in generously heaping tablespoonfuls of batter about 1½ inches/3 cm apart. Let them sizzle for 2–3 minutes, until the underside is nice and brown. Flip. Let them cook on the second side for another 2–3 minutes. Keep going until you run out of batter. Leftover batter will happily sit in the fridge for a day or so.

Serve with a lime-dressed salad, the ponzu dipping sauce and the tōgarashi in the middle of the table. I like to dip the fritters into the wet sauce first, then into the tōgarashi.

Lime & double ginger soba noodles

This recipe uses a lot of lime, which brings amazing zing, backed up by a double hit of ginger and cilantro. I like these noodles with tofu, but any quickly sautéed vegetables, toasted peanuts or cashews would do. Sushi ginger is always in my fridge. It adds freshness and acidity and stands in when I have run out of fresh ginger. It's great in salads, and the liquid it sits in works well in dressings. Any broccoli will work here, I use purple-sprouting broccoli, but regular broccoli would be good too. Remember to chop and use the stalks too—no waste.

———

Bring a large pot of salted water to the boil. Meanwhile, make the sauce: add the lime zest and juice, scallions, ginger, cilantro (stalks and all), honey, 1 tablespoon of soy sauce and 1 tablespoon of the oil to a blender and blitz to a thin, bright green paste with a bit of texture.

Cook the soba noodles according to the package instructions.

Meanwhile, fill and boil a kettle. Once the noodles are cooked, drain, then quickly rinse them with the boiling water to stop them sticking. Off the heat, put the noodles back into the pan they were cooked in, add the lime juice and ginger sauce, and toss to coat.

Drain the tofu, pat it dry, and cut it into matchsticks or ⅜-inch/1 cm cubes. Heat the remaining oil in a large frying pan, add the tofu and the broccoli along with a pinch or two of salt and the seeds, and fry over a high heat for a few minutes, until the tofu is browned on one side. Add a tiny splash more oil if needed, to prevent sticking. Toss gently once or twice, then continue cooking for another minute or so, until the tofu is firm and golden; this should take about 5–6 minutes. Add the remaining teaspoon of soy sauce, take the pan off the heat, toss the tofu and transfer it to another bowl.

Pile the noodles into 2 bowls and top with the tofu, broccoli, seeds, radish, chives and pickled ginger, if using. These are also great cold.

SERVES 2

7 ounces/200 g dried soba noodles
7 ounces/200 g extra-firm tofu
9 ounces/250 g broccoli, stalk thinly sliced, top cut into small florets
⅔ cup/100 g mixed seeds (e.g., black and white sesame, sunflower and pumpkin)
a handful of radishes, cut into thin rounds
a small bunch of chives or garlic chives or chive flowers, finely chopped
2 tablespoons pickled sushi ginger, roughly chopped (optional)

FOR THE SAUCE
the zest and juice of 1 lime, unwaxed or organic
4 scallions, roughly chopped
a large thumb-sized piece of ginger, roughly chopped and peeled
a small bunch of cilantro
1 teaspoon honey or maple syrup
1 tablespoon soy sauce, plus 1 extra teaspoon
2 tablespoons canola oil

Smoky rutabaga carbonara

This is a favorite recipe from my *Guardian* Feast column. This is not, by any stretch of the imagination, an authentic carbonara, but I use the word to give you an idea of what it will look and taste like: crisp-edged morsels of smoky rutabaga offset the instant silky sauce of eggs and Parmesan coating the pasta. Follow the method carefully to make sure you don't scramble the eggs. I use smoked salt here—it's easy to find in supermarkets—but use regular sea salt if you prefer. This is one of the few recipes in the book that does not have a vegan alternative, due to the eggs. I'm sorry.

———

Peel the rutabaga and cut it into roughly ½-inch x 1-inch/1 cm x 3 cm batons. No need to be too precise; the measurement is just a guide.

Heat a little olive oil in a frying pan over a medium heat, add the rutabaga, season with smoked salt or sea salt and add a couple of tablespoons of water. Leave the rutabaga to simmer until the water is all gone, then continue to cook over a medium to high heat until it is golden brown and crisp-edged all over, but soft in the middle (this should take about 15 minutes). Once it's looking good, turn the heat down to very low and keep the pan on the heat.

Meanwhile, bring a large pan of heavily salted water to the boil (the water should be as salty as the sea). Cook the spaghetti according to the package instructions. Crack the eggs into a bowl, add a good grinding (about 1 teaspoon) of black pepper and the Parmesan and mix well.

Once the pasta is perfectly al dente, use tongs to lift it out of the water and straight into the frying pan with the rutabaga, along with a little of the cooking water (scant ½ cup/about 100 ml). This will cool the pan a little, stop the eggs scrambling when they are added and help the sauce emulsify.

Toss the pasta and the rutabaga together and, once the pan has cooled enough that you don't hear any sizzling, add the egg mixture. Toss again until all the pasta is coated in sauce—if you need to, add a little more of the cooking water until you have a thick, silky, creamy sauce that sticks to the pasta. Serve immediately, with more Parmesan and black pepper and a grating of lemon zest.

SERVES 4

1 large rutabaga (about
    1 pound/500 g)
olive oil
a heaping teaspoon smoked salt
    or flaky sea salt
14 ounces/400 g spaghetti
3 medium organic eggs
⅓ cup/30 g vegetarian Parmesan
    or vegan Parmesan-style
    cheese, grated, plus extra
    to serve
the zest of 1 lemon, unwaxed or
    organic

Orecchiette with sweet corn & green chili

SERVES 4

a bunch of rainbow or Swiss
    chard (about 8-9 ounces/
    250 g), stalks and leaves
    separated
2 green chilies
the kernels from 2-3 ears of corn
    or 12 ounces/350 g frozen
    kernels
14 ounces/400 g orecchiette or
    other small dried pasta
extra virgin olive oil
smoked salt or flaky sea salt
1 cup/250 g ricotta or vegan
    ricotta-style cheese (I like
    the Tofutti brand)
the zest and juice of a lemon,
    unwaxed or organic
a large bunch of basil, leaves
    picked

Sweet corn and pasta are not an obvious pairing, but I love the chewiness of the pasta next to the sweet, crunchy pop of sweet corn, which here is backed up by green chili, ricotta and greens. You can use frozen corn if fresh is not around. If you don't have smoked salt, sea salt will do just fine. If you are using frozen corn, defrost it in a heatproof bowl by pouring boiling water over it, leave it to sit for a few minutes, then drain.

———

Bring a large pan of well-salted water to the boil. Finely chop the stalks and shred the leaves of the chard and finely chop your chilies. If you are using frozen corn, put it into a heatproof bowl and cover with boiling water.

Add the pasta to the boiling water and cook according to the package instructions or until al dente.

While the pasta is cooking, heat a tablespoon of oil in a large frying pan over a medium heat, then add the corn (drained if using frozen) and a good pinch of smoked salt or sea salt and black pepper. Cook for 4–5 minutes (a few minutes longer if you are using frozen), until the kernels are tender and beginning to brown.

Next, add the chard stalks and cook for a few minutes more, before adding the leaves and the chilies. Cook for a further 4–5 minutes, until the leaves have wilted.

Drain the pasta once it is cooked, reserving a large mugful of the cooking water. Add the pasta to the frying pan with half the ricotta and half the reserved pasta water and mix well. Turn off the heat, then add the lemon zest and juice. Toss, then, if need be, add more cooking water, so you end up with a silky sauce that coats each piece of pasta.

Toss through most of the basil. Spoon the pasta into bowls, spoon the rest of the ricotta on top and finish with the last of the basil leaves.

Squash & ginger noodle soup

Made creamy with coconut milk and sweetened with squash, this fragrant, makes-you-feel-better soup is perfect for a quick, nourishing meal. The key to this being quick is slicing your squash thinly. If you can't get it thin with a knife, a mandoline or the slicing blade on a food processor will work.

————

Put a tablespoon of oil into a deep saucepan and let it heat up a little, then add the onion, garlic and ginger and cook for 10 minutes, until soft and sweet. Next, add the coriander and cook for 2 minutes, stirring all the time.

While the onion cooks, peel and de-seed the squash, then slice it as thinly as you can. Once the onion has had its time, add the soy sauce or tamari, coconut milk, vegetable stock powder or cube, 3–3½ cups/800 ml boiling water from the kettle and, finally, the sliced squash. Bring to the boil and leave this to simmer gently for 10 minutes or until cooked. It may take a little longer if you cut it thickly. Cook your noodles according to the package instructions.

While the soup is cooking, make the topping. Heat a large frying pan over a medium heat, add a teaspoon of oil, the broccoli and the seeds and cook for 4–5 minutes until crisp at the edges and softened a little. Add the soy sauce or tamari and vinegar and cook for another 30 seconds, then take off the heat.

When the squash is cooked, mash a few pieces into the broth to thicken it. Next, add the greens and miso to the soup, allowing the greens to wilt. Check the seasoning of the soup, adding salt and pepper, as needed.

Drain the noodles, then divide them among four deep soup bowls. Ladle over the soup and broccoli, finishing with some chopped toasted peanuts and a squeeze of lime.

SERVES 4

FOR THE SOUP

flavorless oil for frying
  (I use coconut)
1 red onion, finely chopped
2 cloves of garlic, peeled and
  finely chopped or grated
a thumb-sized piece of ginger,
  peeled and finely chopped
  or grated
1 tablespoon ground coriander
½ a butternut squash
  (about 1¼ pounds/600 g)
1 tablespoon soy sauce or tamari
1 x 13.5-ounce/400 ml can
  unsweetened coconut milk
2 teaspoons vegetable stock
  powder or ½ a vegetable
  stock cube
3½ ounces/100 g flat rice
  noodles (I use brown rice ones)
2 large handfuls of greens,
  shredded
1 tablespoon miso (I use brown
  rice miso)

FOR THE TOPPING

14 ounces/400 g broccoli,
  roughly chopped, stalks and all
4 tablespoons seeds (I use
  a mixture of sesame and
  sunflower)
1 tablespoon soy sauce or tamari
1 tablespoon rice wine vinegar

TO SERVE

a handful of toasted, chopped
  unsalted peanuts
1 lime, unwaxed or organic

Peas, salted lemon & sticky dates

SERVES 4

1 lemon, unwaxed or organic

2½ cups/400 g freshly
    podded peas (about a good
    2 pounds/1 kg in their pods)
    or frozen peas

2 tablespoons extra virgin olive
    oil, plus more for finishing

1 cup/250 g ricotta or vegan
    ricotta-style cheese (I like
    the Tofutti brand)

8 dates

olive oil, for frying

4 large handfuls of pea shoots or
    other delicate salad leaves

TO SERVE

4 slices of sourdough

1 clove of garlic, cut in half

There are few vegetables that please me more than peas. I love them fresh or frozen just the same. There is a childlike quality to them, which I'm sure is why they are so widely loved. This salad with salted lemons, sticky dates, ricotta and leaves is one of my favorite ways to eat them and takes something simple into a world of more classy flavor, and the pan-crisped dates elevate it to another level again.

——

Put a pan of water on to boil. Cut the lemon in half and put half to one side. Quarter the remaining half, picking out any big seeds. Rest the flat side of each quarter on a chopping board and slice the lemon, peel and all, as thinly as you can. Put it into a bowl with a good pinch of salt and mix well to make your own quick preserved lemon.

Blanch the peas in boiling water for 3 minutes. Drain well and, while warm, dress with the 2 tablespoons of extra virgin olive oil and a good pinch of salt, then grate over the zest of the other half of the lemon and set aside.

Season the ricotta with salt and pepper and drizzle with a little extra virgin olive oil.

Pit the dates and tear or chop into pieces. Heat a frying pan over a medium heat, add a splash of olive oil, then cook the dates for a couple of minutes, until they are warm and beginning to caramelize.

Toast the sourdough and rub with one of the cut sides of the garlic clove, then drizzle with extra virgin olive oil and sprinkle with salt.

When you are ready to eat, spread the ricotta over the base of each plate or dot into bowls. Scatter over the peas, then the warm dates and the preserved lemon pieces. Mix the shoots or leaves with the juice from the other half of the lemon and a drizzle of extra virgin olive oil, and lay over the top of the peas and ricotta. Serve with the sourdough.

Flash-fried sticky tofu

SERVES 4

FOR THE RICE

1¾ cups/350 g jasmine rice

FOR THE TOFU

3 tablespoons good black
    bean sauce

a little squeeze of honey or
    maple syrup

2 tablespoons light soy sauce
    or tamari

peanut or vegetable oil

14 ounces/400 g firm smoked
    tofu, cut into ⅜-inch/1 cm-
    thick strips

2 cloves of garlic, peeled and
    thinly sliced

a small thumb-sized piece
    of ginger, peeled and thinly
    chopped

½ teaspoon Sichuan peppercorns,
    bashed and roughly ground in a
    pestle and mortar

1 stalk of celery, stringy bits
    peeled off and cut into thin
    ⅜-inch/1 cm matchsticks

4 scallions, chopped into
    ¾-inch/2 cm pieces

2 big handfuls of green beans
    (about 14 ounces/400 g),
    trimmed and chopped in half

2 tablespoons sesame oil

¼ teaspoon dried chili flakes

TO SERVE

2 scallions, thinly sliced

4 tablespoons toasted sesame
    seeds

I travel round the world in my kitchen on a weekly basis—in recent
months this has become more important than ever—often to Italy, Mexico,
southern India, Indonesia and the Middle East. Until recently, I mostly ate
Chinese food at restaurants, as the Chinese palate of ingredients felt
unfamiliar to me. I have been experimenting more with Chinese flavors
thanks to the books of the brilliant Fuchsia Dunlop. Now I pass by my
local Chinese shop and fill my basket with new intriguing jars, noodles and
vegetables. I'm still learning and cooking with deep respect for the culture
and recipes passed on.

The black bean sauce you use here is important. Ideally I'd use Lao Gan
Ma black bean sauce from a Chinese supermarket, but if you are buying
it elsewhere, get the brand which is the darkest and looks most packed
with black beans—none of the brown sludgy stuff, please.

———

First, make sure all ingredients are washed, chopped and ready to go.
The key to good stir-frying is having everything prepped and at hand.

Start with your rice. Put the rice into a strainer and rinse it really well
under cold running water until the water starts to run clear. Put it into a
saucepan with 4¼ cups/1 liter of boiling water and bring to the boil over
a high heat. Once boiling, give it a quick stir to make sure there aren't
any grains stuck to the bottom. Cook for 8 minutes at a rolling boil, by
which point the surface should look dry and have a few "breathing"
holes. Take off the heat and cover with a lid wrapped in a clean tea
towel for a further 8 minutes.

In a small bowl, mix the black bean sauce with the honey and soy sauce
(or maple syrup and tamari). While the rice is cooking, heat a couple of
tablespoons of oil in a wok over a medium heat. Add the tofu and cook
until crisp and golden. Then add the garlic, ginger and Sichuan pepper
and sizzle for a couple of moments before adding the celery, chopped
scallions and green beans. Turn up the heat and cook for about
4 minutes, until everything is fragrant and hot throughout.

Add the black bean mixture and continue to cook until everything is
coated. Take off the heat and stir in the sesame oil and chili flakes.
Serve with big piles of steamed rice and with some thinly sliced
scallions and toasted sesame seeds sprinkled on top.

Cauliflower & ginger soup with maple spiced cashews

This soup is so comforting, I crave it all year. It's rich and calming but with a hit of warming spice and cheering lemon, which perks it up.

———

Start with the soup. Heat a large pan over a medium heat, add the oil and scallions and cook for 2 minutes until softened. Add the garlic and ginger and cook for another 2 minutes. Add the spices and cook, stirring all the time, for another 2 minutes.

Next, add the cauliflower and the stock and coconut milk to the pan. Taste and season with a little salt (the amount will depend on how salty your stock is). Bring to a simmer and cook for 15 minutes, until the cauliflower florets are soft throughout.

While the soup is simmering, heat a medium frying pan, add 1 tablespoon coconut oil and the roughly chopped cauliflower leaves and fry until they are tender, crisped and golden at the edges. Transfer to a plate.

Put the pan back on a medium heat and toast the cashews until they are golden all over, then add the sesame seeds and toast for another couple of minutes. Add the spices and toss the pan so all the nuts and seeds are covered, then pour in the tamari and the maple syrup. Toss the pan again, then tip the coated nuts and seeds onto a plate to cool.

Once the cauliflower is super soft and breaks easily with the side of a spoon, take the soup off the heat, add the lemon juice and blitz with an immersion blender until creamy and spoonable.

Ladle the soup into warm bowls. Roughly chop the cooled maple spiced nuts and serve them on top of the soup, along with the crispy leaves.

SERVES 4

FOR THE SOUP

1 tablespoon coconut or olive oil, plus 1 teaspoon, melted, for roasting

a small bunch of scallions, thinly sliced

2 cloves of garlic, peeled and finely chopped

a small thumb-sized piece of ginger (about ⅓ ounce/10 g), peeled and finely chopped

1 teaspoon ground coriander

a pinch of ground cinnamon

1 teaspoon ground cumin

1 medium head of cauliflower (about 1⅓ pounds/600 g), cut into large florets, reserving the whole leaves

3 cups/750 ml vegetable stock

1 x 13.5-ounce/400 ml can unsweetened coconut milk

the juice of ½ lemon, unwaxed or organic

FOR THE CASHEWS

1 cup/100 g cashews

1½ teaspoons sesame seeds

¼ teaspoon cayenne pepper or chili powder

½ tablespoon ground turmeric

a pinch of ground coriander

1 tablespoon tamari

1 tablespoon maple syrup

Lemongrass & tofu larb

Larb, the punchy-flavored Lao salad and national staple, is my new obsession. Lemongrass, lime leaf, shallot, and chili flavor hits, paired with some crispy tofu and sticky rice, are hard to beat. Most of the work is done in one pan here, but if you want to serve it with rice you'll need another pan.

———

Spread the grated tofu in a single layer on a clean kitchen towel or pieces of paper towel. Cover with more paper towels and let it stand for 15 minutes, pressing down occasionally, to remove excess moisture.

Next, cook your rice to serve with the larb. Put the sticky rice into a saucepan and cover with 1¼ cups/300 ml of cold water. Bring to the boil, then cover and simmer for 10 minutes, until the water is absorbed. Turn off the heat and allow the pan to stand with the lid on while you get on with the rest.

Heat half the oil in a large nonstick frying pan over a high heat. Add the tofu and cauliflower and cook for 10–12 minutes, stirring every couple of minutes, until the mixture is golden and crispy in places. Tip the cooked mixture into a bowl and set aside.

While the tofu is cooking, mix the dressing ingredients together in a bowl, taste and adjust the seasoning; you may prefer more lime, soy sauce or sweetness. Set aside.

Pour the remaining oil into the frying pan and reduce to a medium heat. Add the shallots, garlic, ginger, lime leaves, lemongrass and chilies and cook for 5 minutes, until softened. Return the cooked tofu mixture to the pan, pour in half the dressing and stir to combine. Cook for another few minutes, until everything has browned and caramelized. Remove from the heat and stir through the cilantro and mint, reserving a handful for the top.

Serve in lettuce leaves with lots of sticky rice and more herbs scattered on top, and the rest of the dressing.

SERVES 4

10 ounces/300 g extra-firm tofu, grated
5 tablespoons peanut or vegetable oil
½ a medium head of cauliflower (about 10 ounces/300 g), grated
2 shallots, peeled and thinly sliced
3 cloves of garlic, finely chopped
a thumb-sized piece of ginger, peeled and grated
3 lime leaves, very finely shredded
2 sticks of lemongrass, outer layer peeled away, bashed and very finely chopped
2 Thai red chilies, thinly sliced (or use normal chilies if you can't find Thai)
a small bunch of cilantro, roughly chopped
a few sprigs of mint leaves, roughly chopped

FOR THE DRESSING
the juice of 3 limes, unwaxed or organic (about 6 tablespoons)
3 tablespoons soy sauce
3 tablespoons vegetarian fish sauce
2 teaspoons Thai chili sauce
3 tablespoons maple syrup

TO SERVE
1 cup/200 g Thai sticky rice
crisp lettuce leaves (iceberg or Little Gem)

Greens & kimchi-fried rice

When I have the time and the inclination I make my own kimchi, but mostly I buy it. Most health food shops and Asian markets will have a decent one. This dish is a good introduction to kimchi if you have found it a bit intense in the past; once mixed with the rice it is mellower. It is a brilliant way to use up leftover rice. When cooking rice, I use a cup measure, as I find measuring rice and water by volume is simpler and gets a better result. I have made this recipe to serve two, as you'd need a huge pan or wok for four, but double it if you like and cook in batches. Vegans can make this without the eggs.

———

If you are cooking your rice, follow the instructions below.

Heat 2 teaspoons of oil in a wok or large frying pan over a high heat, then add the stalks of the greens and a splash of water. Once the water has evaporated, add the sesame seeds and kimchi, cook for about 5 minutes, until the seeds are toasted, then throw in the rest of the greens and cook until wilted. Stir through 2 tablespoons of soy sauce and the cooked rice, mixing everything together.

If you are using them, beat the eggs with 2 more tablespoons of soy sauce, push the rice to one side, and add a teaspoon of oil to the pan. Pour in the eggs and cook for a couple of minutes, until just set. Mix the eggs through the rice with a spatula, then serve with scallions and more kimchi on top, if you like.

To cook perfect rice for 2

Wash 1 cup of rice in a strainer or sieve until the water runs clear. Heat a saucepan over a medium heat, add a little oil and then the rice and fry for a minute to seal the rice. Add 2 cups of water and a good pinch of salt, bring to the boil and simmer for 8 minutes. Then turn the heat off, cover with a lid wrapped in a kitchen towel and leave (without peeking) for 8 minutes. This should give you perfectly cooked rice.

SERVES 2

2 cups/350 g cooked basmati rice or 1 cup/175 g uncooked basmati rice

olive oil

7 ounces/200 g greens (I like spring greens or cavolo nero), leaves pulled from the stalks and torn, then stalks roughly chopped

2 teaspoons sesame seeds

4 heaping tablespoons kimchi (or less, depending on its spiciness—taste it first), plus extra to serve

2-4 tablespoons soy sauce

2 organic eggs (optional)

2 scallions, thinly sliced

Greek olive & herb shakshuka

SERVES 4

olive oil

1 red onion, finely chopped

2 cloves of garlic, peeled and
 thinly sliced

1 teaspoon coriander seeds,
 bashed

1 teaspoon paprika or
 chili powder

2 x 14.5-ounce/400 g cans diced
 tomatoes

⅔ cup/100 g Kalamata olives,
 pitted and halved

1 tablespoon dried oregano

1 teaspoon red wine or
 cider vinegar

6 organic eggs or 7-ounce/200 g
 block of smoked tofu, sliced

¾ cup/75 g feta or vegan feta-
 style cheese (optional)

a small bunch of chopped dill,
 mint or parsley, or a mixture
 of all three

TO SERVE

4 slices of warm bread or
 flatbreads (optional)

A Greek-inspired take on baked eggs. I know I am mixing things up here and that this is not a traditional shakshuka—I use the word so you know the feeling of this baked-egg dish. It's inspired by something I ate at Hand Café in East London, where there is great coffee and clever cooking. For vegans, I make this with crisped-up smoked tofu. If you are making the version with eggs, rather than poaching them in the sauce, I boil them and put them on top of the tomato sauce, making life much simpler, and you get perfect jammy eggs every time.

———

Heat a little olive oil in a large frying pan, add the onion and cook for 10 minutes, until soft and sweet, then add the garlic and cook for another couple of minutes, until the edges begin to brown. Next, add the coriander seeds and toast for a minute with the onion mixture.

Add the paprika or chili powder and cook for a few seconds before adding the tomatoes, half the olives, the oregano, the vinegar and a good pinch of salt and pepper. Half-fill one of the tomato cans with water and add this to the pan too. Simmer over a medium heat and leave the sauce to reduce and thicken a bit, about 10 minutes. While the sauce is cooking, prepare your eggs or tofu.

For the egg shakshuka

For the eggs, put a pan of salted water big enough for all six on to boil, then add the eggs and cook for 5 minutes. Drain, run under cold water, then slightly crack the shells against a hard surface and leave them to cool in the cold water. Once cool, peel and cut in half.

For the tofu shakshuka

If you are using tofu, fry the slices in a little oil until crisp on both sides, then put to one side.

Once the tomato sauce is reduced and thickened, taste and add more salt, pepper and vinegar, if needed. Nestle the cooked tofu or boiled eggs into the sauce, put a lid on the frying pan and leave for a minute or two to warm through. Finally, crumble over the feta, if using, and sprinkle over the remaining olives and chopped herbs. Serve with warm bread or flatbreads, if you like.

Carrot soup with tahini & rosemary

This is the first thing John (my husband) learned to cook, taught to him by his Granny Liz, who at 92 is still making it today (as well as giving Dylan races around the garden and playing football from her wheelchair). It is a humble soup lifted by the perhaps unexpected hit of orange. The crispy chickpeas, tahini and rosemary are my additions—John likes it straight up, Granny Liz-style. So, this one is for you, Granny Liz. I hope with all my heart I am as gracious, sprightly and glamorous when I'm 92.

Heat the oil in a large saucepan over a medium-high heat. Add the onion and cook for about 10 minutes, until soft and sweet. Add a good pinch of salt, the paprika and garlic and cook for another minute or so. Add the carrots, tomatoes and the zest and juice of the orange and cook for 3 minutes more, until everything is bubbling, then add the stock and bring to the boil. Reduce the heat to medium-low, cover and simmer for 20 minutes or until the carrots are very tender.

While the soup is simmering, drain the chickpeas and pat them dry with a paper towel. Put a large frying pan over a medium heat and add about 4 tablespoons olive oil. Once hot, add the chickpeas (be careful, as they may spit to begin with) and rosemary and cook until the rosemary is fragrant and the chickpeas are crisp and popping. Sprinkle with salt and keep warm.

Once the carrots are tender, take the soup off the heat and stir in the sherry vinegar and half the tahini, and purée with an immersion blender.

Serve the soup topped with the fried rosemary chickpeas, with the rest of the tahini and a little extra virgin olive oil drizzled over.

SERVES 4

2 tablespoons olive oil, plus extra for frying

1 large onion, peeled and finely chopped

1 teaspoon sweet smoked paprika

2 cloves of garlic, peeled and roughly chopped

1 pound/500 g carrots, peeled and chopped into ⅜-inch/1 cm-thick rounds

1 x 14.5-ounce/400 g can diced tomatoes

the zest and juice of an orange, unwaxed or organic

4¼ cups/1 liter hot vegetable stock

1 x 15-ounce/400 g can chickpeas

a couple of sprigs of rosemary, leaves picked

1½ tablespoons sherry vinegar

4 tablespoons tahini

a little extra virgin olive oil

Tomato & tamarind bhel puri

Bhel puri is eaten on the streets and in homes all over India. There seem to be a million versions, but most are based on some onion, potato, tomato and crispy puffed rice and some kind of tamarind sauce. Bhel puri is a lesson in how to build texture and flavor. I owe the inspiration for this one to my great friend and insanely good cook, Emily Ezekiel. I use a bhel puri mix of puffed rice, peanuts and crispy gram (chickpea) noodles. You can buy this in any Indian shop and widely online. But if you can't get your hands on it, some crumbled-up poppadoms would do the trick. The recipe makes more dressing than you initially need, but I like to put bowls on the table for spooning over as we eat.

——

In a small saucepan, boil the potatoes over a medium heat until cooked. This will take about 20–25 minutes, depending on their size. Drain and leave to cool.

Put the onion and the zest and juice of the lime into a large bowl and season really well with salt and black pepper. Massage with your hands and give the onions a really good squeeze, then leave to pickle a little.

Put all your dressing ingredients in a small food processor and blend until smooth and a lovely pale green color, then leave to one side.

Once cool, peel off the skin of the potatoes and roughly dice. Add the chopped tomatoes, chopped cucumber and toasted cumin seeds to your pickled onion mixture. Add the chopped potato and toss to combine, then season well with sea salt and black pepper.

Mix the tamarind paste and 2 tablespoons of water in a small bowl until the mixture has a good pouring, sauce-like consistency.

Arrange the potato and tomato salad on a large serving plate with a really generous amount of your herby yogurt dressing and tamarind sauce, and finally the bhel puri mix. Finish with some pomegranate seeds and eat straightaway.

SERVES 4

FOR THE SALAD
7 ounces/200 g small waxy potatoes
1 red onion, finely chopped
the zest and juice of
1 lime, unwaxed or organic
10 ounces/300 g tomatoes, a mixture of sizes and colors, roughly chopped
1 small cucumber, peeled and roughly chopped
1 teaspoon toasted cumin seeds
3 tablespoons tamarind paste

FOR THE DRESSING
a bunch of mint, leaves picked
a bunch of cilantro, leaves picked
1 green chili (de-seeded if you like)
⅔ cup/160 ml yogurt of your choice

TO SERVE
5-ounce/150 g package bhel puri mix
seeds from 1 pomegranate

Carrot & peanut nasi goreng

SERVES 2–4

1 tablespoon coconut or
  vegetable oil
7 ounces/200 g tempeh or firm
  tofu, chopped into bite-sized
  pieces
1 small onion or 2 shallots,
  peeled and finely chopped
a thumb-sized piece of ginger,
  peeled and roughly chopped
2 cloves of garlic, finely chopped
¼ teaspoon ground turmeric or
  a small piece of fresh, peeled
  and grated
2 cups/350 g cooked basmati rice
2 tablespoons soy sauce
1 tablespoon sambal oelek or
  chili oil (depending on the heat
  of your chili oil)
2 carrots, peeled and grated
½ a cabbage or 2 large handfuls
  of other green veg, shredded or
  sliced

TO SERVE
2 organic eggs (optional)
juice of 1 lime, unwaxed or
  organic
a small bunch of fresh cilantro,
  roughly chopped
⅔ cup/100 g roasted unsalted
  peanuts, chopped
2 scallions, thinly sliced
a small handful of crispy shallots
1 tablespoon ketjap manis
  (or 50/50 mix of soy sauce
  and honey)

I spent a month in Indonesia eating nothing but gado-gado (a salad of vegetables, egg, and tofu with peanut sauce) and nasi goreng (Indonesian fried rice)—two of the greatest things you can eat, in my opinion. Check out cookbook author Lara Lee (@LaraLeeFood) for more incredible Indonesian food and recipes.

It's good to have everything prepped and ready to go so you can throw it all into the pan. There are not many things I think crispy shallots don't make better. You can buy them in tubs from supermarkets and Asian grocers or make them yourself (a recipe is below). The rice element of this dish comes together in one pan, but if you want to serve it with eggs and homemade crispy shallots, you'll need an extra pan.

———

Heat a large frying pan over a high heat and add a splash of the oil. Add the tempeh or tofu and cook for about 5 minutes, turning all the time until crisp on all sides. Then scoop out onto a plate. Put the pan back on the heat, add a little more oil and then the onions or shallots. Turn the heat down to medium and cook for 2–3 minutes, until softened, then add the ginger and garlic and cook for another minute or so. Add the turmeric and stir for 1 minute until the spices release their oils and you can smell a toasty fragrance.

Now add the cooked rice to the pan with the soy sauce and chili oil and stir to coat the rice with spices. Add your grated carrots and green vegetables and crispy tempeh and stir-fry for another 2–3 minutes.

Meanwhile, if you are using eggs, fry them in a separate pan until crisped around the edges.

To finish, squeeze over the lime juice, spoon into bowls, top with the fried eggs and sprinkle with the cilantro, chopped peanuts, scallions and the crispy shallots. Serve with a little ketjap manis.

To make your crispy shallots

Heat ⅜-inch/1 cm of vegetable oil in a large frying pan or wok until a sliver of onion dropped into it sizzles immediately. Fry 6 peeled and thinly sliced shallots in batches, stirring constantly, for 3–4 minutes each batch, or until they are crisp and lightly browned. Remove with a slotted spoon and drain in a strainer lined with paper towels. Let them cool. They will keep in an airtight container for about a week.

Greens & caramelized tofu
with XO sauce

This dish is all about the sauce, I have suggested making more than you will need, as it keeps well in the fridge for a few weeks and makes almost anything from sandwiches to salad bowls taste even more delicious.

———

Start with the XO sauce. Heat the oil in a small frying pan over a medium heat. Add the red onion, chopped chilies and garlic and a pinch of salt and fry, stirring occasionally, for 15 minutes, until everything is glossy and completely soft. Stir in the dried chili flakes and smoked paprika and remove from the heat. Add the remaining sauce ingredients and stir well to combine. Reserve 4 tablespoons of the XO sauce for the tofu. The rest of the sauce will keep well in a jar in the fridge for up to 3 weeks.

Heat a splash of oil in a large frying pan over a high heat. Cook the tofu for 3 minutes on each side, until golden and crispy. Add the garlic, ginger and scallions and cook for another minute, then add the soy sauce and cook for about 30 seconds before spooning in the reserved XO sauce. Cook for 3–4 minutes, until everything is thickened and caramelized. Remove from the heat and stir in the cilantro, then put onto a plate.

Wipe the frying pan clean with a paper towel. Pour in a tablespoon of oil and heat to medium-high. Stir in the shredded cavolo nero and corn and add the rice wine vinegar and 1 teaspoon of soy sauce. Cook for 2–3 minutes, stirring a couple of times until the corn is blackened in places and the greens are bright and crisp at the edges. Stir through the tofu.

Serve in warm bowls with cooked brown rice.

SERVES 2

FOR THE TOFU AND GREENS
vegetable oil, for frying
7 ounces/200 g extra-firm tofu,
    cut into ¾-inch/2 cm-thick
    strips
2 cloves of garlic, peeled and
    finely chopped
a thumb-sized piece of ginger,
    peeled and finely chopped
a bunch of scallions, thinly sliced
2 teaspoons soy sauce, plus
    1 teaspoon extra for the greens
a small bunch of cilantro, leaves
    and stalks roughly chopped
1 head of cavolo nero, shredded
the kernels from 1 ear of corn or
    ¾ cup/200 g frozen kernels
1 teaspoon rice wine vinegar

FOR THE XO SAUCE
1 tablespoon flavorless vegetable
    or canola oil
1 red onion, very finely chopped
2 red chilies, finely chopped
4 cloves of garlic, finely chopped
½ teaspoon dried chili flakes
1 teaspoon smoked paprika
3 tablespoons honey or
    maple syrup
1 tablespoon sesame oil
2 tablespoons soy sauce
1 tablespoon rice vinegar
2 tablespoons toasted sesame seeds

TO SERVE
2 cups/300 g brown rice (see
    page 262)

Sweet potato & miso noodle broth

The quickest of soups that uses three of my favorite flavor boosters: coconut milk, miso and tamarind. The coconut cream brings a richness that adds a depth of flavor. The miso brings umami, which creates layers of flavors, and the tamarind adds a sharpness that offsets the coconut. They are ingredients I keep on hand for nights when food needs to be fast. All sit happily in the cupboard or fridge for months. I've purposely left the choice of green veg up to you so you can use what you have and what's in season. Just be sure to cut things that take a little longer to cook into smaller pieces, so everything cooks evenly.

Fill and boil a kettle and put two saucepans on the stove top. Once the kettle has boiled, fill one saucepan one-third full and add the egg noodles. Bring to the boil over a high heat and cook according to the package instructions.

Next, pour scant 1 cup/200 ml hot water into the other saucepan, add the coconut milk and tamarind, grate in the ginger and put over a medium heat. Peel and thinly slice the sweet potato and add to the pan. Simmer over a high heat for 10 minutes or until the sweet potato is cooked.

In a small bowl, mix the miso paste with 4 tablespoons of cold water. Take the broth off the heat and stir in the miso mixture.

Once the noodles are cooked, divide between two bowls. Put the broth back on the heat, add the green vegetables to the broth and allow to simmer for 2-3 minutes, until the vegetables are just cooked and any greens have wilted, then take off the heat. Ladle the soup over the noodles and top with the tōgarashi, herbs, chili and scallions.

SERVES 2

5 ounces/150 g dried egg or rice noodles
1 x 13.5-ounce/400 ml can unsweetened coconut milk
1 tablespoon tamarind paste
a small thumb-sized piece of ginger, peeled
1 medium sweet potato
2 tablespoons miso paste
2 large handfuls of green vegetables (I use a mixture of shredded greens, broccoli and green beans)

TO SERVE
2 tablespoons tōgarashi seasoning
a small bunch of basil or mint, leaves picked
1 red chili, finely chopped
2 scallions, thinly sliced

Saag aloo shepherd's pie

SERVES 6

FOR THE RAJMA MASALA BASE

2 tablespoons ghee or coconut oil

1 onion, peeled and
    finely chopped

4 cloves of garlic, chopped

a small thumb-sized piece of
    ginger, peeled and finely
    chopped

1 green chili, finely chopped

½ teaspoon ground turmeric

½ teaspoon chili powder

1 teaspoon garam masala

1 teaspoon cumin seeds

2 x 15-ounce/400 g can pinto or
    borlotti beans

1 x 14.5-ounce/400 g can diced
    tomatoes

FOR THE SAAG ALOO TOP

2 pounds/1 kg small new or red-
    skin potatoes, large ones cut
    in half

1 pound/500 g cauliflower,
    broken into small florets, stalk
    roughly chopped

3 tablespoons/50 g ghee or
    unsalted butter

1 teaspoon cumin seeds

1 teaspoon ground turmeric

7 ounces/200 g baby spinach,
    washed

This is not as quick as the other recipes in this chapter, but it comes together pretty quickly, most of the cooking time is in the oven and it's so good I wanted to include it. This is one of those recipes that made me do a victory dance when I got it out of the oven. I could tell before I ate it from the smell and from the bubbling filling and crispy top that it was going to be everything I had wanted it to be.

—

Add a little oil to a large pan, add the onion and cook for 10 minutes over a medium heat until soft and sweet. Add the garlic, ginger and chili and cook for another 5 minutes.

Add the spices to the pan and stir for a couple of minutes until all smells fragrant. Next, add the canned beans and their liquid, the tomatoes and 1⅔ cups/400 ml (a can's worth) water.

Simmer for 25 minutes, until the tomatoes are broken down and you have a thick, flavorsome gravy.

Meanwhile, preheat the oven to 400°F/200°C and put the potatoes into a large saucepan (leaving enough space to add the cauliflower later). Cover with boiling water, add half a tablespoon of salt and bring to the boil. Cook for 15–20 minutes, until the potatoes are almost cooked, then add the cauliflower for the last 6 minutes. Drain well.

Put the empty saucepan back on the heat, add 1 tablespoon of ghee or butter and the cumin and turmeric, cook for a minute or so, then add just under ½ cup/100 ml water, the potatoes and cauliflower and half the spinach. Stir to wilt the spinach and use the back of a spoon to crush the potatoes a little.

The beans should be thickened by now. Stir in the other half of the spinach, then spoon into your baking dish. Top with the potato, cauliflower and spinach mixture, drizzle with oil or melted ghee and put into the oven for 30–40 minutes, until the filling is bubbling and the top is brown and crunchy in places.

Rhubarb & stem ginger fool

SERVES 4

FOR THE RHUBARB

2 stems rhubarb, thinly sliced
   (see below for alternatives)
1 heaping tablespoon superfine
   sugar

FOR THE FOOL

1¼ cups/300 ml heavy cream or
   vegan cream
scant ½ cup/100 ml thick Greek
   or coconut yogurt
6 balls stem ginger, 4 finely
   chopped, 2 thinly sliced,
   plus 1 tablespoon of syrup
   from the jar
the zest of ½ lemon, unwaxed
   or organic

This fool, spiked with stem ginger, is so light and pillowy, and so pleasingly neon. I find it hard to think of a dessert I'd rather eat. The rhubarb brings a welcome sharpness and pop of bright pink. Vegan cream may not whip to soft peaks—just whip it as much as you can.

———

In a pan, cook the rhubarb and sugar for 2 minutes, until the juices turn the sugar into a pink syrup but the rhubarb still holds its crunch. Set aside to cool in the pan for 20 minutes.

Whip the cream or vegan cream a little shy of soft peaks, then fold in the yogurt. Add the finely chopped ginger and stir it through with the ginger syrup and lemon zest.

When it has cooled, stir half the cooked rhubarb into the cream.

Top the dessert with the thinly sliced ginger and the rest of the rhubarb.

Seasonal variations

— Strawberries, raw, sliced
— Raspberries, raw, crushed
— Pear, raw, thinly sliced
— Plums, cooked with a little sugar
— Gooseberries, cooked with a little sugar

You can adjust the amount of sugar to the sweetness of your fruit.

Fig & halva sundae

4 ripe figs (see below for
    alternatives)
2 tablespoons honey or
    maple syrup
4 scoops of good vanilla ice cream
    or vegan ice cream
2 ounces/55 g halva, crumbled
1 small handful of pistachios
    (about 3 tablespoons/20 g),
    roughly chopped

The magic of a sundae never gets old. They always take me back to knickerbocker glories in too-high glasses on holiday. Here, the fruit gets mashed to make the sundae sauce, so if your fruit is not super-ripe and mashable, you might want to chop it up a little first. If you are vegan, check that the halva you buy is vegan—most is, but some has honey in it.

——

Peel and mash 2 of the figs and stir in the honey. Cut the remaining figs into quarters.

Take two glasses or glass bowls and spoon in a quarter of the mashed figs, top with a scoop of ice cream, a crumble of halva, a couple of quarters of fig and some chopped pistachios. Then repeat the process, finishing with the final pieces of fig and the last of the pistachios.
Eat immediately.

Seasonal variations

— Raspberries
— Strawberries
— Ripe peaches or apricots
— Very ripe plums

ONE PLANET II

How you can support biodiversity & soil health / What foods should fill your plate / Consider food miles / How to live with less plastic / Cooking with the seasons

How you can support biodiversity & soil health

Biodiversity is the variety of life on Earth, in all its forms and all its interactions, from single-cell organisms to blue whales. Biodiversity is complex and layered. It starts with genes, but also includes individual species, communities of creatures and entire ecosystems, such as forests or coral reefs. It's these infinite interactions that have made the Earth habitable for millions of years.

A more wide-ranging way of viewing biodiversity is that it represents the knowledge learned by evolving species over millions of years about how to survive through the vastly varying environmental conditions Earth has experienced. As Darwin said, everything in nature is connected.

For many people living in towns and cities, wildlife is often something you watch on a David Attenborough documentary. But in reality, the air you breathe, the water you drink and the food you eat all rely on biodiversity. We all know that without plants there would be no oxygen and without bees to pollinate there would be no food. Biodiversity is also central to the coral reefs and mangrove swamps that help to shield us from cyclones and tsunamis and to the trees that absorb air pollution.

When scientists explore ecosystems, they find countless interactions, all honed by millions of years of evolution. If undamaged, these produce a finely balanced, healthy system that contributes to a sustainable planet. The sheer richness of biodiversity also has more direct human health benefits.

Many new medicines are harvested from nature, from a fungus that grows on the fur of sloths potentially helping to cure malaria, to the slime from a sea slug being used to fight cancer.

Where are we now? Thanks to factory farming, overfishing and monocultures, and the farming of just one crop (at the expense of others) in certain areas, as well as changing land use (clearing forests and farming), the crucial biodiversity that this planet relies on is under threat. Species of plants, animals and seeds are being lost. The rate of extinction of all species over the last 100 years is greater than the average of the previous two million years. Alarming to say the least.

Food & biodiversity

"Today, farming rather than hunting is our most lethal activity," says Carolyn Steel in her excellent book *Sitopia: How Food Can Save the World*.

By selectively choosing certain plants or animals to grow on our farms at the expense of others, we are destroying the habitats of those plants and animals not in our food or domestic circle while also drastically reducing the number of wild animals. And we have ended up with only a few crops feeding the planet: by the end of the twentieth century, 12 plant species and 5 animals account for 75% of global food supply. Hard to believe when you consider that there are around 3,000 edible plant species.

The world's capacity to produce food is being undermined by our failure to protect biodiversity. In the first UN study of the plants, animals and microorganisms that help to feed us, approximately 20% of the earth's vegetated surface has become less productive over the last two decades (http://www.fao.org/state-of-biodiversity-for-food-agriculture).

Plant & seed biodiversity

While we rely heavily on 12 species of plants, or crops (see below), heirloom growers, small farmers and seed banks are working to keep less popular plants from extinction. We have become so reliant on the 12 crops that for many of us it might feel like a step out of our comfort zone to cook and eat more unusual foods. But supporting your local farmers and buying more unusual varieties of fruits, vegetables, herbs, grains and pulses is a key way we can support biodiversity.

The world relies heavily on these crops to feed us:
— Sugarcane
— Maize (corn)
— Rice
— Wheat
— Potatoes
— Soybeans
— Cassava (a starchy tuberous root)
— Tomatoes
— Banana
— Onions
— Apples
— Grapes

Growers, farmers, chefs and those engaged with soil and biodiversity all over the world are doing great work to bring back more variety in our food choices. Over the last 10 years, more farmers in the UK have started offering heritage varieties and native produce, and have grown with the land to help the soil to regenerate, known as sustainable agriculture. The tide is changing slowly: but as it stands, only top restaurants and well-off and informed consumers can get their hands on this produce.

Our food buying habits have a part to play in farmers' choices—think about a "trendy" food like quinoa that has become popular. Yet only a few of the thousands of varieties native to South America are cultivated. This has meant farmers now choose to grow a tough, nutritious variety that will protect them from future diseases or extreme weather, but this has put other varieties in danger of becoming extinct.

The food system's reliance on one type or species of food or crop (a monoculture) means cheaper food can be produced more efficiently but leaves crisis in the food system if that particular crop fails or is hit by disease. In her book *The Way We Eat Now*, Bee Wilson points out our reliance on the Cavendish banana, which became the banana of choice when the superior-flavored Gros Michel banana got hit by disease. While there are more than a hundred varieties of banana, 47% of the world relies on the Cavendish: in the UK, it's almost 100%. You can see a similar pattern when you look at apples—we eat 4 or 5 of a possible 6,000 varieties native to the UK that have specific flavors as different as flower varieties, and nutrients to match.

As well as affecting how we farm and grow, the narrow list of foods the world relies on is also not helping our health or helping us to prevent obesity and undernutrition.

While eaten as part of a balanced diet, most of these foods are perfectly healthy. But if we limit ourselves, we are missing out on a range of nutrients that come from a widely balanced diet. My approach to nutrition has always been to vary the types of fruit, vegetables, grains, pulses, herbs and spices that I eat, making sure that most days there is a rainbow of each on offer. By eating a wide range of foods, we are making sure our nutritional net is cast as wide as possible and we are helping to protect biodiversity.

A heartening story is that of chef Dan Barber, who is trying to change how we grow food from the kitchen. He works with growers and plant breeders to grow for flavor and develop new species that can be grown not just for restaurants but for supermarkets, too, so that the new varieties are accessible to all. His sweeter, smaller honeynut squash is now available in supermarkets all over the U.S.: "democratizing flavor," as Barber puts it. This approach, which links chefs, growers, supermarkets and shops, seems a smart way forward.

Soil health

A single spoonful of soil contains 10,000 to 50,000 different types of bacteria. Soil is essential. It is a combination of minerals, organic matter, air, water and living organisms. We need it to sustain life. But our soils are degrading at an alarming rate. We have taken soil for granted and now one-third of the world's arable soils are degraded. The situation becomes even more urgent when we consider that it can take a thousand years for just one centimeter of topsoil to form.

In as little as 60 years we will no longer be able to feed ourselves if we continue to grow, farm and consume as we do now. Soil, home to 98% of life on Earth, is being lost 40 times faster than it is being made. Industrial farming is the leading cause of deforestation and greenhouse gas emissions. It is generally accepted that if nothing is done, we have only 60 harvests left. We lose the equivalent of 30 football fields of soil every minute to degradation. If we do not radically change how we grow and produce food now, our children will not be able to feed themselves.

So why is soil so important?

Combat climate change
Not only does soil help combat climate change, it also helps reduce the effects of climate change. Healthy, well-managed soil captures carbon dioxide and stores it. In the UK, our soils hold an estimated 9.8 billion tons of carbon, making them an essential resource in reducing our greenhouse gas emissions and tackling climate change.

Feed the planet
Without lots of healthy soil it would be impossible for farmers to produce food.

Prevent flooding and drought
Healthy soil is essential for water storage and helping to prevent floods and droughts. It stores water so that crops have a longer life when a drought kicks in, and improves water quality by filtering out pollutants. Healthy soil also has better structure and can reduce erosion through water damage.

Supports biodiversity
Soil also supports biodiversity above the ground. It provides food for birds and other small animals in the worms and insects that live in healthy soil.

How can we help?

Grow your own

Whether in your own back garden or on a shared allotment or on a balcony in a grow bag, growing your own is the most environmentally friendly way to get your food. Be careful to buy peat-free compost and to avoid chemical pesticides and insecticides.

Leaving soil bare is not good for its health; rain can wash away soil's nutrients—and even the soil itself. Growing different vegetables and plants in your garden helps recycle nutrients back into the soil, with the added benefit of reconnecting you with where your food really comes from. Adding compost to your soil will help the soil's health, as will growing soil-friendly plants that pull nitrogen from the air.

Support soil-friendly farming

Some farmers are changing the way they grow. The conservation or regenerative agriculture movement means no plowing or turning the soil, instead keeping the ground covered with crops all year-round and growing a wide variety of plants.

Regenerative agriculture works in harmony with nature, encouraging wildlife and other species of plants to grow alongside crops. Its aim is to restore the soil and, in turn, help to reverse carbon emissions. In fact, some scientists believe that by switching to regenerative agriculture we could dramatically reduce carbon emissions.

You can help by switching your shopping habits. Choose to buy produce from growers practicing conservation (though these are still quite few and far between). If that is a bridge too far, consider buying organic—

your money will be supporting farmers and farming methods that put soil health at the core of their business.

Organic farmers do not use artificial fertilizers and pesticides that can harm life in healthy soil. Looking to natural ecosystems to inform agricultural practices helps maintain healthy soil and protects the delicate balance of life within it.

I appreciate that these are choices that not everyone can make, and that most people who can buy these foods come from a position of privilege (myself included). But I don't think that's a valid reason not to encourage those who can to search out this produce. The more of us who support it, the more chance it has of being grown more widely and becoming affordable and accessible to all.

Having spoken with many farmers trying to do things differently, I have come to understand that the regenerative farming model relies on animals as a part of it— to naturally till the land, to move seeds and crops and to provide natural fertilizer. It's something I am thinking and learning about. While I choose not to eat meat, it would feel fraudulent not to make this point. I have been asked a number of times about my support for regenerative farming as a vegetarian. It is clear to me that this way of growing is the best way to repair our soil and in turn our planet. It does not mean that I need to eat that meat—there are literally billions of people overeating meat in the world who can do that for me. And I am buoyed by advances made in the biodynamic farming community researching vegan practices that could replace this on some farms.

What foods should fill your plate

When deciding what to buy and eat, you should become aware of how your food is produced. There is an abundance of foods we can eat. In fact, there are over 30,000 edible plants. But, thanks to our current food systems and a lack of diversity in our diets, 60% of our global calorie intake comes from rice, white flour and corn. Add sugar and soy, and that total is 75%.

There are fruits and vegetables which thrive and grow easily and cheaply in UK and U.S. soil, but we just don't eat enough of them. For instance, squashes are an enormously diverse and delicious crop, but most of us are familiar only with the butternut.

Woven into the fabric of what we eat are many things that, day to day, we might not consider—from slave labor to cartels, to deforestation and loss of wildlife to an impact on biodiversity and GM foods. When you look into the environmental impact of some of the food we eat, the picture is really complicated and a little overwhelming.

We are living in the age of convenience in terms of buying pre-prepared foods that we fancy at any time we like, but also homogeneity—that is, breeding only the strongest crops, and losing the biodiversity that is so crucial to the health of the planet. We are making our everyday lives easier but steadily destroying the planet.

Our reliance on a limited number of "staples" came into sharp focus during the coronavirus pandemic, when pasta, flour, eggs and other basics were in short supply. My hope is that this crisis allowed us all to be a little more open and flexible in how we eat—if we ever needed an example of the urgent need for us to diversify the food we eat, this was it. According to Bee Wilson, in the Western world particularly, we have access to more foodstuffs than ever before "of a freshness and variety our grandparents could not have imagined" (*The Way We Eat Now*, page 19). Especially in our cities, many foods once considered exotic are now easily available and often affordable too: from asparagus in winter to ready-cut mango and strawberries in December. Though many of us might want to eat a peach in January, it is not going to taste as good or be affordable. Buying ingredients at their peak moment in season means their environmental impact is lowest too.

We have also become very trend-led when it comes to how we eat. When a food becomes a trend, supply pressure increases, and production processes become focused on money, speed and quantity rather than sustainability or ethics. Avocados are an obvious example. According to the U.S. website Eater, the price of a wholesale box of Mexican avocados was $84.25 in the summer of 2019, compared to $37 at around the same time in the previous year. Avocados have helped to pull people out of poverty in Mexico, but have also been linked to cartels.

The "superfood" quinoa is a less clear but much-publicized example of a food fad. Our love for this little seed—which is gluten-free, protein-rich, low in carbohydrate and contains all nine essential amino acids—was widely reported to have stripped local Peruvians and

Bolivians of their everyday nutritious staple, but it also helped farmers grow their businesses and support their families. So, as with most things in the world of sustainability, nothing is simple.

So what foods should we fill our plate with? If we know that following trends and mass mono-cropping is, for the most part, damaging to the planet, then we need to be doing the opposite—thinking about simple, locally grown whole foods that are good for our bodies and treating anything imported as a treat. If you eat dairy, then buying organic and using it in small quantities as creamy, tangy or rich accents to balance or accentuate other ingredients is a good way of working. The same goes for anything imported that we use in small quantities but can make a huge difference to taste—soy sauce, harissa, preserved lemons, etc.

Variety and creativity are key to this mindset. I recommend investigating community-supported agriculture (CSA) baskets, as they easily tick some of these boxes and aren't necessarily unaffordable. (If CSA veg baskets are out of the question, try your supermarket and look for local or misfit veg.) There are many great veg box programs that support farmers and sustainable agriculture. It might seem daunting to be presented with unusual fruits or vegetables, especially if they appear week after week, but hopefully some of the recipes in this book will help to give you the inspiration and confidence to embrace unfamiliar ingredients.

The U.S. is also proving to be the ideal climate to explore growing ingredients such as quinoa more sustainably and ethically. U.S. growers and suppliers are doing fantastic things to make non-native foods available to us in more sustainable ways.

Tread lightly

These are crops that for a variety of reasons have a negative impact on the planet or on the people who produce them. Some are things most of us might use very little of and consider a "treat." When buying from this list of foods, consider the sustainability of the producer (if that is information you can find) and, where possible, buy Fairtrade (see page 227); this is about making judgments based on your value system and what is important to you.

— Almonds
— Avocados
— Cashews (buy Fairtrade)
— Imported quinoa
— Soy
— Cane sugar (buy Fairtrade)
— Bananas (buy Fairtrade)
— Corn
— Chocolate (buy Fairtrade)
— Coffee (buy Fairtrade)
— Tea (buy Fairtrade)
— Rice (buy Fairtrade)
— Palm oil

Fill your plate

Try to fill your plate with seasonal fruit and veg and legumes and pulses grown in your home country.

Fill up on your country's grains and accent them with nuts, seeds, herbs and flowers for extra nutrients, flavor and color. In the U.S. and Canada, native grains include maize (corn) and wild rice; but you will also find many small-scale farms that grow oats, heirloom varieties of wheat, spelt, and many others.

Foods to fill your plate with

Seasonal fruit and veg
See the chart on pages 232-233.

Cereals, grains and flours
Swapping your normal wheat flour for spelt or a more unusual grain will help support biodiversity. I switch up the flours I use as much as the veg I eat. Buying the whole grain cuts down on waste too; bleached refined flour uses only a small part of the grain and throws away the most nutritious part, so veer toward whole grain and more unusual varieties if you can.

— Rye
— Wheat
— Barley
— Spelt
— Oats
— Einkorn
— Amaranth
— Buckwheat
— Emmer wheat
— Khorasan wheat or kamut
— Millet
— USA- or Canada-grown quinoa
— Teff

Beans and pulses
Beans and pulses make up a huge part of my diet, and if I were to back a food that will help us combat climate change, it would be humble pulses. They are super-economical nutritional powerhouses, need less water to produce than other proteins, and are nitrogen-restoring, which means they help fix the soil (see page 214). They are also easy to cook from scratch and freeze,

or to buy in jars (which are, in my opinion, always superior) or cans.

— Beans: fava beans, organic soybeans
— Lentils: red, green, yellow, Puy
— Peas: Carlin, marrowfat, large blue peas, yellow split peas, chickpeas

Nuts and seeds
Nuts and seeds are nutritionally rich and full of essential fats. Soaking nuts in cold water before eating them makes them easier to digest. Some of the nuts available in the U.S. are imported, so be sure to buy Fairtrade.

— Cashews (buy Fairtrade)
— Hazelnuts
— Hemp seeds
— Flaxseeds
— Walnuts
— Sesame seeds
— Sunflower seeds
— Pumpkin seeds
— Almonds
— Brazil nuts (buy Fairtrade)

Sugar and sweet things
The rule with sweet things is the same as for most other foods: the simpler and less processed, the better. Look for unprocessed sugars like rapadura (panela) or jaggery, and use natural syrups and dried fruit to sweeten.

— Unrefined sugar
— Blackstrap molasses
— Dates and date syrup
— Maple syrup
— Honey

Oils
Good oil can transform a dish. I use a cheaper olive oil for cooking and a good extra virgin for dressing and finishing

food. I also use a canola oil (it's important to buy organic here) for cooking as well as a Fairtrade coconut oil for frying at high temperatures (olive oil is not good for very high temperatures, as heat damages it and produces free radicals). Hemp oil is also great for dressings.

— Coconut oil
— Extra virgin hemp oil
— Extra virgin olive oil
— Extra virgin canola oil (organic)

Foraged food

My connection with food and nature comes when I head out to the marshes near my house and pick from the local thickets. Where I live in the UK, it's quite easy to forage. But it is wise to be cautious if you are not sure what you are looking for. There are books and courses you can take if you'd like to learn more. It might sound a bit whimsical, but it's a great thing to do: to connect with the source of our food, to pick our own food, when lots of us are so removed from that. Foraged foods are wild, nutritious and totally free. Here are a few of the ones I love to find.

Nettles
Instantly recognizable for its ragged leaves; remember to wear gloves when picking and preparing. Once blanched, the leaves lose their sting. *Season:* best picked from February to June; go for the younger-looking leaves.

Elderflowers
The little cloud-like flowers are distinctive and you'll be able to smell them too. I pick mine on Hackney Marshes. Pick the ones higher up and, if you can, ones that face

the sun. *Season:* May to early July if you're lucky.

Wild garlic (Ramps)
Long, flat deep green leaves, found in pretty much every British woodland or on riverbanks; you'll be able to smell it if you've picked the right stuff. *Season:* late winter to mid-spring.

Crab apples
Tiny little apples, green with blushing red cheeks, which deepen in color as they ripen. They are the wild ancestors of the apples we eat today. Trees are found throughout the UK but are also easy to plant in your garden. *Season:* August to October.

Blackberries
So easy to find on the east and west coasts of the U.S. and in certain regions of Canada; look for them in less urban areas. A good tip is to take an umbrella with a hooked handle with you to hook brambles and bring them closer to you. Avoid roadsides and berries that are low down. *Season:* late summer to autumn.

Sloes (Blackthorn berries)
Dusty, inky-blue berries that are found on bushes, on and near beaches and in woodland. Their bushes have spiky thorns and the berries have short stems and hug the branches. *Season:* pick from the end of September to December; some people say to wait until after the first frost for the best flavor.

Consider food miles

Food miles are a huge part of the discussion around sustainability. But it's often hard to know exactly which foods are high on the food miles scale and what impact that has on the overall carbon footprint of that food.

Often, packaging can be hard to decipher and misleading. If you are buying food with more than one ingredient, it is hard to track them all. An easy solution is, of course, buying seasonal, local whole foods. It's much easier to trace the source of a potato than a factory-made item with 20 ingredients, for instance. But I know that's not realistic all the time. Remember: if you are eating a predominantly plant-based diet, you have already significantly improved your carbon footprint.

Some imported foods have become a huge part of how we eat. For me, that's things like coconut milk, miso and even lemons. It can be confusing to try to work out where something is coming from and if you are making a good decision.

The way I approach it is to think about where the food originates and what season it might be there right now. Is that food in season if it's fresh and, if it's packaged, how long will it last and how quickly will it need to reach its destination to stay in good condition? Foodmiles.com is a good resource to use for checking distances here.

Common sense in most cases will tell you if an ingredient has come on a boat (several weeks' travel) or a plane (a day's travel). As an approximation, food that is air-freighted can generate more than one hundred times the carbon emissions per kilometer of food that travels by ship (shrinkthatfootprint.com/food-miles).

This is not a foolproof method by any means, as some things, like bananas, for instance, are picked green, shipped on a boat then ripened locally, but you might assume they are flown over and hence have a much higher carbon footprint. In general, if something is jarred, canned or dry, it will have come on a boat and therefore have a significantly lower footprint.

There are some good steps being taken to help us be more aware about food miles. In 2020, Quorn became the first major UK-based brand to introduce carbon labeling on its products. Quorn's "farm to shop" carbon footprint data, certified by the Carbon Trust, is already available online for some of their products, and hopefully other brands in the UK and North America will follow suit (https://www.quorn.co.uk/carbon-footprint).

A deeper dive into food miles

The distance food travels, and the transportation used to deliver it, while a small piece of the overall footprint, can add significantly to its carbon footprint. A 100 g box of blueberries grown locally or imported by boat will produce around 100 g of carbon dioxide. If it is flown in, that increases by ten times, pushing its carbon footprint up to more like 1 kg (independent.co.uk/news/food-miles-carbon-footprints-climate-change

-sustainability-a9050406.html). The last mile is often forgotten, but it's one we have direct control over: How did we get to the shop and take the food home?

It is also important to look at the whole supply chain. How a food is grown, the fertilizers and pesticides used by the farmer and the fuel used by harvesting machinery, as well as the amount of water used during production, contribute a far more significant percentage to the overall life cycle of a food than just how it is transported.

I was surprised to learn that some foods grown in season, in Europe or even farther afield like Brazil, then transported to the UK by boat, actually have a lower carbon footprint than those produced out of season in the UK. For example, tomatoes grown in the natural sunshine in Spain have a lower carbon footprint than those grown in UK polytunnels or greenhouses that require substantial energy to heat. "According to government data, buying a tomato grown in the UK has three times the footprint of a tomato grown in Spain." Similarly, with some apple varieties, including Braeburn, buying New Zealand apples out of season, which have been shipped in, rather than buying UK ones, which have been stored in fridges all year, results in fewer emissions.

If you are buying foods from abroad, knowing whether a particular food is in season in the country of origin is useful to know but not always easy to find out. I have included a chart of seasonal foods on pages 232-233. But, as a guide, if foods are out of season in the U.S., then they are also likely to be out of season in countries with similar climates.

Hotter countries closer to the equator, with warm climates throughout the year, are more likely to harness the sun's energy than to use greenhouses or polytunnels and carbon-intensive synthetic heating methods. So a soft fruit that is out of season in parts of the U.S., such as strawberries, is far more likely to be flown in and is therefore best avoided.

People

The people who farm, process and produce our food are such an important piece of the conversation we are having here. They feel the effects of climate change on their crops and livelihoods and are critical in making changes to how we farm. Around 2 billion people are employed in agriculture. It is our duty as consumers to support farming practices that benefit the lives of farmers, especially those closest to the poverty line, as well as marginalized groups and women who are key to sustainable economies. Buying Fairtrade is a brilliant way of supporting these systems.

Another consideration is human rights issues, such as gender discrimination and modern slavery, which are sadly still prevalent in the food industry. Companies have a responsibility to ensure ethical working conditions have been used in the production of the goods they sell. While this area is complex, there are tools to help: viewing company websites, requesting information via social media and looking at comparative benchmarks like Oxfam's Behind the Barcodes initiative, which ranks the supermarkets on how they line up on human rights.

Fairtrade

By buying Fairtrade you are guaranteeing fair prices and providing a premium to invest in local communities, so farmers can provide a better future for themselves and their families. Remembering that we are cooking with a precious ingredient, that takes a lot of resource to grow, to produce and to transport, makes every recipe even more of a luxury. Buying Fairtrade ingredients means you are sending a clear message to the food system that you care about the people who grew or made your food.

As well as securing a fair price for the farmer, the Fairtrade organization requires farmers to adhere to greenhouse gas emissions limits, soil and water quality and biodiversity protection, waste management and a ban on GMOs, among other things. They also train farmers in moving toward more environmentally sound ways of growing. It is also a way of ensuring your food is traceable and honestly produced. Look out for the mark of the Fairtrade foundation.

Food you should try to buy Fairtrade:
— Cashews
— Cane sugar
— Bananas
— Chocolate
— Coffee
— Tea
— Rice

Supporting communities with the food you buy

While I base my shopping on local and seasonal food as much as I can, we live in a world with a global food system.

Buying foods from communities on the other side of the planet can help support and regenerate local economies and good farming and hence the environment.

Some guidelines for imported food:
— Eat in season when you can—see the seasonality chart on pages 232-233.
— Try to avoid air-freighted fresh produce; check labels and use common sense.
— Look at the whole picture—from how your food is grown, processed, transported, cooked and stored, to the waste it produces.
— Prioritize local dry goods over imported.
— Give yourself a break; no one is perfect and this can be a confusing area to navigate.
— Support Fairtrade where you can.

How to live with less plastic

It seems that the tide is finally beginning to turn against plastic. As the full realization of what we are doing to our oceans begins to hit us, it's time to look at the wealth of alternatives out there, which often actually work better (and look nicer) than their plastic counterparts.

Plastic is a tricky issue, not in the least because consumers have (quite rightly) become a lot more aware of it in the last year or two, but the packaging industry has yet to catch up properly with viable alternatives for the majority of our food. The facilities needed to process seemingly more environmental alternatives often don't exist yet, especially in the UK and U.S., and there is a wealth of confusing plastic alternatives which may not be any better, or could potentially be even worse, for the environment.

Plastics do a very good job of keeping food protected and fresh and so can reduce waste, especially with delicate things like salad leaves and soft fruit. Some supermarkets have started using compostable trays for berries and cellulose tops instead of plastic; these can be recycled, unlike plastic wrap. They are hard to find, though, and tend to be more expensive. As with all the issues surrounding sustainability, it's not black and white.

For good reason, there has been a huge focus on reducing plastic these last few years, and some of my friends are evangelical about it. While I think it's incredibly important for us to tread as lightly as possible, I also think it's important that we keep a wide focus on all the issues affecting our health and the health of the planet, not just one.

So pick your battles, and try your best to avoid single-use plastic, bags, bottles, plastic-lined coffee cups, etc. But if you are going to use something hundreds of times (like a plastic Tupperware), that's a different thing. If you have something in your kitchen already that is plastic, use it and replace it (preferably with a non-plastic alternative) only when it's worn out.

It's taken me a long while to change my habits in the kitchen, and I am still far from perfect. I started buying in bulk many years ago, then I got reusable water bottles and coffee cups. Next, I reduced the plastic packaging my food came in, then I moved away from plastic wrap and finally I have tried to reduce the packaging I buy when I am traveling (which I have to say is the hardest bit). And I still end up buying containers of berries in plastic and the occasional bag of salad. But I try my best.

I also wanted to note that it's not possible for everyone to do this. I am in a position of privilege as someone with enough money, information and resources to be able to make these choices. It's about doing what you can.

Some of the suggestions here might be things you have already made part of your life, but if you are anything like me, it's always good to have a gentle reminder.

In the kitchen

Buy in bulk
Wherever you can, buy dry goods and spices in bulk, but make sure you are being realistic about the amounts: overbuying and waste are also not the aim here. Save

your old glass jars to refill with loose grains, lentils, nuts and seeds. If you can take them with you to the shop and fill them there, all the better.

Bottled water

I keep glass bottles to fill with tap water, which I then keep in the fridge to save running the tap if I want cold water. I use a cheap charcoal filter inside the bottle to make the water taste better or run it through my water filter (I use a Berkey one) first. If you buy a lot of bottles of sparkling water, you could consider a SodaStream to carbonate your own drinking water.

Buy loose, unpacked fruit and veg

Where you can, in the supermarket or the greengrocer's, opt for loose, packaging-free fruit and veg. Use canvas bags or clean totes to store vegetables in the fridge or freezer. This stops freezer burn and helps keep vegetables from drying out. This way you'll be more likely to buy what you need and in turn reduce your waste too. For soft fruits and veg, like berries and tomatoes, this can be harder, but some places use compostable paper containers and compostable wrappers.

Storage containers

If you need new ones, go for glass rather than plastic (obviously don't throw away existing plastic ones; use them until they fall apart). Glass is a safer material to use for storing food, as plastic can taint food. Also consider enamel storage pots or baking trays, which can go straight from the oven into the fridge. More often than not, though, I use an old jar or a bowl with a plate on top.

Cling wrap

This is one where I use my judgment, since food waste is potentially more harmful than using plastic wrap. And there are really no viable alternatives for plastic wrap in restaurant kitchens just yet. At home I use beeswax wraps instead, and they work really well for covering cheese, sandwiches and bowls. They work less well for oily or tomato-based sauces, as they can be hard to clean. Health-food stores and bulk shops sell beeswax wraps and they are easy to find online—a simple recipe for how to make them is below. For wrapping pastry and dough while it rests, use a clean, damp tea towel. Reusable zip-lock bags are also now available and really useful for freezing and storing things where you might have used a throwaway zip-lock bag.

Beeswax wraps

YOU WILL NEED:

The ends of some burnt-down candles, grated, or beeswax beads
Clean fabric (ideally with a tight weave)
Scissors (fabric ones if you have them)
A brush

METHOD:

Preheat the oven to its lowest setting. Cut your fabric with pinking shears into the sizes you want to use.

Line a large tray with parchment paper, lay down the fabric flat and sprinkle it with a scattering of beeswax beads or grated wax.

Put it in the oven and let it melt for 5–10 minutes (or you can use your iron on a low setting). Take it out and use your brush to spread the beeswax evenly. Cut into useful sizes for what you need. Between uses, wash with warm water and drip dry. Don't use soap.

Straws

Try straws actually made from straw (which is what they were named after in the first place) or stainless steel straws. Single-use plastic straws are now banned in England, but paper ones are not really much better for the environment and are mostly not bio-degradable. Also, be mindful that some food outlets use plastic lids and non-plastic straws, which obviously is not a win for anyone.

Bowl covers

Linen or fabric bowl covers are a great way to avoid plastic wrap, and they look nice, too.

Cleaning cloths

You can buy reusable cloths, which go in the washing machine, rather than J Cloths and sponges (though these can be washed in the washing machine too, they just don't last as long). Ones made of natural fabrics are obviously the best choices. Use wooden-handled brushes for scrubbing pans and veg.

Make your own all-purpose cleaning spray

I use an old spray bottle and fill it with a homemade kitchen cleaning spray—I mix 2 cups/500 ml (depending on the size of the spray bottle) of boiled water with ¼ cup/60 ml of white vinegar and a few drops of essential oils.

Out and about

On the whole I think life would be all-around better if we took the time to drink a coffee, or to sit down and eat our lunch in a café. This of course means no takeaway waste. It's not always possible, but I try to do it when I can.

Bags

In the U.S., regulating single-use plastic bags has made a big difference. But, you need to use sturdier plastic bags at least eight times before its carbon footprint is lower than an ordinary plastic bag's. Even an organic cotton tote bag must be used 149 times (for the thinnest, most basic ones) and over a thousand times for a sturdier one for it to be worth it. I keep totes in all the most useful places to make forgetting them harder.

Coffee cups

This is a very obvious one, but use a reusable coffee cup. I keep one in my handbag and one in our car. My general rule is if I don't have the cup I don't buy a coffee; it makes me remember it. Try and avoid "compostable" packaging, too, as it is sadly not the green option we had all hoped for just yet.

Water bottles

Again, an obvious one, but I use a stainless-steel water bottle instead of buying bottled water, a simple but vital step we should all be taking. If you forget yours, most coffee shops and restaurants will give you a glass.

Food shopping

Lots of shops now let you bring your own containers to fill with loose veg or cheese from the deli counter or dry goods.

Plastic cutlery

I try and avoid using these. If there is a choice, I'll eat in, or there are lots of affordable wooden options. Don't forget to pack kitchen flatware for picnics.

When recycling

Pay close attention to the item or package you are getting rid of—clean everything well. You will need to separate a label from a can, or a cardboard header from a pouch. Putting trash in the correct bin is important and helps your recycling actually get recycled.

COOKING WITH THE SEASONS

SUMMER — arugula / asparagus / baby carrots / beets / broccoli / carrots / cauliflower / chicory / chilies / cucumber / eggplants / fava beans / fennel / garlic / green beans / kohlrabi / lettuce / mushrooms / new potatoes / peas / peppers / potatoes / radishes / scallions / sea beans / snow peas / sorrel / summer squash / sweet corn / Swiss chard / tomatoes / watercress / zucchini / apricots / blueberries / cherries / damsons / first apples / edible flowers / gooseberries / greengages / loganberries / peaches / plums / red currants / strawberries / tayberries

SPRING — artichoke / arugula / asparagus / beets / cabbage / carrots / chilies / collard greens / cucumber / endive / fava beans / kale / leeks / lettuce / morel mushrooms / new potatoes / parsnips / peas / peppers / purple-sprouting broccoli / radishes / ramps / scallions / sea beans / spinach / spring greens / sorrel / Swiss chard / turnips / watercress / blackberries / elderflowers / lemons / rhubarb

Produce varies widely in the U.S. and Canada due to geography, climate, and different growing seasons. Here is a very general guide to seasonal fruits and vegetables.

For more information about what grows in your region, visit seasonalfoodguide.org or canadianfoodfocus.org/whats-in-season/.

AUTUMN — arugula / beets / broccoli / Brussels sprouts / butternut squash / carrots / cauliflower / celeriac / celery / chard / chicory / chilies / collard greens / cucumbers / eggplants / endive / fennel / garlic / green beans / kale / kohlrabi / leeks / lettuce / onions / parsnips / peas / peppers / potatoes / pumpkin / radishes / rutabaga / scallions / sea beans / snow peas / sorrel / spinach / squash / sweet corn / sweet potatoes / Swiss chard / tomatoes / turnips / zucchini / apples / blackberries / cranberries / damsons / elderberries / figs/ greengages / medlar pears / pears / plums / loganberries / quince / raspberries / red currants

WINTER — beets / Brussels sprouts / carrots / cauliflower/ celeriac / celery / collard greens / endive / Jerusalem artichokes / kale / leeks / onions / parsnips / potatoes / pumpkin / purple-sprouting broccoli / red cabbage / rutabaga / Savoy cabbage / scallions / squash / sweet potatoes / Swiss chard / turnips / winter tomatoes / apples / chestnuts / clementines / pears / quince

ONE
TRAY

Rhubarb & potato traybake

Forced rhubarb shows up exactly when we need it. These neon-pink stems, the color of Brighton rock (a traditional seaside treat of hard candy), are forced from the ground in dark sheds in Yorkshire and cheer me on in the kitchen until the first greens of spring. Whatever rhubarb you use, though, its spiritual home is under a sweet rubble of brown sugar crumble, but it also has enough acidity to stand up to savory flavors—the richness of cheese or a crisp-edged roasted potato. This is a painting of a dish, which I finish off with some buttery toasted oats and almonds. Serve this straight from the roasting tray on the table. Vegans should use a vegan feta-style cheese and maple syrup instead of honey, and olive oil for butter.

———

Heat the oven to 425°F/220°C. Cut any large potatoes into halves or quarters, and tumble them onto your largest sheet tray. Add a good pinch of salt and pepper, most of the rosemary, the bay leaves and fennel seeds. Mix the vinegar, honey or maple syrup and 3 tablespoons of oil, and pour half of it over the potatoes, saving the rest for later. Toss everything together to coat the potatoes, then roast for 25 minutes, until they are beginning to turn golden.

Once the potatoes have had their time, take them out of the oven, add the feta and rhubarb, gently toss to mix, and roast for another 15–20 minutes.

While this cooks, heat the butter in a frying pan with the remaining rosemary and add the oats, chopped almonds and a good pinch of salt. Move everything around the pan until the flakes are golden and smell buttery and toasty, then transfer to a bowl to cool.

The bake is ready when the rhubarb has softened but is still holding its shape and the potatoes are burnished and crisp. Pour the rest of the honey dressing over the tray and toss to coat everything. Sprinkle the oats over the top and serve in the middle of the table with some greens.

SERVES 4–6

1⅔ pounds/750 g waxy potatoes
a few sprigs of rosemary
4 bay leaves
1 tablespoon fennel seeds
2 tablespoons cider vinegar
2 tablespoons runny honey or
    maple syrup
olive oil
7-ounce/200 g block of feta or
    vegan feta-style cheese, cut
    into rough cubes
10 ounces/300 g rhubarb, cut
    into ¼-inch/5 mm-thick slices
2 tablespoons butter or olive oil
½ cup/50 g rolled oats
¼ cup/25 g almonds, toasted and
    roughly chopped

Pea, mint & preserved lemon phyllo tart

SERVES 6

1 pound/500 g fresh or
    frozen peas
olive oil
a bunch of scallions, sliced
1 x 15-ounce/400 g can small
    white beans, drained
4 ounces/125 g spinach, wilted
1 preserved lemon, flesh
    removed, rind finely chopped
a handful of green olives, pitted
    and roughly chopped
a good pinch of dried chili flakes
a small bunch of mint, leaves
    picked and roughly chopped
a small bunch of parsley, leaves
    picked and roughly chopped
7 ounces/200 g phyllo pastry
½ cup/50 g shelled pistachios,
    roughly chopped

A quick tart made in a frying pan with not much fuss but all the flavor. Most of the things in this tart I have on hand in the freezer or in my cupboards—a couple of bunches of fresh herbs liven things up. For very little work this looks impressive too. A crumble of feta on top would not hurt, if that's your thing. This tart is vegan, provided you use vegan phyllo, which happens to be the most common.

——

Heat the oven to 400°F/200°C. Boil the peas (fresh or frozen) in well-salted water for 3–4 minutes, then drain and put to one side.

Heat a tablespoon of olive oil in a cast-iron frying pan about 10 inches/24–26 cm (you will use this for your tart) and sauté the scallions with a good pinch of salt until soft.

In a bowl, mash the beans and peas roughly to make a chunky paste. Add the spinach, the preserved lemon, olives, chili flakes, mint, parsley and scallions, then season well and mix. Drizzle a little oil all around your frying pan.

Unwrap the sheets of phyllo and lay them one by one over your frying pan (which we will be using like a round roasting pan), leaving a little overlap around the edges (you'll fold this in later). Drizzle with oil, then keep layering and drizzling with oil until you have a good, sturdy layer of four sheets—you may need to patch it together piece by piece if you have small sheets.

Drizzle the whole lot with a bit more olive oil, then use a pastry brush to spread the oil all over the pastry. Spoon the filling into the middle, spread it evenly across the base and fold the excess phyllo back over the filling to form a wavy edge. Brush a little oil on top. Scatter over the roughly chopped pistachios. Put the pan over a medium heat and cook for 3–4 minutes to crisp up the pastry from the bottom.

Put in the bottom of the oven and bake for 15 minutes, or until golden and crisp. Check halfway through and rotate the pan to ensure the pastry cooks evenly. Allow to cool, then carefully transfer to a chopping board. Serve in generous slices with lemon-dressed salad leaves.

Quick squash lasagna

SERVES 6

2¾ cups/690 g tomato passata/
   purée/crushed canned
   tomatoes

2 tablespoons extra virgin
   olive oil

2 cloves of garlic, peeled
   and chopped

a good pinch of dried chili flakes

2 x 15-ounce/400 g cans green
   or Puy lentils, drained (or
   9 ounces/250 g home-cooked)

½ a butternut squash (about
   1⅓ pounds/600 g), peeled
   and grated

⅓ cup/50 g black olives, pitted
   and chopped

2 tablespoons capers

the zest of a lemon, unwaxed or
   organic

a small bunch of basil,
   leaves picked

2 x 4-ounce/125 g balls of
   mozzarella or vegan-style
   mozzarella

9 ounces/250 g dried lasagna
   sheets

Pasta has my heart like nothing else. My love affair with it was cemented when making stuffed agnolotti, caramelle and everything in between in restaurant kitchens, but it started with something simpler: my mum's lasagna. This lasagna is something slightly different but still as nostalgic and comforting. It is the quickest I've made, ready for the oven in 10 minutes (not the hour it normally takes), yet there is still a rich deep tomato sauce and those crisp baked edges to fight over. I don't pre-cook my lasagna sheets, as they cook in the sauce and I like them a little al dente. If you prefer them softer, you could use fresh pasta sheets here. This recipe was originally inspired by one of my all-time favorite cooks, Heidi Swanson of 101cookbooks.com.

———

Heat the oven to 400°F/200°C.

In a large bowl or jug, mix the passata (or purée/crushed canned tomatoes) with the oil, half a teaspoon of flaky sea salt, the chopped garlic, chili flakes, drained lentils, grated squash, chopped olives, capers and lemon zest. Tear the basil leaves in half.

Spoon a quarter of the sauce into an ovenproof dish roughly 8 inches x 12 inches/20 cm x 30 cm (I use an oval roughly the same size), tear over a third of one of the balls of mozzarella, then cover with pasta sheets. Repeat for another two layers: a quarter of the sauce, a third of a ball of mozzarella, a layer of pasta.

Finish with a final layer of sauce, then tear over the whole second ball of mozzarella, sprinkle with salt and pepper, top with the basil, and drizzle with a little more olive oil.

Bake for 30–35 minutes, until the mozzarella is deeply golden. Serve with a sharply dressed salad (I mix lemon juice, cider vinegar, mustard and extra virgin olive oil, and toss through a bowl of green leaves).

Spiced olive-oil roasted tomatoes with yogurt & herbs

Tomatoes and olive oil are the culinary equivalent of Fred and Ginger— they just work. Here, the tomatoes are roasted in the oil, making them buttery and the oil vine-scented and sweet. I add spices, but they'd be just as good on their own. Serve warm with yogurt for a welcome hot-cold contrast and some bread for mopping up the juices. Don't be put off by the amount of oil; it's what makes this dish what it is.

I serve this for dinner but also as a sharing starter or snack when I have people round. The oil is insane and prime for bread dipping, which I think makes a good start to any meal.

———

Heat the oven to 300°F/150°C. While the oven is heating up, toast the spices in a deep 12-inch x 8-inch/30 cm x 20 cm roasting pan (large enough to hold all the tomatoes) in the oven for a few minutes until they smell toasty. Then add the tomatoes to the tray, leaving on any stalks or vines.

Slice the tops off the garlic bulbs and nestle them among the tomatoes. Season well with salt. Pour in the olive oil, making sure it comes two-thirds of the way up the tomatoes. Roast for 2 hours.

Let the tomatoes cool a little, then squeeze the soft garlic from the papery skins and add back to the tomato pan.

To serve, put a few spoonfuls of yogurt on each plate and top with some still-warm tomatoes and garlic. Scatter some basil and dill over the top, followed by a little grated lemon zest and a drizzle of the tomato oil. Serve with the warm, toasted sourdough bread.

Ways to serve your tomatoes

— Add some cannellini or butter (lima) beans for the last 30 minutes for a more hearty meal
— Toss the tomatoes through pasta, with ricotta and basil
— Pile on top of toast and top with a 6-minute egg
— Blend into a sauce to use with pasta/pizza/to enrich a stew
— Stir through rice with lots of toasted cumin and chopped mint

SERVES 4–6

1 teaspoon mustard seeds
1 teaspoon coriander seeds
2 pounds/900 g tomatoes, a mixture of sizes, shapes and colors
2 whole bulbs of garlic
1½ cups/350 ml extra virgin olive oil

TO SERVE
scant 1 cup/200 ml plain yogurt of your choice
a small bunch of basil
a small bunch of dill
the zest of a lemon, unwaxed or organic
plenty of toasted sourdough

Baked dhal with tamarind-glazed sweet potato

SERVES 4

1¼ cups/250 g split red lentils

2 tablespoons coconut or peanut oil

1 onion, peeled and finely chopped

a large thumb-sized piece of ginger, peeled and finely chopped

2 cloves of garlic, peeled and finely chopped

1 teaspoon cumin seeds

10 cardamom pods

1 teaspoon ground turmeric

a pinch of dried chili flakes

1 x 14.5-ounce/400 g can diced tomatoes

3 cups/750 ml hot vegetable stock

1 x 13.5-ounce/400 ml can unsweetened coconut milk

1⅔ pounds/750 g sweet potatoes

3 tablespoons tamarind paste

2 limes, unwaxed or organic, halved

In every book I write there is a recipe that I love a little more than the rest. I don't feel good about it. Kind of like having a favorite child, no one wants to admit it. And this is it. Turmeric, cardamom and ginger-heavy dhal, topped with tamarind-glazed sweet potato, the stuff of my dreams. Luckily, I have only one actual child.

———

Preheat the oven to 400°F/200°C. Wash the lentils in cold water, until the water is no longer milky, then leave to drain.

Warm the oil in a wide, shallow ovenproof pan over a medium heat, add the chopped onion and cook until it is soft and pale gold, so about 10 minutes. Stir the ginger and garlic into the onion and add the cumin seeds. Continue cooking for 2–3 minutes.

Meanwhile, crack open the cardamom pods, take out the seeds, grind to a coarse powder, then stir into the onion together with the turmeric and chili flakes. Add a good grind of black pepper and half a teaspoon of flaky sea salt, stirring for a minute or two.

Add the tomatoes, lentils, stock and coconut milk, then bring to a simmer for a few minutes until everything has come together. You don't need to cook the lentils here, as they will cook under the sweet potato in the oven.

While the lentils simmer, cut the sweet potatoes into long slices about ¼ inch/5 mm in thickness. Season them with salt and pepper, then place on top of the lentils to form a lid (don't worry if the first few sink), brush the top with the tamarind paste and put into the oven to bake for 30–40 minutes, until the lentils are tender and have thickened and the sweet potatoes are crispy. Finish with a squeeze of lime over the top.

Roasted squash with
lemongrass, peanut & lime

SERVES 4

2 medium butternut squash

5 tablespoons olive or coconut oil

2 tablespoons coriander seeds

4 cardamom pods, seeds
removed

3 sticks of lemongrass, very
finely chopped

3 red chilies, roughly chopped

4 limes, unwaxed or organic

a thumb-sized piece of ginger,
peeled

1 cup/250 ml thick Greek or
coconut yogurt

TO SERVE

1 cup/150 g roasted unsalted
peanuts, roughly chopped

a large bunch of cilantro leaves,
roughly chopped

A one-tray dinner that takes roasted squash in an unexpected flavor direction: heady lemongrass, crunch from roasted peanuts, punchy ginger and lime and chili with some yogurt for acidity. For the really hungry, some brown or basmati rice here would work, but I eat this just as it is.

———

Heat the oven to 400°F/200°C. If your squash is a butternut or thin-skinned variety, there is no need to peel it. Halve it, scoop out the seeds and cut into thick slices or boats. Lay them on a roasting tray and drizzle with the oil.

Bash the coriander and cardamom seeds in a mortar with a pestle. Add the chopped lemongrass and bash again to break it down a little. Scatter half this mixture over the squash with a good pinch of salt and the chopped chilies, keeping the other half of the lemongrass mixture for later.

Use a fine grater to zest 2 of the limes over the top of the squash, then cut the 2 limes in half and squeeze the juice over as well. Toss everything together and put the lot into the hot oven for 45 minutes, or until the squash is golden.

Meanwhile, make the sauce. Put the reserved lemongrass mixture into a bowl with the zest and juice of the remaining limes, finely grate in the ginger, add the yogurt and mix well.

Once the squash is roasted perfectly, lay it on a serving platter, sprinkle over the peanuts and cilantro leaves and serve the yogurt on the side for spooning over.

Lemon, asparagus &
Israeli couscous traybake

Here, everything is cooked under the broiler rather than baked in the oven, to give a charred flavor and to spice things up. Asparagus quickly sears under the broiler, bringing out its nutty character, and slices of lemon char and sweeten. You do have to cook the couscous on the stove top first. Any leftover cooked grain would work well here. Israeli couscous is the same thing as giant couscous, pearl couscous, or moghrabieh.

———

First, cook your couscous in boiling water and a good pinch of salt until al dente, probably a couple of minutes less than the package instructions.

Preheat your broiler to high. Snap the woody bottoms from the asparagus and discard them or keep for a stock. Roughly shred the spring greens. Put the lot onto a sheet tray, grate over the zest of both lemons and sprinkle with the chili flakes and the garlic. Cut the zested lemons into thin slices.

Once the couscous is cooked, add it to the tray and toss with a generous amount of olive oil. Season with salt and pepper, then lay the Halloumi and the lemon slices on top.

Put the sheet tray under the broiler and cook for 10 minutes, turning from time to time until the asparagus has lost its rawness and the Halloumi is browned.

Finish with the chopped dill, a drizzle of oil and a sprinkle of sumac, and serve right away.

SERVES 4

7 ounces/200 g pearl or Israeli couscous
14 ounces/400 g asparagus, halved lengthways
1 head of spring greens (about 5-7 ounces/150-200 g)
2 lemons, unwaxed or organic
a generous pinch of dried chili flakes or 1 teaspoon Turkish chili flakes
2 cloves of garlic, peeled and thinly sliced
olive oil
7-ounce/200 g block of Halloumi or vegan Halloumi-style cheese (sometimes called "Mediterranean-style"), thickly sliced, broken into small pieces
a bunch of dill or mint, chopped
1 teaspoon sumac

Creamy parsnip, leek & white bean crumble

SERVES 4

6 medium leeks (about
    1⅔ pounds/750 g), trimmed,
    washed, halved and cut into
    ¾-inch/2 cm lengths
4 medium parsnips (about
    1½ pounds/700 g), 2 peeled
    and roughly chopped into
    ¾-inch/2 cm pieces, 2 coarsely
    grated
3 tablespoons olive oil
a small bunch of thyme,
    leaves picked
scant 1 cup/200 ml crème fraîche
    or vegan oat crème fraîche
2 cloves of garlic, peeled and
    finely chopped
the zest of a lemon, unwaxed or
    organic
1 teaspoon cider vinegar
½ cup/125 ml vegetable stock
1 x 15-ounce/400 g can navy
    beans, drained and rinsed

FOR THE CRUMBLE TOPPING
¾ cup/75 g jumbo rolled oats
3 tablespoons/40 g cold butter,
    cubed, or olive oil
½ cup/60 g all-purpose flour
2 tablespoons/30 g pumpkin seeds
¼ cup/20 g vegetarian Parmesan
    or vegan Parmesan-style
    cheese, finely grated

TO SERVE
crusty bread
lemon-dressed salad or greens

I gave my son a bite of parsnip the other day. "Mum, that's too sweet," he said—and I know what he means. Parsnips sometimes have a sweetness that needs offsetting, and they are at their finest paired with umami flavors (ever tried tossing your parsnips in a bit of Marmite before roasting?). This crumble does that well, with the sharpness of lemon and crème fraîche and heady thyme. A filling, all-in-one meal that's gracing our table at least once a week this winter.

———

Heat the oven to 400°F/200°C. Toss the leeks and chopped parsnips with the olive oil in an 8-inch x 6-inch/20 cm x 15 cm pie dish or roasting pan (I use a similar-sized round one). Sprinkle over half the thyme leaves and season well. Roast for 35 minutes or until the leeks are soft and buttery, and the parsnips are soft all the way through.

Meanwhile, mix all but ½ cup/50 g of the grated parsnips in a bowl with the crème fraîche, chopped garlic, lemon zest, cider vinegar, stock and navy beans. Taste and season with salt and pepper, if needed.

In a separate bowl, make the crumble topping. Using your fingertips, rub the oats, butter or olive oil, flour and pumpkin seeds together with the remaining grated parsnip and thyme leaves so that it starts to clump and looks like chunky breadcrumbs. Chill in the fridge until needed.

Once the leeks and parsnips have softened, remove from the oven, toss through the bean and crème fraîche mixture, then tip back into the pan.

Remove the crumble topping from the fridge, sprinkle it over the filling, sprinkle over the cheese and return to the oven for 30 minutes.

You can put the crumble together, cover and chill in the fridge up to 24 hours before you bake it. Serve with warm, crusty bread and lemon-dressed salad or greens.

Halloumi, lemon & caramelized onion pie

I dream about this pie. Greek flavors of dried mint and Halloumi, lemon and sesame seeds. This is a pie that's good cold and travels well, so it is perfect for a picnic. In summer I eat it with tomatoes and lemony green salad, and in winter I serve it with buttered greens with nutmeg and little crisp, lemony roasted potatoes. I have given two filling options here, one for vegans (using vegan Halloumi-style cheese and chickpeas in place of the eggs) and one with Halloumi.

———

Preheat the oven to 400°F/200°C.

While the oven is warming, heat the olive oil in a large frying pan over a medium heat, and when it's hot, add the onions. Add a pinch of salt and use a wooden spoon to break them up a bit and stir so every piece has touched the oil. Turn the heat down to low and cook for 20 minutes, until the onions are completely soft. Add the brown sugar and cook for another 5 minutes, until the onions begin to color. Finally, squeeze in the lemon juice and continue to cook for another 5 minutes, until the onions are glossy and golden all over.

Lightly grease an 8-inch x 12-inch/20 cm x 30 cm sheet tray or tart pan with removable bottom with olive oil and line with parchment paper (the oil will keep the paper stuck to the sides and will prevent a wobbly pastry). Unroll the pie dough and press it down into the base of the tray or pan and up the sides. Lay another sheet of paper over the top and fill with ceramic baking beans, dried uncooked pulses or rice. Place in the preheated oven to bake blind for 15 minutes, then lift out the beans (or pulses/rice) and paper and return the pastry to the oven to cook the base through for another 4–5 minutes (the pastry should look pale and dry all over, with no raw gray patches).

While the pastry is baking, mix your filling.

For the vegan filling

In a mixing bowl, blitz the half-can of chickpeas and half the liquid from the can together with an immersion blender until smooth. Stir in the dried and fresh mint, Dijon mustard, garlic and lemon zest. Grate in most of the Halloumi-style cheese and stir to combine. →

SERVES 6

FOR THE ONIONS

2 tablespoons olive oil, plus a
    little extra for greasing
6 white onions, thinly sliced
¼ teaspoon soft brown sugar
the juice of ½ lemon, unwaxed or
    organic

FOR THE VEGAN PIE

12 ounces/320 g ready-rolled pie
    dough (most brands are vegan
    unless "all-butter" is stated on
    the packaging), thawed
half a 15-ounce/400 g can
    chickpeas, drained and half
    the liquid from the can reserved
1 teaspoon dried mint
leaves from most of a small
    bunch of mint, picked and
    roughly chopped
1 teaspoon Dijon mustard
1 clove of garlic, grated
the zest of a lemon, unwaxed or
    organic
7-ounce/200 g block of
    vegan Halloumi-style
    cheese (sometimes called
    "Mediterranean-style")
1 teaspoon black sesame seeds →

← FOR THE HALLOUMI PIE

12 ounces/320 g ready-rolled
  pie dough, thawed

3 organic eggs, beaten

1 teaspoon dried mint

leaves from most of a small
  bunch of mint, picked and
  roughly chopped

the zest of a lemon, unwaxed or
  organic

½ pound/225 g Halloumi

1 teaspoon sesame seeds

FOR THE GREEN OLIVE SALSA

4 scallions, white and
  green parts thinly sliced

12 green olives, pitted

leaves from a few sprigs of
  mint (use the rest from
  the bunch above)

1 teaspoon red wine vinegar

½ teaspoon honey or agave

TO SERVE

green salad (optional)

red wine vinegar-dressed
  tomatoes (optional)

← Season well with pepper (you shouldn't need salt, as the chickpeas and cheese will be quite salty already).

For the non-vegan filling

In a mixing bowl, combine the beaten eggs together with the dried and fresh mint and lemon zest, then grate in most of the Halloumi. Season well with black pepper.

Spread the caramelized onions over the par-baked pastry and use a spatula to help the onions reach all four corners. Spread your filling over the top of the onions and, again, spread out with a spatula (the pastry should hold the filling snugly), then grate over the last bit of Halloumi and sprinkle the sesame seeds over the top. Return to the oven and bake for 35 minutes.

Meanwhile, soak the scallions in cold water to remove some of their intensity. Drain, then place in a mixing bowl. Roughly chop the olives and mint, add these too, then stir in the vinegar and honey or agave.

Remove the pie from the oven and leave for 5 minutes before topping with the green olive salsa.

Piquant smoked paprika pasta bake

SERVES 6–8

2 tablespoons extra virgin olive
oil, plus extra for greasing
1 large white onion, peeled and
finely chopped
1 bulb of fennel, finely chopped
3 cloves of garlic, finely chopped
1 teaspoon fennel seeds
a small bunch of parsley,
roughly chopped
3 red peppers from a jar, sliced
and chopped
¼ cup/40 g green olives, pitted
and roughly chopped
1 x 14.5-ounce/400 g can diced
tomatoes
1½ tablespoons sherry vinegar
2 teaspoons smoked paprika
14 ounces/400 g pasta (penne,
fusilli, conchiglie, casarecce)
1 teaspoon vegetable stock
powder or 1⅔ cup/400 ml hot
vegetable stock

FOR THE TOPPING
½ cup/40 g breadcrumbs
¼ cup/30 g Manchego or vegan
cheese, finely grated

I can't get enough of baked pasta. There are far fancier things to eat for dinner, but almost nothing that is more comforting. Sauce bubbling at the edges, a crisp golden top. This pasta bake has its heart in Italy but has borrowed a few Spanish flavors too. It is made often. The pasta goes into the bake uncooked here, saving a little time.

———

Preheat the oven to 400°F/200°C.

Grease an 8-inch x 12-inch/20 cm x 30 cm deep baking dish with olive oil. Toss the onion, fennel, garlic and fennel seeds in the baking dish with 2 tablespoons of olive oil and half a teaspoon of flaky sea salt and place in the hot oven for 15 minutes, until starting to soften but not yet coloring.

While the onions and fennel are cooking in the oven, get your other ingredients together and boil a kettle.

Keep a handful of parsley back for the breadcrumb topping and add the remaining ingredients, except the vegetable stock powder, to the baking dish with the onions and fennel. Season well with salt and pepper and stir to combine. Put the stock powder into a measuring jug and top with 1⅔ cup/400 ml boiling water. Pour over the filled baking dish, so the liquid comes to just below the level of the pasta. Cover the tray tightly with foil and return to the oven for 45 minutes.

Mix the breadcrumbs and Manchego together with the reserved parsley.

After the pasta has had its time in the oven, lift it out, remove the foil and scatter the breadcrumb mixture over the top. Return to the oven for 10–12 minutes, until golden and crisp on top. Allow the pasta bake to rest out of the oven for at least 10 minutes before serving. This will help the sauce to thicken (and the pasta won't burn your mouth as you eat it!).

Leek & potato traybake
with quick romesco

SERVES 4

1 pound/500 g baby new
   potatoes, large ones halved
2 large leeks, washed, halved
   and sliced into ¾-inch/2 cm-
   thick pieces
1 x 15-ounce/400 g can
   chickpeas, drained
2 cloves of garlic, bashed
4 sprigs of oregano or thyme,
   leaves picked
zest of ½ orange, unwaxed or
   organic
olive oil, to drizzle

FOR THE ROMESCO
⅓ cup/50 g almonds or hazelnuts
1 thick slice of stale sourdough
   or good white bread, torn
   into chunks
1 teaspoon sweet smoked
   paprika
5 ounces/150 g jarred roasted
   red peppers, drained
1 tablespoon sherry or
   red wine vinegar
4 tablespoons olive oil

TO SERVE
a small bunch of parsley,
   roughly chopped

This potato traybake packs in lots of flavor, considering it is so quick to make. Most meals I make come together in less than 30 minutes these days. This quick version of romesco adds a punch to a tray of quickly roasted veg. You could add more greens here, too, if you like.

———

Heat the oven to 400°F/200°C. Toss the potatoes, leeks and chickpeas with the garlic, oregano or thyme leaves, orange zest, a good drizzle of olive oil and plenty of salt and pepper on your largest sheet tray. You might want to spread the vegetables on two trays so they have enough space to crisp up. Roast for 20 minutes.

Meanwhile, start on the romesco. Toast the nuts and bread on a sheet tray for roughly 6–7 minutes, until they are a little colored.

Blitz the nuts and bread with the smoked paprika in a food processor, until you have a rough crumb. Add the peppers, vinegar, oil and a tablespoon of water, then season and blitz again, until you have a slightly textured but silky sauce.

Once the vegetables have had their 20 minutes, take them out of the oven and toss them with half the romesco. Return them to the oven for a further 5 minutes, or until golden and beginning to crisp. Serve with extra romesco, if you like, and sprinkle with parsley.

Preserved lemon & herb-baked orzo

I have been trying to find an authentic recipe for this since I heard about Syrian yogurt-baked orzo from a friend. I couldn't find a recipe that sounded like the one my friend Holly O'Neill described, so I made this up. I am sure it is a long way from the traditional recipe, but it has all the things I want to eat with orzo. I'm still in search of the Syrian version. Please do get in touch if you have a good recipe.

—

Preheat the oven to 450°F/220°C.

In an 11-inch/28 cm baking dish (I use a round one), toss the leeks with the olive oil, half the lemon juice, the coriander, fennel and chili and season well with salt and pepper. Cover tightly with foil and cook in the hot oven for 15 minutes.

Meanwhile, toss the spinach in a large mixing bowl with the orzo, half the herbs and all the remaining ingredients. Season well with salt and pepper.

Remove the baking dish from the oven and stir through the yogurt, spinach and orzo mixture. Pour over 1¾ cups/400 ml boiling water and stir again to combine. Cover the dish with foil (or a lid if it has one) and return to the oven for 25 minutes.

After this time, remove the foil, squeeze over the remaining lemon juice and return to the oven for 5–7 minutes, until the top is crisp and beginning to turn golden at the edges.

Remove from the oven and allow to sit for 5 minutes before sprinkling over the remaining herbs, scallions and lemon zest.

SERVES 6

2 medium leeks, washed, trimmed and thinly sliced
2 tablespoons olive oil
the juice of a lemon, unwaxed or organic
1 teaspoon coriander seeds, roughly ground in a pestle and mortar
½ teaspoon fennel seeds
1 green chili, finely chopped
3½ ounces/100 g baby spinach, washed
12 ounces/350 g orzo pasta
4 generous handfuls of mixed soft herbs (I like parsley, tarragon, mint and dill)
1¾ cups/400 ml plain yogurt of your choice
1 organic egg, beaten, or ¼ cup/30 g ground flaxseed
½ large preserved lemon, flesh discarded and rind finely chopped
1 teaspoon sumac

TO SERVE
4 scallions, thinly sliced
zest of 1 lemon, unwaxed or organic

Sticky sesame-baked cauliflower

SERVES 4

FOR THE CAULIFLOWER

1¼ cups/120 g spelt flour

2 tablespoons rice flour

a clove of garlic, grated

1 tablespoon sesame seeds

1 large head of cauliflower
  (about 1¾ pounds/800 g)

FOR THE SAUCE

3 tablespoons soy sauce
  or tamari

2 tablespoons maple syrup

1 tablespoon toasted sesame oil

1 tablespoon rice vinegar

1 tablespoon tomato purée

1 tablespoon chili paste
  or chili sauce

2 cloves of garlic, peeled
  and grated

a small thumb-sized piece of
  ginger, peeled and finely grated

3 tablespoons sesame seeds

TO SERVE

2 cups/300 g cooked brown rice
  (see opposite)

2 heads of Little Gem lettuce,
  shredded

1 tablespoon sesame seeds

4 scallions, thinly sliced

I crave food like this: sticky, crunchy, with the right balance of sweetness from maple and acidity and heat from some chili. I serve this with simple rice and lime-spiked crunchy lettuce and crispy onions.

——

Preheat the oven to 400°F/200°C. Line 2 sheet trays with parchment paper. To cook your rice, rinse it under cold water until the water runs clear, then put it into a pan, cover with 3 times the amount of water and bring to the boil. Cook for 20–40 minutes, depending on the type of brown rice you are using.

In a large bowl, whisk the flours, ⅔–¾ cup/150–200 ml water, grated garlic, sesame seeds and a good pinch each of salt and pepper. Your batter should be like a pancake batter, thick enough to coat a piece of cauliflower and not run off. If the batter is too thick, add a drop of water until you reach that consistency.

Cut the cauliflower into small florets. Toss the cauliflower florets in a good pinch of salt, then drop them into the batter and stir until all the pieces are coated. Use 2 forks to transfer the battered cauliflower to the sheet trays, leaving a bit of space around each floret. Bake for 20 minutes, until golden brown.

While the cauliflower is baking, make the sauce. In a small saucepan, combine the sauce ingredients. Bring the sauce to a gentle boil on the stove over a medium heat. Simmer for a couple of minutes or until slightly reduced. Set aside.

When the cauliflower is golden and crisp, remove it from the oven and let it cool slightly. Once it is cool enough to handle, transfer the par-baked cauliflower to a large bowl. Cover the cauliflower with all but 3 tablespoons of the sesame sauce. Toss to thoroughly coat the cauliflower.

Put the cauliflower back on the sheet trays and back into the oven for another 10–15 minutes, or until the edges are starting to darken. Remove from the oven. Serve with the shredded lettuce and cooked rice. Finish with the remaining sauce, extra sesame seeds, and scallions.

Celeriac & red wine stew
with Cheddar dumplings

Celeriac is a bit of a beast to look at, but looks aren't everything. Beneath that gnarly, knobby exterior lies creamy white flesh with a sweet, nutty, super-savory flavor. We eat it raw, in thin shavings, in salads with a mustardy dressing, or cut into steaks brushed with herbs and griddled, and sometimes roasted whole. Here, though, I use it as the base for a stew with some Cheddar-spiked dumplings on top. Food for dark evenings with red wine. Be sure to peel your celeriac thickly to get rid of any green tinges around the edge and any leftover muddy traces.

———

Heat a Dutch oven on a medium-high heat and add a good glug of olive oil. Add the onions and garlic and cook for 5 minutes or so until beginning to brown.

Meanwhile, peel and chop your veg, making sure you set aside ¼ pound/100 g of the celeriac for the dumplings. Once the onions have had their time, add the carrots and celeriac to the pot and cook for another 5 minutes, stirring from time to time.

Next, pour in the wine, stock, herbs, harissa and a good pinch of salt and put the lid on. Transfer to a low oven, 350°F/180°C, and cook for 1 hour and 15 minutes.

Make your dumpling mixture. Grate the reserved celeriac and the butter into a bowl and crumble in the Cheddar in small pieces. Add the flour and strip in the leaves of the thyme. Season with salt and pepper. Add 2 tablespoons of very cold water and use your hands to bring the dumpling mixture together until you have a nice dough (if it looks dry you could add a few drops of water). Roll into 12–16 balls.

The stew is ready when the vegetables are soft and yielding and the wine has reduced. Stir through the beans and the greens, plus the Marmite, and purée and place the dumplings on top, brushed with a little egg yolk if you like, leaving a little room in between for them to increase in size. Cook in the oven (no lid this time) for another 25–30 minutes, until browned on top. Serve with lemon-dressed greens and mustard.

SERVES 6–8

FOR THE STEW
olive oil
2 red onions, sliced
1 head of garlic, cloves peeled but left whole
3 carrots, peeled and cut into ¾-inch/2 cm-thick slices
2 pounds/900 g celeriac, peeled and chopped into ¾-inch/2 cm pieces
½ a bottle of red wine
2½ cups/600 ml vegetable stock
2 bay leaves
a few sprigs of rosemary
1 heaping tablespoon harissa
1 x 15-ounce/400 g can white beans, drained (I use navy)
5 ounces/150 g cavolo nero, de-stemmed and roughly chopped
1 teaspoon Marmite
1 teaspoon tomato purée

FOR THE DUMPLINGS
3½ ounces/100 g celeriac saved from the stew quantity
½ cup/100 g cold butter or vegan butter
½ cup/50 g crumbly Cheddar or vegan Cheddar-style cheese
1¾ cups/200 g self-rising flour
a few sprigs of thyme
egg yolk for brushing (optional)

TO SERVE
greens and mustard

Fig, thyme & goat cheese galette

I think my favorite smell is fig leaf. There are a few heavy-leaved trees in parks and gardens near where I live, and when I pass, I stop to scrunch then sniff the leaves. Local bakers pick them for custards and ice creams. I make this galette with hazelnut pastry and a caper and herb goat cheese filling.

This is a pretty tart. I make it with a couple of substantial salads for a summer lunch for 6; with a green salad it would serve a hungry 4. Roasting the figs will bring out their jammy nature, so you can get away with using them lightly under- or over-ripe here.

———

First, make the dough. Put the hazelnuts into a food processor and blitz until you have fine crumbs; be careful not to overdo it, as they will turn into a nut butter. Add the flour and half a teaspoon of flaky sea salt, then pulse a few times so everything is evenly mixed.

Now add the butter and pulse again until it looks like breadcrumbs. Then, with the motor running, add 2–3 tablespoons of ice-cold water one tablespoon at a time until it comes together to form a ball of dough. Remove the dough from the processor, flatten into a rough disc, then wrap in a clean kitchen towel or plastic wrap and place in the fridge to chill for half an hour.

Preheat the oven to 450°F/220°C.

Using the same food processor, add the goat cheese, honey, the leaves from 4 sprigs of thyme or oregano, capers, parsley, lemon juice and zest to the bowl and blitz for a few seconds until creamy and flecked with herbs and capers. Season with some black pepper.

Once the dough has chilled, remove from the fridge and line a large sheet tray with parchment paper. Drizzle some olive oil into the center of the paper.

Roll out the dough onto a floured surface to about 12 inches/30 cm round and ⅜-inch/1 cm thick, turning it as you roll to make sure it stays circular. Roll it up onto the rolling pin and carefully transfer to the prepared sheet tray. →

SERVES 4–6

FOR THE PASTRY
3 tablespoons/25 g hazelnuts
2 cups/225 g white spelt flour or
    all-purpose flour, plus extra for
    dusting
9 tablespoons/125 g very cold
    butter or vegan butter, cubed

FOR THE FILLING
1¼ cups/300 g soft goat cheese
    or vegan soft cheese
1 teaspoon honey
a small bunch of thyme or
    oregano, leaves picked
3 tablespoons capers
a small bunch of parsley, leaves
    and stalks roughly chopped
the juice and zest of ½ lemon,
    unwaxed or organic
extra virgin olive oil
8 figs, sliced
1 organic egg, beaten, or a splash
    of plant milk
⅓ cup/50 g hazelnuts, toasted
    and chopped

TO SERVE
some lemon-dressed salad leaves

← Spread the goat cheese mixture onto the dough, leaving a 1½-inch/4 cm border to fold over later. Top with the figs, being generous, as they'll shrink in the oven slightly.

Next, fold the edges of the dough over the figs to hold them in, brush the edges with the beaten egg or plant milk, then season all over with salt and pepper.

Bake in the oven for 45-50 minutes until golden, scattering over the ⅓ cup/50 g of chopped hazelnuts for the last 5 minutes to toast. Cool on the sheet tray for 10 minutes, then top with the remaining thyme or oregano leaves. Serve with lemon-dressed leaves.

Halloumi, broccoli & chickpea bake

A variation of this goes into our oven at least once a week. I pinched this way of cooking Halloumi from my friend and brilliant cook Georgina Hayden. Ras el hanout is a North African spice mix that I always have on hand, but if you don't have it, try a mixture of ground cinnamon, cumin, and smoked paprika or chili powder. Vegans could swap the Halloumi for a block of firm tofu rubbed with more ras el hanout and olive oil, or use vegan-style Halloumi in the same way.

Heat the oven to 450°F/220°C. Spread the chickpeas on a large sheet tray, sprinkle with the ras el hanout and the zest and juice of half the orange (grate the remaining zest into a bowl), drizzle with olive oil and season. Roast for 10 minutes. Meanwhile, score the top of the Halloumi block with ¼-inch/5 mm-deep crisscrosses, then set aside. In a bowl or jar, mix the tahini, remaining orange zest and juice, and a tablespoon of olive oil—if your tahini is thick, it might need a really good stir.

Once the chickpeas have had 10 minutes, take them out of the oven and turn on the grill. Add the Halloumi, broccoli and pumpkin seeds to the tray, toss everything together, so it is all coated in the orangy spiced oil, then put under the grill for 10 minutes, until the Halloumi is golden, the broccoli spears are softened and the florets are crisp.

Sprinkle over the pomegranate seeds and parsley, drizzle over the tahini mix, then drizzle the Halloumi with honey. Serve with flatbreads.

SERVES 4

2 x 15-ounce/400 g cans
    chickpeas or
    1 x 1½-pound/700 g jar,
    drained
1 heaping teaspoon ras el hanout
1 orange, unwaxed or organic
olive oil
7 ounces/200 g block of
    Halloumi or vegan Halloumi-
    style cheese (sometimes called
    "Mediterranean-style")
3 tablespoons tahini
9 ounces/250 g purple-sprouting
    or Tenderstem broccoli
a large handful of pumpkin seeds
seeds from 1 pomegranate
a small bunch of parsley,
    leaves picked

TO SERVE
1 heaping teaspoon honey or
    maple syrup
4 flatbreads

Gobi Manchurian

SERVES 4–6

peanut or coconut oil

3 cloves of garlic,
   roughly chopped

small thumb-sized piece of
   ginger, peeled and roughly
   chopped

2 red peppers, de-seeded and
   cut into ⅜-inch/1 cm pieces

1 stick of lemongrass,
   finely chopped

½ bunch scallions,
   finely chopped

1 green chili

1 tablespoon tomato purée

2 tablespoons peanut butter

1 tablespoon miso
   (I use brown rice miso)

1 tablespoon soy sauce

1 tablespoon vinegar

1 large cauliflower (about
   1¾ pounds/800 g), head
   broken into florets, leaves
   roughly shredded

1 x 15-ounce/400 g can
   chickpeas, drained

a pinch of dried chili flakes

FOR THE CUCUMBER

½ cucumber

2 teaspoons toasted sesame oil

1 teaspoon light soy sauce

1 thumb-sized piece of ginger

TO SERVE

a handful of cilantro leaves,
   chopped

brown rice (see page 262)

1 lime, unwaxed or organic, cut
   into wedges

Gobi Manchurian crosses the boundaries between Indian and Chinese cooking, to my mind the ideal cross section of the Venn diagram. The traditional recipe is for deep-fried cauliflower in a sticky-sweet sauce, but my version has spiced roasted cauliflower and a peanut and miso-rich sauce with freshness from chili and lemongrass. Wildly untraditional I am sure, but I like it.

⸻

Preheat the oven to 350°F/180°C.

First, make your sauce. Find a large sheet tray (it needs to be big enough to fit the cauliflower and chickpeas on it) and add a splash of oil, then add the garlic, ginger, peppers, lemongrass, scallions and whole green chili and cook in the oven for 5–10 minutes, until the peppers have lost their rawness. Transfer the lot into a bowl. Add the tomato purée, peanut butter, miso, soy sauce, vinegar and 2 tablespoons of water, then blitz with an immersion blender or in a food processor until a smooth sauce forms. Set aside.

Increase the oven temperature to 450°F/220°C. Put the cauliflower florets and leaves on the sheet tray. Make sure the chickpeas are well drained (transfer to a plate lined with paper towels if needed), then add to the cauliflower. Season with salt and drizzle with a little oil, then sprinkle over the chili flakes and toss well. Roast in the hot oven for 25 minutes, until the cauliflower is soft throughout and crisp on the outside and the chickpeas are starting to blister.

Meanwhile, whack the cucumber a few times with a rolling pin (this breaks down the fibers), then slice thinly and toss in a bowl with the sesame oil and soy sauce. Grate the ginger onto a plate, then gather it in your hands and squeeze out the ginger juice over the cucumber. Discard the ginger pulp and toss the cucumber to combine.

Once the cauliflower-chickpea bake is ready, take it out of the oven. Pour the sauce into the bottom of a serving bowl and tumble the cauliflower-chickpeas on top. Taste and check the seasoning, adding a little more soy sauce, chili or vinegar if needed.

Top with the cucumber salad and cilantro, and serve with rice and lime wedges for squeezing over.

Biryani with saffron & golden veg

Biryani is feasting food. It feels extravagant with saffron, rosewater and a lineup of warming spice. It takes a little bit of preparation, but once it's in the oven you can leave it to steam and cook. Rosewater splits opinion; I love it, but for some people it's a bit too like Granny's perfume. Here, the bold spice tempers its sweet florals. If you are still not convinced, leave it out.

This is a grand dish that I would argue can be eaten on its own with chutneys and pickles. But it would be equally good next to a few curries, which is how I make it when there are a few more to feed.

———

Preheat the oven to 450°F/220°C.

Put the cardamom pods, cinnamon, cloves, nutmeg, fennel seeds, bay leaves and saffron into a pan with 3¼ cups/700 ml water. Bring to the boil, turn off the heat, then cover and allow to infuse. Once cool, add the rosewater (if you are using it).

Add 1 tablespoon of the ghee or butter to a large Dutch oven. Pop the pot into the oven briefly to melt the ghee (or alternative), then add the onions and return to the oven for 10–15 minutes, until the onions are light brown and beginning to crisp. Add the ginger and garlic to the onions in the Dutch oven and return to the oven for 2 minutes.

Add the turmeric, garam masala and grated root vegetables to the pot and stir around, adding a little more ghee or butter if needed. Return to the oven for 5–10 minutes, until just softened, transfer to a bowl, add the herbs and season well with salt and pepper. Wipe out the Dutch oven with a paper towel.

Melt the remaining ghee (or alternative) in the Dutch oven by putting the dish briefly in the oven as before, then add the rice and heat in the oven for a few minutes, until shiny. Strain two-thirds of the spice-and-bay liquid into the dish. Cover, put in the oven and cook for about 5–6 minutes, or until the liquid has been absorbed by the rice. Remove from the oven. →

SERVES 4–6 AS A MAIN MEAL,
MORE AS PART OF A SPREAD

8 cardamom pods
1 small stick of cinnamon
4 cloves
a few gratings of nutmeg
1 teaspoon fennel seeds
3 bay leaves
a large pinch of saffron strands
1–2 teaspoons rosewater
  (optional)
4 tablespoons ghee, butter or
  coconut oil
4 onions, peeled and thinly sliced
a small thumb-sized piece of
  fresh ginger, peeled and finely
  chopped
3 cloves of garlic, peeled and
  finely chopped
1 teaspoon ground turmeric
½ teaspoon garam masala
14 ounces/400 g root vegetables,
  such as carrots, butternut
  squash and potato, grated
2 sprigs of mint, leaves picked
  and roughly chopped
a small bunch of cilantro,
  roughly chopped
1½ cups/300 g basmati rice
1¼ cups/50 g sliced almonds

← Now, assemble your biryani. This will take a bit of concentration, but stick with me. Transfer two-thirds of the rice from the dish to a bowl, leaving a third layered on the bottom of the Dutch oven. Sprinkle over all the remaining strained spice-and-bay liquid.

Spoon over a third of the vegetable mix into the Dutch oven. Layer another third of the rice over the top, then top with the other third of the vegetable mixture.

Finish with the final third of the rice and then the vegetables, then dot the almonds on top. Cover with a tight-fitting lid and cover the dish tightly with foil, to allow the rice to steam.

Put in the oven for 40 minutes, reducing the heat to 375°F/190°C after 20 minutes. Fluff and mix with a fork before serving.

Baked feta with tomato & smoky peppers

SERVES 4

2 green peppers or 8 smaller
  Turkish peppers
2 x 7-ounce/200 g blocks feta or
  vegan feta-style cheese, each
  cut into 5 slices
2 handfuls of cherry tomatoes,
  halved (I use different
  colored ones)
2 teaspoons coriander seeds,
  bashed in a pestle and mortar
a pinch of dried oregano
olive oil

TO SERVE
green salad
flatbreads

This is my take on Greek feta bouyiourdi, although I char my peppers first, as I like how it intensifies the smoky hum. I use the pale yellow-green Turkish peppers: they are long and thin, sweeter and milder than their deeper green-pepper cousins, but if you can't find them, don't worry. These are also great cooked on the coals of a barbecue. I have found a good vegan feta-style cheese from Follow Your Heart, or Violife in supermarkets, that works well for this recipe.

———

If you have a gas stove, use this to char your peppers. If not, turn your broiler up as hot as it will go. Cook the peppers directly on the flame or under the grill, turning them all the time with some tongs, until they are blackened all over. Take off the heat and, once cool, peel away most of the black skin and cut the flesh into slices, discarding the stems and seeds.

Preheat the oven to 450°F/220°C. Put the blocks of feta on a piece of foil large enough to wrap around them. Top with the charred peppers, tomatoes, bashed coriander seeds, oregano and a drizzle of olive oil. Wrap the foil around and seal at the top to make a little parcel. Put the packet on a sheet tray and bake for 15 minutes.

It is ready when the feta is soft, and the tomatoes are sticky and roasted. Serve with a green salad and flatbreads for mopping up the juices.

Crispy caper & slow-roasted tomato pappardelle

A bowl of tomato pasta is pretty much my favorite meal. It's often thought that having people over means you have to make fancy food. Not true. Almost everyone will breathe a sigh of relief when a massive bowl of pasta thuds onto the table. This tomato one takes some beating, thanks to roasting them until sweet and the level up of crispy fried capers and marjoram.

——

Preheat the oven to 350°F/180°C. Arrange the tomatoes in a large, deep baking dish with the garlic, chili and chopped marjoram. Pour over the oil (this may seem a lot, but trust me) and season well with salt and pepper. Use a slotted spoon to mix everything together. Place the baking dish in the middle of the oven for 90 minutes, shaking the pan every 20 minutes to prevent the tomatoes from catching and burning.

Once cooked and cooled a little, drain the tomatoes through a strainer suspended over a bowl to catch the oil. Pour the oil into a sterilized jar and set aside. Lift out the chili and garlic and discard. Tip half of the tomatoes into a blender and blitz until smooth. Mix the blended tomatoes with the whole tomatoes in a very large, heatproof mixing bowl with lots of room for the pasta and keep warm in a low oven.

Pour 6 tablespoons of the reserved tomato oil into a medium frying pan and place over a medium heat. Spread the capers on a piece of paper towel and pat dry before tipping into the hot tomato oil. Be careful, as the oil will spit initially. Using a slotted spoon, move the capers around the oil and fry for about 4–6 minutes or until popped and crispy. Remove with a slotted spoon, drain on a plate lined with paper towels, and set aside.

Fill a large pot with water and place over a high heat. Season well with salt. When the water is boiling, cook the pasta for 2 minutes if fresh, or 1 minute less than package instructions if dried. When the pasta is cooked but still al dente, lift out with tongs and transfer to the warm tomato bowl. Toss the pasta in the sauce, adding a little of the starchy pasta water with a drizzle of the tomato oil.

Scatter over the ricotta and half the crispy capers. Put the rest in a bowl for the table and serve the pasta in warm bowls with lots of black pepper.

SERVES 6

4½ pounds/2 kg mixed cherry tomatoes (I like a mixture of colors)
1 head of garlic, peeled (about 14 cloves)
1 red chili, sliced in half lengthways
a bunch of marjoram (or oregano or thyme)
1 cup/250 ml extra virgin olive oil
6 tablespoons baby capers
1½ pounds/650 g fresh pappardelle or 1 pound/450 g dried pappardelle if you are vegan
1 cup/250 g fresh ricotta or vegan ricotta (I like the Tofutti brand)

Melon, potato, herb & roasted feta salad

I am always chasing a melon as perfectly sweet as the ones I remember from markets on French and Spanish vacations. But when a melon is a little less than perfect, I have ways to soften the blow. This salad with roasted feta and new potatoes makes a meal of a melon; the lemon, honey and herbs bring out the flavor of even a lackluster fruit. You can use any melon you like for this, or a mixture; I love the contrast of bright pink watermelon, the peach of a cantaloupe and the off-white of a sweet Piel de Sapo. I buy good Greek or Italian oregano, which is much more fragrant, so get your hands on some if you can.

——

Heat the oven to 400°F/200°C. Chop any large potatoes in half and keep the smaller ones whole, then transfer to a large sheet tray. Use a Y-shaped peeler to peel the zest from the lemon in long strips, then add to the tray. Bash the head of garlic until the cloves are slightly split, then add to the tray with the olive oil and oregano. Season well, then roast for 20 minutes.

Peel the melons and cut into thin half-moon slices and bite-sized pieces, removing the seeds as you go.

After the potatoes have had 20 minutes, take them out of the oven, then squash them down with a potato masher until broken apart and flattened. Break over the feta, then return the tray to the oven for a further 20 minutes, or until the feta is golden and crisp all over.

Remove from the oven, toss with the juice of half the lemon, then add the melon, basil and mint. Finish with a little honey or agave, if you like, and a drizzle of olive oil.

SERVES 4–6

2 pounds/1 kg small new
   potatoes
1 lemon, unwaxed or organic
1 whole head of garlic
3 tablespoons extra virgin
   olive oil, plus extra for
   drizzling
1 tablespoon fresh oregano
2 pounds/1 kg melon (I use a mix
   of watermelon, cantaloupe and
   Piel de Sapo or Santa Claus
   melon)
7-ounce/200 g block feta or
   vegan feta-style cheese
a small bunch of Greek basil
   leaves
a small bunch of mint, leaves
   picked

TO SERVE
1 tablespoon runny honey or
   agave (optional)

Roasted rainbow carrots
with beans & salsa rustica

SERVES 4–6

FOR THE CARROTS

2 x 14-ounce/ 400 g bunches of
   carrots with tops (a mixture of
   colors looks nice), scrubbed
olive oil, for drizzling
a few sprigs of rosemary
½ lemon, unwaxed or organic

FOR THE SALSA RUSTICA

1 shallot, very finely chopped
2-3 tablespoons red wine vinegar
½ cup/50 g pistachios, shelled
3 cloves of garlic, peeled
3 tablespoons capers
10 green olives, pitted
a small bunch of mint
a small bunch of parsley
1 tablespoon apple cider vinegar
½ teaspoon honey or agave
1 lemon, unwaxed or organic
½ cup/120 ml extra virgin
   olive oil

FOR THE WHITE BEANS

2 tablespoons extra virgin
   olive oil
2 cloves of garlic, thinly sliced
1 x 1⅓-pound/600 g jar white
   beans
2 bay leaves
the juice of ½ lemon, unwaxed or
   organic

This dish is all about glory cooking—cooking for adoration and praise. We all know a glory cook; they cook only all-out meals on a weekend, often on a barbecue or high-tech cooking device. They are rarely seen in the kitchen on a Wednesday night. They live for the oohs and aahs as they carry their food to the table. A riot of color looks super impressive, so will undoubtedly result in sighs of adoration.

Salsa rustica is a flavor-packed herb salsa somewhere between salsa verde and pesto. I make the most of the leftover carrot tops to make it here, but if your carrots are without tops, then some parsley will stand in.

———

Preheat the oven to 450°F/220°C.

Break the carrot tops off with your hands. Discard all but a handful of the tops. Halve the carrots lengthways, then toss them in a sheet tray with enough olive oil to coat, and add the rosemary and some salt and pepper. Add half a lemon to the tray and place in the hot oven for 40 minutes, until the carrots are soft to the point of a knife and catching at the edges. Keep the oven on, but reduce the heat to 325°F/160°C.

While the carrots are roasting, make the salsa rustica. Put the shallots into a small bowl and cover them with the red wine vinegar, then let them macerate for about 20 minutes.

Place the reserved carrot top leaves in a small heatproof bowl and fill and boil a kettle. Pour the boiling water over the carrot tops for 10 seconds, then drain and run under cold water to preserve the bright green color. You can skip this bit if you are short on time.

Squeeze out as much moisture from the carrot top leaves as you can, then place in a food processor with the pistachios, garlic, capers, olives, herbs, apple cider vinegar and honey or agave in that order.

Add the juice from half the lemon and pour in half the olive oil. Continue adding the olive oil, a little at a time (you may not need it all), pulsing until you have a chunky pesto consistency. →

← Taste and adjust the seasoning, adding a little more lemon if you like. Drain and stir in the shallots.

To make the white beans, place the sheet tray you used for the carrots on the stove top and heat the oil and fry the garlic until it's soft and fragrant, moving it around to make sure it doesn't catch and burn. (If it's difficult to do this on your stove top with a tray, then you can use a large frying pan.) Add the beans, with a couple of tablespoons of the liquid from the jar, the bay leaves and a squeeze of lemon juice. Cook for 15 minutes, pushing down regularly with a wooden spoon to break down the beans to a smooth and creamy consistency, adding a little more liquid from the jar if needed. Season with lots of black pepper (you shouldn't need any salt, as the jarred beans are salty enough) and perhaps a squeeze more lemon juice.

Spread the white bean dip on a platter, arrange the carrots over the top and spoon over a quarter of the salsa rustica, with the rest in a bowl on the side for spooning over.

Chocolate, olive oil & rosemary cake

MAKES 1 LOAF, TO SERVE ABOUT 8

2½ cups/300 g light spelt or all-purpose flour

1½ cups/125 g superfine sugar or light muscovado sugar

1½ teaspoons baking powder

1½ teaspoons baking soda

3 organic eggs and ⅔ cup/150 ml milk or ⅔ cup/150 ml sparkling water

1 cup/250 ml olive oil, plus extra for greasing

2 sprigs of rosemary, needles only, finely chopped

1 cup/150 g dark chocolate (70% cocoa solids), chopped into ⅜-inch/1 cm pieces

1 tablespoon demerara sugar

This is one of my all-time cakes, peppered with flecks of rosemary and chunks of chocolate and which uses olive oil instead of butter. The rosemary and chocolate are an unexpectedly subtle pairing, which I adore. This is a less sweet cake, almost fudgy, with a delicate herbal back-note. It's so good that, if I got married again, I'd have it as a layer in my wedding cake. It's an old favorite from my *Guardian* column. You can use a standard olive oil here; it doesn't need to be extra virgin. It pairs wonderfully with rosemary, but I have also made this by nestling a few bay leaves in the top of the batter instead. You could also replace the rosemary with orange zest or the seeds from a vanilla pod.

Heat the oven to 350°F/180°C. Grease and line a 9-inch x 5-inch/900 g loaf pan. Put the flour, sugar, baking powder, baking soda and a good pinch of sea salt into a large bowl and use a whisk to mix together, making sure there are no lumps.

For the non-vegan cake

In another large bowl, whisk the eggs, then add the olive oil, milk and rosemary, and mix. Now fold the oil mixture into the dry ingredients, gently mixing until just combined, but no more: for a light cake, don't overmix.

For the vegan cake

If you want to make a vegan cake, instead of using eggs and milk, add the olive oil and rosemary to the flour mixture, and whisk again. Add the sparkling water, gently mixing until just combined, but no more: for a light cake, don't overmix.

Stir in most of the chocolate pieces. Pour the mixture into the pan and smooth the surface. Scatter over the rest of the chocolate, pushing the pieces down a little into the mixture so they are half covered, then sprinkle over the demerara sugar for a crunchy finish.

Bake for about 40 minutes, or 45 minutes for the vegan version, or until it is golden brown and a skewer inserted in the cake comes out clean. Cool for 10 minutes in the pan, then transfer to a wire rack.

Pistachio & tahini fridge tiffin

MAKES 8 RECTANGLES

1 cup/120 g all-purpose flour

¼ cup/30 g rice flour

½ cup/100 g cold unsalted butter
or vegan butter

¼ cup/50 g superfine sugar

1 ounce/30 g stem ginger in
syrup, very finely chopped

1¼ cups/200 g dark chocolate
(70% cocoa solids)

¾ cup/100 g tahini

3 tablespoons syrup from the
stem ginger jar

⅔ cup/80 g pistachios, shelled
and roughly chopped

¼ cup/40 g dried cherries

¼ cup/40 g sultanas

3 tablespoons/30 g pumpkin
seeds, toasted

My sister Laura loves tiffin. And I am with her. Growing up, she ate it
wherever she could get her hands on it. It's that combination of biscuit,
nuts and dried fruit, giving crunch, snap and chew. All the textures.
This one is an upgrade from those of our childhood, though, with
tahini, stem ginger, pistachios and a quick homemade ginger biscuit.
In America, tiffin seems to be called fridge cake. I can't work out the
difference and I like the word *tiffin* better, but this is also a cake you
make and keep in the fridge.

——

Preheat the oven to 350°F/180°C.

Sift the flours into a mixing bowl. Add the butter and rub together with
your fingers until the butter is soft and no large lumps are visible. Stir
through the sugar, ¼ teaspoon of salt and the stem ginger to combine.
Line an 8-inch x 8-inch/20 cm x 20 cm pan with parchment paper and
pack the biscuit mixture into the base. Prick a few times with a fork,
then place in the hot oven to bake for 18 minutes until golden. Remove
from the oven and allow to cool completely.

While the biscuit is cooling, break the chocolate into ¾-inch/2 cm
pieces and place in a heatproof bowl with the tahini and stem ginger
syrup. Pour a ¾-inch/2 cm depth of water into a saucepan and bring to
a gentle simmer. Place the chocolate bowl over the top of the saucepan,
making sure the base of the bowl doesn't touch the water. Stir until
the chocolate is melted. Remove from the heat and mix through the
pistachios, dried fruit and seeds.

When the biscuit is completely cool, roughly chop it directly in the
pan before tipping and stirring it into the melted chocolate, leaving
the parchment paper in the pan to use again. Pour the chocolate
mixture back into the parchment-lined pan, cover with cling wrap
and chill in the fridge for at least 3 hours or overnight.

Slice into eight 2-inch x 4-inch/5 cm x 10 cm rectangles and serve.

Chocolate & almond butter swirl brownies

Chocolate and nut butter, a flavor friendship rarely bettered. If you can't have nuts, then sunflower seed butter will work here, too. To make your own nut butter, blitz raw or roasted nuts for a minute or two until you have a coarse powder, scrape down the sides and blitz again until you have a smooth paste. If it looks dry at that point, add a little coconut or peanut oil, and blitz again. Sweeten with a little honey, maple syrup or vanilla, if you like.

———

Heat the oven to 350°F/180°C and line an 8-inch x 8-inch/ 20 cm x 20 cm cake pan with parchment paper.

For the non-vegan brownies

For the chocolate batter, melt 1 cup/150 g of the chocolate (saving the rest for the top) with the oil in a small saucepan over a low heat. Whisk together the dry ingredients. Create a well in the center of the dry ingredients and add the eggs and vanilla. Stir to combine. Pour in the melted chocolate and give the batter another stir until the chocolate is mixed through. Make the almond butter batter by whisking together the sugar, baking powder and a pinch of salt in a large bowl. Add the egg and vanilla, whisk again, add the almond butter, stir until well combined and set aside. The batter will be thick.

For the vegan brownies

Follow the steps above, replacing the eggs with the flaxseed. For the chocolate batter, mix 8 teaspoons of ground flaxseed with 6 tablespoons of warm water in a separate bowl. For the almond butter, mix 4 teaspoons of ground flaxseed with 3 tablespoons of warm water in a separate bowl. For both mixtures, leave to thicken for 15 minutes before using.

Dollop alternate heaped spoonfuls of each batter into the cake pan. Once all the batter is in, use a butter knife to swirl it in a figure-eight motion. Top with the remaining chocolate, pressing each piece slightly into the batter, then sprinkle with a pinch of flaky sea salt. Bake for 25–30 minutes, until the brownies are just set with a little wobble and the almond butter swirls are golden. Take out of the oven and leave to cool in the pan completely before cutting into 16 squares.

MAKES 16 SQUARES

FOR THE CHOCOLATE BATTER
1¼ cups/200 g dark chocolate, chopped into ¼-inch/5 mm chunks (1 cup/150 g for melting, the rest for the top)
½ cup/100 g coconut oil
½ cup/100 g white spelt flour
½ cup/100 g superfine sugar
½ teaspoon baking powder
2 organic eggs, or 8 teaspoons flaxseed
1 teaspoon vanilla extract or paste

FOR THE ALMOND BUTTER BATTER
⅓ cup + 1 tablespoon/75 g superfine sugar
½ teaspoon baking powder
1 organic egg, or 4 teaspoons ground flaxseed
1 teaspoon vanilla extract or paste
⅓ cup + 1 tablespoon/100 g smooth almond butter

Strawberry & labneh semifreddo

Halfway between ice cream and fruit and yogurt. This is a lazy person's ice cream, no churning, no custards. I actually love the less-sweet fruit and the slight tartness of the yogurt. If you can find really thick pre-strained Greek-style yogurt (also known as labneh) in the shops, there is no need to strain it either—saving you an (admittedly very easy) step. This is all I want for pudding.

———

Begin with straining the yogurt. Pour the yogurt into the center of a cheesecloth or clean kitchen towel, gather up the sides around the yogurt and secure with an elastic band. Suspend the yogurt in a strainer set over a bowl and set aside for 4 hours.

An hour before the yogurt straining time is up, heat the oven to 400°F/200°C. Arrange the strawberries on a small sheet tray in a single layer and sprinkle over the superfine sugar and cardamom. Toss to combine. Roast the strawberries in the hot oven for 15 minutes until juicy and soft. Discard the cardamom pods and set aside to cool completely.

Line a 9-inch x 5-inch/900 g loaf pan with parchment paper on all sides.

Tip the strained yogurt into a large mixing bowl and stir in the honey or maple syrup. Squeeze in the lemon juice if you are using coconut yogurt and maple syrup. When the strawberries are completely cool, mix most of them into the labneh with all their juices from the tray (saving a little to spoon over at the end), making no more than three or four turns with the spatula so the strawberries and their juices are rippled through the labneh.

Pour into the lined loaf pan and use a spatula to even out the top. Cover with parchment paper and chill in the freezer for 4–5 hours. Lift the semifreddo out using the parchment paper and invert onto a serving plate. Serve in slices with the remaining strawberries.

Seasonal variations

— Autumn—plums
— Winter/early spring—frozen berries

SERVES 6

4 cups/900 ml thick Greek yogurt, or 3 cups/700 ml coconut yogurt

14 ounces/400 g strawberries, hulled, larger ones halved or quartered

2 tablespoons superfine sugar

8 cardamom pods

5 tablespoons/100 g honey or maple syrup

the juice of a lemon, unwaxed or organic, if using coconut yogurt

Chocolate & muscovado fudge cake

MAKES 1 CAKE, SERVES 10

FOR THE FROSTING

½ cup/100 g olive, coconut or
   vegetable oil
⅓ cup/65 g dark muscovado
   sugar
2 tablespoons cocoa powder
7 ounces/200 g dark chocolate,
   finely chopped

FOR THE CAKE

2 cups/200 g all-purpose or light
   spelt flour
1½ teaspoons baking soda
⅔ cup/75 g cocoa powder
1¼ cups, packed/250 g dark
   muscovado sugar
¾ cup/75 g olive, coconut or
   vegetable oil, plus extra for
   greasing
1½ teaspoons vinegar
   (I use cider)

My insatiable sweet tooth knows almost no bounds, so cake is something I take very seriously. This dense, gooey (and incidentally vegan) chocolate cake made with coconut oil is as much of a hit with my two-year-old as it is with my vegan brother. It was passed on to me by a kind American friend, hence oil rather than butter in the batter. It is such an easy cake to make: no creaming, no sifting. Be sure to use a tight-fitting springform pan, as the batter is quite wet and will run out if there are any gaps.

———

Heat the oven to 350°F/180°C. Grease an 8-inch/20 cm round springform pan with oil and line the base with parchment paper.

Put all the frosting ingredients except the chocolate into a saucepan with ¼ cup/60 ml cold water. Heat until everything is melted, making sure the mixture doesn't boil, then turn off the heat, add the chocolate at once and leave it to sit. After about a minute, the chocolate should have melted. Whisk until you have a thick frosting and set aside. It should be cool by the time the cake has baked and cooled.

For the cake, whisk the flour, baking soda, a good pinch of sea salt and the cocoa powder together in a bowl. Make sure there are no lumps of baking soda.

In a separate bowl, mix the sugar, 1½ cups + 1 tablespoon/375 ml of just-boiled water, the oil and vinegar. Stir the mixture into the dry ingredients, then pour into the prepared springform pan (it will be quite a wet batter). Bake for 30–40 minutes.

When it is ready, the cake should have pulled away from the edges of the pan and a skewer inserted into the center will come out clean. Cool for 30 minutes in the pan, then transfer to a wire rack to cool completely. Spoon over the frosting and decorate as you like.

Decoration ideas

— Grated chocolate
— Fresh flowers
— Chopped candied nuts
— Chopped stem ginger
— Crumbled chocolate
— Flakes of sea salt

Double ginger & apple cake

I'm cheating a bit here, as this isn't strictly a one-tray dish but more a cake cooked in a tray. It's my favorite cake of the last couple of years, so I had to find a way to get it into this book. This is such an easy cake, with a double hit of ginger. This way of using the apple to top the cake is inspired by the brilliant cook and writer Anja Dunk. If you are a ginger-lover like me, you could add another couple of balls of stem ginger.

——

Grease a square 9-inch/23 cm springform pan. Heat the oven to 350°F/180°C. Put all the dry ingredients, except the dark brown sugar and 1 teaspoon of the ground ginger, into a bowl. Whisk to combine.

For the non-vegan cake

Melt the butter in a pan, then whisk in the dark brown sugar and chopped stem ginger. Leave to cool slightly, then beat in the eggs one by one, until emulsified. Fold through the dry ingredients and pour into the prepared cake pan.

For the vegan cake

To make a vegan version, melt the coconut oil in a pan, then whisk in the dark brown sugar and stem ginger pieces. Add the coconut oil mix to the flour mixture and whisk to combine. Now, with the whisk running, add the sparkling water and mix until the batter is smooth and light. Pour into the prepared cake pan.

Peel, halve and core the apples, then very thinly slice about two-thirds of the way down each half, leaving the last third uncut to hold the apple together. It is much like a hedgehog or a Hasselback potato. Arrange the apple halves cut side up on top of the batter, brush with some of the ginger syrup, then sprinkle over the demerara sugar and the remaining teaspoon of ground ginger. Bake on the middle shelf of the oven for 45–50 minutes, until golden and cooked through. Test the thickest part of the cake with a skewer: if it doesn't come out clean, put the cake back in for another 5 minutes.

Remove the cake from the oven and pour over the remaining syrup. Cool in the pan for 10 minutes, then remove and cut into 9 squares to serve. This is best eaten on the day it's made, but will keep well for up to 3 days, wrapped inside an airtight container.

MAKES 1 CAKE, SERVES 9

1¾ cups/200 g all-purpose flour
1 teaspoon baking powder
1½ teaspoons baking soda
2 teaspoons ground ginger
½ cup + 6 tablespoons/200 g unsalted butter or ½ cup + 2 tablespoons/150 g coconut oil, plus extra for greasing
¾ cup/150 g dark brown soft sugar
5 balls of stem ginger (2½ ounces/75 g), finely chopped, plus 2 tablespoons syrup from the jar for brushing and drizzling
3 medium organic eggs or ¾ cup/180 ml sparkling water
5–6 small eating apples
1 tablespoon demerara sugar, for sprinkling

Brown butter double-chip cookies

1 cup + 2 tablespoons/250 g
   unsalted butter or vegan butter

1 cup/200 g superfine sugar

1 cup, packed/200 g light soft
   brown sugar

2 organic eggs and 2 organic
   egg yolks, or 3 tablespoons of
   ground flaxseed

3⅓ cups/400 g all-purpose or
   plain spelt flour

1 teaspoon baking powder

1 teaspoon baking soda

½ cup + 1 tablespoon/50 g
   cocoa powder

7 ounces/200 g dark chocolate
   (70% cocoa solids), chopped
   into chunks

2 teaspoons flaky sea salt

These are my ideal cookies, chewy in the middle, crisp on the outside, like the edges of a brownie and with a double hit of chocolate. This recipe leaves you with a lot of dough; I bake half right away and then freeze the other half for later. Knowing I am only ever minutes away from eating one of these cookies is the root of my happiness.

———

Put the butter into a small saucepan and start to melt it over a medium heat. When it begins to foam, turn the heat down a bit and let it continue to foam for about 5 minutes, until it turns golden brown and smells like caramel. If you are using vegan butter, it may not brown like dairy butter. If it just melts, that's okay. Be careful not to take it too far, otherwise the butter will burn. Take off the heat and allow to cool for a few minutes.

Preheat the oven to 350°F/180°C and line 2 large sheet trays with parchment paper. If you are using flaxseed instead of eggs, mix it with 6 tablespoons of cold water and leave to sit.

Add the cooled brown butter and both sugars to a stand mixer or add to a mixing bowl and use an electric hand mixer to whip the butter for about a minute, until light and fluffy. Now add the eggs and egg yolks one at a time, mixing after each one, until you have a smooth batter. If you are using flaxseed, add it bit by bit, mixing after each addition.

In another bowl, whisk the flour, baking powder, baking soda and cocoa powder, to get rid of any lumps. Mix into the butter, then stir in the chocolate chunks with a wooden spoon, making sure they are evenly distributed.

Scoop heaping tablespoons of the dough onto the lined sheet trays, making sure they have space to spread. I'd suggest a maximum of 8 on a standard sheet tray.

Bake for 11 minutes (for dough at room temperature), 15 minutes (for dough from the fridge) and 18–20 minutes (for dough from the freezer). Then remove from the oven and sprinkle each with a little flaky sea salt.

To freeze any leftover dough, roll into golf-ball-sized balls, wrap in plastic wrap and freeze.

Honey, almond & cardamom drizzle cake

This cake is based on a recipe cooked by my friend Alex Hacking from 26 Grains, the London restaurant. For days after eating this cake, I could think of very little else. This is my version. It makes a large loaf and is quite rich, so you'll get a lot of slices out of it.

———

Heat the oven to 350°F/180°C.

Grease a 9-inch x 5-inch/900 g loaf pan and line with parchment paper. Put the flour, almonds, baking powder and a good pinch of sea salt into a large mixing bowl and whisk until there are no lumps of baking powder.

In a stand mixer fitted with a paddle attachment, or with an electric hand mixer, beat the butter, sugar and honey until creamy and combined. Add both orange and lemon zests, then the eggs one by one, mixing well between additions.

Add the dry ingredients a large spoonful at a time, again mixing between additions. Tip the mixture into the prepared pan and smooth out the top with the back of a spoon. Bake for 55 minutes to 1 hour, until the cake is dark golden on top. It will sink a little in the middle.

Take the cake out of the oven and leave in the pan. Bash the cardamom pods in a pestle and mortar to release the seeds, then put the seeds into a small saucepan with all the remaining drizzle ingredients. Bring to a simmer and reduce to a thin syrup—it will thicken a little more as it cools.

Prick the cake a few times with a skewer and pour over the syrup, then leave the cake in the pan until cooled completely. Serve in thick slices, with yogurt mixed with honey.

MAKES 1 LOAF, TO SERVE ABOUT 8

FOR THE CAKE

1¾ cups/200 g light spelt or
    all-purpose flour
1½ cups/150 g ground almonds
2 teaspoons baking powder
1 cup + 2 tablespoons/250 g
    unsalted butter, softened, plus
    extra for greasing
scant 1 cup/200 g
    demerara sugar
⅔ cup/150 ml honey or
    maple syrup
zest of an orange, unwaxed or
    organic
zest of a lemon, unwaxed or
    organic
4 medium organic eggs

FOR THE DRIZZLE

4 cardamom pods
4 tablespoons honey or
    maple syrup
1 teaspoon orange blossom water
2 teaspoons toasted sesame seeds
1 teaspoon fennel seeds
1 teaspoon coriander seeds

TO SERVE
plain yogurt of your choice
a good drizzle of honey or
    maple syrup

Cherry & smoked salt clafoutis

SERVES 6-8

2 tablespoons/30 g
  unsalted butter
3 cups/400 g pitted frozen
  cherries, defrosted
⅔ cup/75 g all-purpose flour
½ cup/100 g superfine sugar
2 medium organic eggs
1 teaspoon vanilla extract
  or 1 teaspoon vanilla paste
⅔ cup/150 ml whole milk

TO SERVE
flaked smoked salt
1 tablespoon demerara sugar
cream or crème fraîche

The smoked salt adds a brilliant flavor note here, but normal sea salt will work well too. The frozen cherries are already pitted, so are perfect for a clafoutis. For a boozy version, soak the cherries in a little kirsch and sugar for an hour before you start, then drain and follow the recipe. I love this recipe, but I haven't found a reliable vegan alternative for the eggs yet, so it is one of the few non-vegan recipes in this book.

———

Heat the oven to 350°F/180°C and grease a 9-inch/23 cm cast-iron frying pan or pie dish with half the butter. Lay the cherries in the base of the pan or dish (they can be layered in places). Melt the remaining butter in a saucepan over a medium heat.

To make the batter, whisk together the flour and sugar, then whisk in the eggs one by one, followed by the vanilla extract or paste, milk and melted butter.

Pour the mixture over the cherries and bake for 40–45 minutes, until puffed and lightly golden. Remove from the oven and sprinkle with the smoked salt and demerara sugar. Serve warm with cream or crème fraîche.

WASTE LESS

Using up / Vegetable dressings / Frittatas / Soups / Herb pestos, sauces & smashes

Using up

Plant milk & yogurt

Nut milk (makes about 4 cups/1 liter)

Making your own non-dairy milk at home is easy, more nutritious, cheaper and uses less packaging than buying it. All you need is a decent blender and a nut milk bag (a muslin bag made for draining nut milk) or a clean piece of cheesecloth or a thin kitchen towel.

Take 1 cup of your chosen nuts, seeds or oats and place in a bowl. Cover with a cup of cold (ideally filtered) water and leave to soak for 8 hours; this will allow the nuts to release all their nutrients. Once the soaking time is up, rinse and drain the nuts, discarding the soaking water, and place in a blender. Add 4 cups of fresh, cold (ideally filtered) water to the blender and blitz until you have a thin, smooth, cloudy mixture. You can add flavorings at this point if you like: a teaspoon of vanilla paste or seeds from a pod, a few dates or a tablespoon of runny honey. Spices like cinnamon (a teaspoon) and cardamom (half a teaspoon) also work well. Once added, blitz again. Put a nut milk bag or several layers of cheesecloth over the mouth of a jug and pour the nut milk through. Allow it to sit and drip into the jug for 5-10 minutes, then use your hands to squeeze out as much moisture from the nuts as you can. Pour the milk into a clean bottle; it will keep in the fridge for 3-4 days. The leftover nut pulp can be added to hummus. Tip: if you don't have time to soak nuts, use cashews or macadamias, which do not need soaking.

Oat milk (makes about 4 cups/1 liter)

Place ¾ cup/75 g of oats in a bowl, cover in double the amount of cold water and leave to soak for at least 2 hours or ideally overnight. Drain and rinse with cold water. Blend the rinsed oats and about 4 cups/950 ml of water for 1 minute on high. Strain through a nut milk bag (failing that, a sieve lined with cheesecloth or a clean kitchen towel) over a bowl, then squeeze the bag until as much milk as possible has been extracted and the pulp is dry. The milk will keep for 5 days in the fridge.

Hemp milk

Use the oat milk recipe, replacing the oats with the same amount of hulled hemp seeds.

Flavored and sweetened plant milk

Add flavors to your mixture after straining and blend again.
— almonds/strawberry/vanilla
— pumpkin seeds/cardamom/vanilla
— cashew/cocoa/dates
— sunflower seeds/cinnamon/maple syrup

Oat cream (makes 1½ cups/350 ml)

Cover ½ cup/50 g of oats with 1¼ cups/300 ml of boiling water and leave to soak for 30 minutes. Blitz with 2 tablespoons of olive/sunflower/canola oil and a pinch of salt until smooth. Keeps for 5 days in the fridge. Mix well before you use.

Plant yogurt (makes 2 cups/500 ml)

Soak 12 ounces/350 g of nuts overnight in double the amount of water. The next day, drain (reserving the liquid) and rinse the nuts well. Put the nuts in a blender with some of the soaking water and ¼ cup/50 g of live store-bought plant yogurt. Blend on high until very smooth, adding some flavorings if you like. Pour into a jar and refrigerate overnight. It will be ready to eat the next day and will keep for up to 2 weeks in the fridge.

Pulses

Perfect home-cooked pulses

The length of time it takes to cook a dried pulse will depend on its age. The older it is, the longer it will take to cook. Buy pulses from places where they are likely to be fresh—loose pulses that you buy by weight are a good option.

Soaking

Most beans need an overnight soak in double their volume of fresh, cold (ideally filtered) water. Soaking them makes them much easier to digest and reduces their famous side effects as well as their cooking time; it also allows them to cook more evenly. If you don't have time to soak them, don't fret, as there are a couple of other options. Give them a quick soak, for as much time as you have but ideally for 2 hours, or cook them without soaking. In my experience, the time you save by not soaking them will only be replaced by the extra time they take to cook.

Soaking & cooking times

Quick—lentils, moth and mung beans, split peas. Soak 30 minutes; cook 30-40 minutes.
Short—adzuki beans and black-eyed peas. Soak 2-3 hours; cook 30-40 minutes.
Medium—borlotti, butter (lima), cannellini, navy, kidney and pinto beans. Soak 4 hours; cook 1-1½ hours.
Long—chickpeas, fava and soybeans. Soak 8 hours or overnight; cook 1½-3 hours.

Cooking

Drain the soaked pulses, put them into your largest pot, and cover with cold water to about 1¼ inches/3 cm above the level of the pulses. Bring to the boil, then boil steadily for 5 minutes (10 for kidney beans)—this is important, as it deactivates the toxins in the pulses—and after that, turn down the heat to a very gentle simmer and cook until tender and creamy. Cooking on a low heat like this will make sure the skins stay intact and that your pulses cook evenly. It is better to shake your pan rather than stir with a wooden spoon, as stirring will break the skins. A cooked pulse should remain intact but will collapse into a buttery, creamy mush when squeezed. Chickpeas will remain a little harder but should still be soft throughout. I season my pulses once they are cooked, as seasoning them while cooking is said to toughen them.

Seasoning

Mix 3 tablespoons extra virgin olive oil with 2 tablespoons cider or white wine vinegar and a good pinch of sea salt. Use this to dress and season warm cooked beans. Leave them to sit at room temperature for about 30 minutes for the flavors to meld, then put them in the fridge. They will keep in the fridge for 5 days.

Freezing

You can freeze your cooked and cooled pulses in their cooking liquid, in portions, just like those in a can, but I prefer to freeze them without it. I season them well, then drain the liquid and leave the pulses to cool before freezing them in meal-sized bags. If I have time, I freeze them on a tray first, to stop them sticking together, and bag them up once frozen.

Pickles & ferments

How to pickle any vegetable
(makes 2 medium jars)
I use this basic brine to pickle any vegetable. My favorites are cauliflower (with mustard seed), carrots (with coriander seed), red cabbage (with caraway seed) and radishes (with slices of fresh ginger). Harder, crunchier vegetables are best cut thin.

Prepare and finely chop 1 pound/500 g of vegetables. Put 1 cup/250 ml of vinegar and scant ½ cup/100 ml of cold water into a saucepan with 1 tablespoon of salt and 1 tablespoon of sugar and bring to the boil. Once at a rolling boil, turn off the heat and add the sliced vegetables and any spices you want to add (fennel, coriander, mustard, caraway, cumin seeds and star anise all work well). Carefully spoon the veg while still hot into sterilized jars and top with the brine. Store in a cool place until needed; once open, keep in the fridge.

Quick pickled vegetables (makes 1 pound/ 500 g depending on the veg you use)
Put about 4 cups of shaved or thinly sliced veg in a medium bowl, then add 1 teaspoon of sea salt and 6 tablespoons of cider or white wine vinegar. Mix well and use your hands to massage the veg—this will speed up the pickling. Taste and add more salt or vinegar or a pinch of sugar as needed. Ready to eat right away. Store in the liquid in the fridge for up to 2 weeks.

Fermented krauts (makes about 1 kg)
Kraut creates its own brine, so I recommend using a little cabbage in the mix of veg, as it ferments well and makes a good brine. Combine about 3 pounds/1.5 kg of sliced or grated veg in a large bowl with any spices or seasonings you might like (think ginger, turmeric, shallots) and about 5 teaspoons of salt. Use clean hands to mix the veg together and to squeeze the salt into the vegetables until they are juicy and wilted. Transfer bit by bit to a large jar or fermentation crock and press down with your hands, then finish with the liquid from the bowl. The liquid should cover the veg; if it does not, then you can make a quick salt brine (see recipe below) to top it up. Place a cabbage leaf on top of the veg and weight it down to keep it submerged. Put in a cool place for 10 days. Remove the lid and weight and taste. If it is as tangy and complex as you would like, transfer to the fridge. If not, leave it for another day and keep checking until you like the flavor.

Lacto-fermented vegetables
(makes about 1 pound/400 g)
Don't be put off by the name; this is not complicated. Lacto-fermentation refers to the lactic acid created when good bacteria found on veg skins is released.

Put 4 teaspoons of sea salt into a bowl, add 1 cup/250 ml of just-boiled water and mix. Cut (or leave whole, depending on your veg) about 1 pound/400 g of veg (carrots and radishes are favorites) and put them into jars, leaving 1 inch/2.5 cm at the top. Add herbs or whole spices and cover with the brine. Push down to release any air bubbles, then use a glass lid or small weight to hold the veg under the brine. Secure the lid and leave on a plate in a cool place for up to a week. When you open it, be careful and do it slowly, as gases from fermentation might have built up. Taste, and if they are fermented enough and you like the flavor, put them in the fridge; if not, leave them for a little longer. Once you are happy with the flavor, store in the fridge for up to 6 months.

Squeezed lemons

Preserved lemons

These can be made from already squeezed lemon halves, unwaxed or organic. You also preserve oranges in the same way. Save your squeezed citrus halves in the fridge until you have eight. Mix 5½ tablespoons/100 g of sea salt with 8 tablespoons/100 g of sugar and sprinkle a pinch of the mixture into the bottom of a clean glass jar. One by one, sprinkle the salt mixture into the middle and around the outside of a lemon half, then put in the jar. Repeat until you have done all the lemons, then push them down. The juice from the lemon (there will still be some) should come up to cover the lemons (you can top up with a little water if not). Put in the fridge and leave for a week before eating. They will keep in the fridge for 2–3 months.

Natural citrus cleaner

Fill a jar with squeezed lemon, orange, grapefruit, blood orange or lime halves or pieces. It's good if some still have their zest, as that's where all the oil is. Cover with white vinegar and leave for 2 weeks for the limonene (natural oils) to be released. Then decant into a spray bottle, use to clean all around the house and compost the leftover citrus peels.

Easy citrus cordial

Start with a bowl or large jar of squeezed citrus halves. Weigh all the citrus first, add the same weight of superfine sugar and stir well to release the oils. Cover and leave overnight. You'll have a tangy, citrusy cordial collecting in the bottom of your bowl or jar. Strain the liquid through a sieve into a jug, squeezing out as much flavor from your citrus as possible (you can compost the citrus halves afterward). Pour the cordial into sterilized bottles and store in the fridge for about a month.

Vegetable stock

Saving vegetable trimmings for stock

I keep a big resealable bag in my freezer with vegetable peelings, odds and ends and vegetables that have wilted beyond saving, the green parts from leeks, even onion skins, peelings from carrots and, in spring, asparagus ends. Once this bag gets full, I use the contents to make stock. Avoid starchy vegetables like potatoes, turnips and parsnips. Beets are not the best and zucchini, green beans and green-leafed veg make a bitter stock, so avoid those too.

Easy veg trimming stock (how much it makes depends on your veg leftovers)

Put your vegetable trimmings into a pot and cover with about the same volume of water; you want roughly a 1:1 ratio. Add a good pinch of salt and any other aromatics or herbs you have, like bay leaves or thyme, peppercorns, kombu seaweed, etc. Bring to the boil and simmer for 1 hour, until full of flavor. You can add more water if it begins to concentrate too much. Strain and store in the fridge for up to a month and for up to 3 months in the freezer. You can make this with whole vegetables if you don't have trimmings.

Homemade stock powder (makes 1 pound/500 g)

Pulse about 1 pound/500 g of veg (I use carrots, leeks, fennel, celery) and 2 peeled cloves of garlic in a food processor until they are roughly chopped. Now add 1 tablespoon/20 g of fine sea salt and pulse until you have a fine paste (it will still be quite wet). Freeze in a Tupperware container until needed. Because of all the salt, this will remain quite powdery when frozen, so you can spoon it straight from the freezer. I use 1 teaspoon to 1 tablespoon per 4¼ cups/1 liter of water, depending on what I am making. This keeps in the freezer for up to 6 months.

Vegetable dressings

Dressings are one of the key things I have on hand to make vibrant, tasty meals. I use these veg-based dressings with salad leaves, grains and steamed roasted vegetables and to spread on sandwiches. They also work well as dips if you make them a little thicker. They are easy to make in a good blender and are a great way to use up any sad or lone vegetables at the bottom of the veg drawer. Use your instincts to guide you as you choose flavors to match. Sticking to families of those you know go together is a good place to start.

MAKES ABOUT 1 CUP/250 ML

Vegetables

2 medium zucchini
2 medium carrots, peeled
2 ears of corn, kernels cut off
1 medium bulb fennel
1 medium cooked beet

Put one of these in a blender. Add ¼ cup/60 ml of good extra virgin olive oil.

Nut/Butter/Tahini

1 tablespoon tahini
⅓ cup/40 g (a small handful) of nuts (I like cashews/almonds/pine nuts/walnuts)
1 tablespoon natural nut or seed butter

Choose one of these for creaminess.

Aromatics/Herbs

1 scallion, chopped
½–1 garlic clove
small piece fresh turmeric or ginger, peeled & chopped
large handful of parsley, mint, cilantro, or dill
small handful of tarragon, or chives
½ red or green chili

Add 1 or 2 of these for flavor.

Spices

pinch of dried chili flakes
pinch of cayenne
pinch of ground cumin
pinch of turmeric

Add one of these if you like or leave out for a cleaner dressing.

Citrus

the juice of ½ a lemon, lime or orange (about 1 tablespoon), plus the zest
½ tablespoon cider or white wine vinegar

Add one of the above for acidity.

Seasoning/Water

½ teaspoon sea salt
1 teaspoon miso
1 tablespoon soy or tamari sauce

Finish with a salty element. Then add cold water; start with ¼ cup/60 ml, adding up to ½ cup/120 ml until you have a thin spoonable consistency. Taste and adjust seasoning. The dressings will keep up to 4 days, stored in the fridge.

Frittatas

Frittatas are the best way to use up leftovers. Here is a flexible choose-your-own-adventure recipe that is the base for all of mine. Use up what you have and use your instincts to guide you. Cooking times will differ, depending on whether you use eggs or chickpea (gram) flour.

SERVES 4–6

Choose base	Choose flavor	Herb/Aromatic	Spice
6 eggs, beaten with a little salt and pepper	onions 2, finely sliced	thyme, a few sprigs	1 teaspoon cumin seeds
2¼ cups/200 g chickpea flour mixed with 1½ teaspoons baking powder, and a pinch of salt and pepper, then whisk in 1½ cups/350 ml of cold water and leave to sit	scallions 2, finely sliced	rosemary, a couple of sprigs	1 teaspoon coriander seeds
		sage, 10 leaves	1 teaspoon smoked paprika
		oregano, a few sprigs	1 teaspoon dried chili flakes
		if using the leaves later, basil/cilantro stalks	1 tablespoon mustard seeds
			1 teaspoon harissa
			1 teaspoon chipotle paste

Choose the base for your frittata.	Put your choice of onions into a 10-inch/26 cm ovenproof frying pan with some olive oil and fry over a medium heat for 10 minutes.	Add the herb or spice to the pan and cook for a couple of minutes to release the flavors. Then take off the heat and tip into a bowl.	Choose 1 or 2. If using, add these to the pan at the same time as your herb or aromatic.

Main vegetable	Second vegetable	Begin to cook	Choose topping
potatoes, cooked and chopped	red peppers, roasted		feta
parsnips, cooked and chopped	spinach or greens, wilted and drained		goat cheese
sweet potato, cooked and chopped	peas, cooked		Parmesan
cauliflower florets, cooked and chopped	chopped soft herbs		vegan cheese
zucchini, roughly chopped and sautéed until cooked	fava beans, cooked		chopped nuts
grated root veg, roughly chopped and sautéed until cooked	asparagus, sliced		seeds
leftover cooked pasta	green beans, cooked and chopped		toasted whole spices
a drained can/jar of chickpeas or beans	ramps, wilted and chopped		chili flakes
			chopped soft herbs
			sliced scallions

Begin to cook

Preheat your oven to 400°F/200°C. Once the onions and other veg are cool, add to the egg or chickpea flour mixture and mix well. Wipe out the frying pan and put it back on the heat with a generous amount of olive oil (about 3 tablespoons).

Once hot, add the mixture and cook on a medium heat until crisp around the edges. This will take about 4 minutes for eggs and up to 10 minutes for the chickpea mixture.

Choose topping

Top your frittata with any of the above. Put the frittata into the hot oven and cook until the top feels firm and set. This will take about 8–10 minutes for the eggs and about 30 minutes for the chickpea mixture. Leave to cool in the pan, then slide onto a board and cut into slices.

Second vegetable

Choose a second vegetable. Add both vegetables to the bowl with the onions and mix well.

Main vegetable

Choose main vegetable filling (about 1 pound/500 g).

Soups

This is a choose-your-own-adventure recipe and is my blueprint for soup. Soup is the savior of leftovers. As a rule, I try to choose flavors that are from the same family. The idea here is that the recipe is flexible and a good way to use any vegetables and leftovers that might otherwise be wasted, so use this as a guide and follow your instincts.

SERVES 4–6, DEPENDING ON WHAT YOU ADD

Choose base	Herb/Aromatic	Spice	Main body
1 onion or leek, 2 shallots or 4 scallions, finely chopped	a few sprigs of thyme	1 tablespoon cumin, coriander or mustard seeds	butternut squash
2 stalks celery, ½ a head fennel, trimmed and finely chopped	a couple of sprigs of rosemary	3 cardamom pods, bruised	sweet potato
2 carrots, roughly chopped	sage, 10 leaves	½ cinnamon stick	peas
2 cloves of garlic, peeled and finely chopped	bay leaf, 2–3 leaves	1 tablespoon smoked paprika	celeriac
	a few sprigs of oregano	1 tablespoon garam masala	parsnips
	lime leaves, 2	1 teaspoon ground turmeric	tomatoes
	lemongrass, 1 stick, bruised	1 teaspoon dried chili flakes	carrots
	ginger, finely chopped		broccoli
	if using the leaves later, basil or cilantro stalks		cauliflower

Choose base: Sweat on a medium heat with a little olive oil for about 10 minutes until soft and sweet.

Herb/Aromatic: Add depth with woody herbs or aromatics such as the above.

Spice: Add the herbs and/or spice and sizzle for a couple of minutes to release their flavor.

Main body: You can use 1 or 2, the total combined weight should be about 2 pounds/1 kg. Add enough hot stock to cover and simmer for 20–40 minutes until cooked.

Add substance	Second vegetable	Smooth/Textured	Choose topping
quinoa, a handful	spinach (add at the very end)		roasted seeds or nuts
drained 15-ounce/400 g can of beans or chickpeas	peas		toasted whole spices
small or smashed-up pasta, 2 handfuls	fava beans		dukkah
rice, 2 handfuls	ramps		quick croutons
red lentils, a handful	chopped soft herbs		crispy breadcrumbs
torn-up bread (best added at end)			crispy fried onions
			yogurt or tahini
			harissa
			chopped soft herbs
			herb oil or pesto
			chopped scallions
		It's your call. Some soups, in my opinion, taste better smooth (pea soup), while others (minestrone) taste better with some texture remaining.	quick pickled onions
			lemon/lime/orange zest or juice
This is optional. These will add texture and make it more filling, and your soup will go further. If using, add a couple of handfuls with your stock.	Choose a backup vegetable if you would like to. Add a couple of handfuls and simmer for 5 more minutes.	Blitz now if you want a smooth soup. I often blitz half and keep half textured (and finish with something different) for another meal so one batch of soup can feel like two meals.	Top with 1 or 2 of these options and a drizzle of olive oil and eat. Any leftover soup can be kept in the fridge for up to a week and the freezer for up to 6 months.

Herb pestos, sauces & smashes

Herb sauces and pastes are one of the easiest, most effective and labor-saving ways I know to give a flavor boost to a dish. They are also a brilliant way to get extra life out of languishing bunches of herbs or peppery salad leaves. From pesto to salsa verde, chimichurri to zhoug, there are herb pestos, smashes and sauces the world over. Use this flavor map to make your own. Think in flavor families: I group together ingredients that feel similar in terms of flavor notes or a style of food.

MAKES ABOUT 1 CUP/250 ML

Nut Base

almonds, pumpkin seeds,
   walnuts, pistachios,
   hazelnuts, or pine nuts

If you want a pesto, start with a nut base; if not, skip to the herbs. Start with about ½ cup/50 g of one of the above.

Herb Base

a large bunch of mint, basil,
   parsley, dill, cilantro, arugula,
   watercress or other peppery
   salad leaves
or a smaller bunch of marjoram,
   oregano, tarragon or chives

Choose a combination of two or three. Go for the ones you know work together.

Citrus/Acidity

lime or lemon juice
orange juice
balsamic vinegar
rice vinegar
white wine vinegar
cider vinegar

Add about 2 tablespoons of one of the above for acidity.

Vegetable/Nut Oil

avocado or avocado oil
olive oil
canola oil
walnut oil

Add about 4 tablespoons of one of these oils.

Accent/Flavor

Parmesan, grated, a small
   handful grated ginger, a small
   piece grated garlic, a small
   clove
red or green chili, ½–1,
   finely chopped
pecorino, grated, a small handful
honey or maple syrup, a dash

Add one of the above for flavor.

Seasoning

salt
soy or tamari sauce
ground black pepper, if needed

Add seasoning, then taste and adjust with more salt, acid, etc., as required until balanced.

Index

Acknowledgments

I always leave this "saying thank you" bit to the very end of the writing process, as it's my favorite part, remembering the people who helped and lifted me up. While my name is on the cover, this book is thanks to many people.

First of all, thank you to my family. To **John**, the kindest person I have ever met. You have sailed us through some stormy seas these last few years. You are a daily grounding force who cracks me up and lifts us higher. You are everything. **Dylan**, thanks for being my guiding force and my biggest fan. Being your mum is the great joy of my life; nothing else comes close. Thank you for showing me what matters, for being the funniest, wildest, coolest person I have ever met. This is all for you.

To **Mum, Dad, Laura and Owen**. I'll never be able to quite put into words the immense love and safety knowing I have all of you as my family brings. We are woven together like a blanket. And I love that. **Mum and Dad**, thank you for being (grand)parents all over again to Dylan. We are so grateful and could not do it without your help and guidance. Thank you for your sage advice and calming words when things get a bit much and for it all. No words will ever come close. **Laura**, as ever, my sounding board and my heart. Too far away, but we are still two halves of the same. So much excitement to come. To **Owen**, carving your own path as ever and inspiring me as you do it. Good things are on the way.

To the team at **4th Estate**. My editor **Louise**, you have, with your usual grace and wisdom, guided this book to what it is. Your patience and support and belief in me are humbling and I am, as ever, so grateful to have you at the helm of this book and that I get to do this for the fourth time. Thank you to **David** for always cheering me on; I am hugely grateful to be published by 4th Estate. **Michelle**, as ever, thank you for your friendship, your unwavering belief in me and your refreshing approach to the world of books. You are flying. **Matt**, thank you for your creative thinking and for all that is to come. I know you have big plans. Thanks to **Sarah and Katy** for all your support in the day to day of the book. It's been a joy to work with you both. To the Sales team headed by **Paul**, and the Rights team headed by **Tara**: huge thanks for all you do to get this book out into the world.

To **Louise Tucker**, how lucky I am to have you work on another book. Very safe and very brilliant hands to be in. To **Annie Lee**, we are close to double figures on the books we have worked on together now. Always in your debt, thank you.

Tegan, thank you for your graceful and beautiful design; I have long been a fan of your work, so it has been a total joy to work with you, finally. Your care, attention to detail, perfectly neat notebooks and friendship are all stand out. Thanks to **Rachel Vere** for your discerning eye and ideas at the beginning of the shoot, as ever invaluable and on point.

To my little team: **Jess and Rachael**. You are two of the nicest people I have ever met and I consider myself incredibly lucky to have you both around. **Jess**—is there anything you can't do? Your creativity, kindness and loyalty are so treasured. **Rachael**, I'm so grateful that you have my back, for your commitment to fighting the good fight and for all the great things you bring into my life, from art to avocado dyeing. Two of the most brilliant women.

Felicity and all at CB, thanks for guiding me through with such wisdom and grace, for believing in me and for having my back way beyond the remit of being my agent. So much love for you and your family.

Alice, KJ, Daisy: I love being part of the **Found** family. Thanks for believing in me and cheering me on.

To the incredible team of women who turned my words into pictures. **Issy**, thanks for your beautiful pictures, and for your patience when I asked to shoot things a hundred ways. To **Emily**, thanks as ever for being my sounding board and my second sis. Love you both beyond. To **Christina**, you are the nicest person and the kindest; you light up everything around you. **Kitty**, I mean 10/10, what a babe.

Holly O'Neill, thanks for being an all-round wise woman and letting me dip into the font of food knowledge that is your brain.

Emma Lee, thanks for letting us use your incredible house to shoot in—when can we all move in? The recipe testers who made sure everything was in shape—**Christina** (again), **Kitty** (again), **Anna Shepherd, Daisy Shayler, Nena Foster, Elly Kemp**, as well as the crew of people who answered my callout on Instagram to test the recipes. Your feedback was invaluable. To the kind souls who offered up their time to do work experience on the shoot—**Jemima Davies, Susannah Hunt, Kathy Slack** and **Helena Anderson**.

My editors and supporters at *The Guardian*, though I have moved on, I want to thank **Mina Holland, Anna Berril** and all my fellow Guardian Feast writers; it's been so good being part of that food family. Thanks to Allan and all at OFM for their unwavering backing since day one.

Thanks to the sustainability experts who helped me navigate the very complex world of sustainable eating—to **Emmanuelle Hopkinson, Sonja Vermeulen** and **Lauren Davies**. Your help and wisdom were invaluable. I salute you all.

To the incredible makers and artists who helped the book come to life. Fabrics came from **Ros Humphries** of **The Natural Dyeworks, Tessa Layzelle, Flora Duke, SZ Blockprints** and **Victoria Bain** and her **Eleanora** napkins. Incredible marbled paper came from **Florence Saumarez** of **Inq.Ink**. The beautiful ceramics from **Pip Hartle, Skandihus, Rebecca Proctor** and **Jono Smart**. Thanks to **Crane Cookware** and **Le Creuset** for the most beautiful pans. Thanks to **The New Craftsman** for the loan of some of their incredible works of art.

For the food, thanks to **Calyxta** from the incredible **Flourish Produce** for her next-level produce and to **Natoora**, too. To all the other cooks: there are too many to mention who inspire me. The London food community is filled with the best people.

But most of all, thank you to you for reading my words and cooking my recipes and supporting what I do. I am so grateful to each and every one of you. It means the world that these recipes are cooked in your homes and feed you and your families.

Anna Jones is a cook, writer, and stylist. Dubbed the
"Queen of Greens" by *The Guardian*, she is widely recognized
as being the voice of modern vegetarian cooking. She is the
author of *The Modern Cook's Year*, *A Modern Way to Eat*, and
A Modern Way to Cook. *The Modern Cook's Year* won the
Observer Food Monthly Best New Cookbook Award and The
Guild of Food Writers Cookery Book Award. Her previous books
have been nominated for the James Beard, Fortnum & Mason
and André Simon Awards. She lives in Hackney, East London,
with her husband and young son.